Presidential
VETOES
1792-1945

Presidential
VETOES
1792 -1945

By

CARLTON JACKSON

University of Georgia Press
ATHENS

To My Parents

MR. AND MRS. L. H. JACKSON

Contents

PART II

VETO PROVISIONS

"Every bill which shall have passed the House of Representatives and the Senate, shall, before it become a law, be presented to the President of the United States; if he approves he shall sign it, but if not he shall return it, with his objections, to that House in which it shall have originated, who shall enter the objections at large on their journal and proceed to reconsider it. If after such reconsideration two-thirds of that House shall agree to pass the bill, it shall be sent, together with the objections, to the other House, by which it shall likewise be reconsidered, and if approved by two-thirds of that House it shall become a law. But in all such cases the votes of both Houses shall be determined by yeas and nays, and the names of the persons voting for and against the bill shall be entered on the journal of each House respectively. If any bill shall not be returned by the President within ten days (Sundays excepted) after it shall have been presented to him, the same shall be a law, in like manner as if he had signed it, unless the Congress by their adjournment prevent its return, in which case it shall not be a law.

"Every order, resolution, or vote to which the concurrence of the Senate and the House of Representatives may be necessary (except on a question of adjournment) shall be presented to the President of the United States; and before the same shall take effect, shall be approved by him, or being disapproved by him, shall be repassed by two-thirds of the Senate and House of Representatives, according to the rules and limitations prescribed in the case of a bill."—The Constitution of the United States, Article I, Section 7.

Preface

By using the veto, a President emphasizes, for the most part, a positive position in government. He can force the Legislature to materially change a bill so that it will be acceptable to the Executive, thus allowing him to participate in the legislative process. Or he can force a quorum of Congress to repass a bill by a two-thirds vote rather than by a simple majority. Finally, a bill can be killed altogether, activating a congressional-executive "culling" system, in which many possibly unsatisfactory laws are kept from becoming part of the governmental process. All of the above alternatives, springing from the veto power, are examples of positive action in the relations between the President and the Legislature. Actually, there is little negativism in the presidential veto, except in instances when Presidents such as Andrew Jackson used it as an instrument of personal malice.

The veto fits into the pattern of flexibility embodied in the Constitution because it allows several alternative actions on legislation. Often it makes possible a compromise between opposing legislative forces, or between the Legislature and the President. Most of the Presidents in this study realized the value of the veto as a means of effecting compromise. Jackson and Andrew Johnson, and to an extent Franklin Roosevelt, were the only ones who made little use of the compromising possibilities of the veto.

Another evidence of the positive character of the veto is its suspensive rather than absolute nature. By vetoing a bill, a President cannot totally destroy the chances for its ultimate passage, as can happen in a close contest when one member of the Legislature votes against a certain measure. Defenders of the veto have always cited this suspensive feature, pointing out that in the American government Congress and the Supreme Court are the only bodies with absolute vetoes. Those who have argued that a President may aspire to monarchy through a veto (notably Jackson, Tyler, and Franklin Roosevelt) have been told that this is impossible under the Constitution because a veto merely orders Congress to reconsider a bill rather than to destroy it completely.

The veto clause also states that, in addition to bills, "every order, resolution, or vote to which the concurrence of the Senate and House of Representatives may be necessary" shall be presented to the President for his approval or rejection. This, of course, has prevented the enactment of laws under the camouflage of resolutions. The only area in which this is not applicable is that of amendments to the Constitution.

The clause (which, incidentally, does not mention the word "veto") places no restrictions on the reasoning of a President when he disapproves a bill. It simply directs him to return it with his objections. No demand is made that the Constitution alone be the basis for approval or rejection. The clause's vagueness, no doubt deliberate, has led to many controversies over the nature of the veto power. James Madison felt that the veto was intended to check the instability of the legislative department by preventing hasty and ill-timed laws. Thomas Jefferson viewed the power as a protective device by the Executive, the Judiciary, and the State Legislatures against the National Congress. But neither of these men explained whether constitutionality or politics, or both, should be the rationale for presidential action.

Another aspect of the veto clause has been controversial. The clause requires only that the house to which a bill is returned enter the President's objections in the house journal and proceed to reconsider. But when? Immediately? At the pleasure of the house? By the whole house? Or could the reconsideration go to a committee, either standing or select, which would then make recommendations to the whole membership?

Ante-bellum opponents of the veto usually argued that a reconsideration could come up in the due course of Congress's business and that it should be given no preference over other impending legislation. To these people it was also proper for a reconsideration to go to a committee for recommendations. By using these devices the Whigs, during Tyler's administration, were able to show their disdain for the President by preventing a vote on the reconsideration which they knew would be against them, thereby giving themselves time to gain additional support. The Democrats constantly charged the Whigs with unconstitutional manipulations in this regard. The Reconstruction Congress acted similarly to the Whigs of Tyler's time. The members not only referred many vetoed bills to a committee, but sometimes they simply tabled, and subsequently forgot them. These questions were fully answered only after the Civil War. It became the practice for Congress to reconsider vetoed legislation after other matters were attended to, and the referral to a committee for specific recommendations became the rule rather than the exception.

In all, there were 1,762 bills returned during the period under consideration: Washington vetoed 2 bills; Madison, 7; Monroe, 1; Jackson, 12; Tyler, 9; Polk, 3; Pierce, 9; Buchanan, 7; Lincoln, 6; and Johnson, 29. All Presidents since the Civil War have exercised the veto power: Grant, 94; Hayes, 13; Arthur, 12; Cleveland (both terms), 583; Harrison, 44; McKinley, 42; Theodore Roosevelt, 82;

Taft, 39; Wilson, 44; Harding, 6; Coolidge, 50; Hoover, 37; and Franklin Roosevelt, 631.

The veto was used sparingly until Jackson's administrations. The first 10 vetoes were applied primarily to issues wholly constitutional in nature or to issues of constitutional interpretation. Most of the vetoed bills were returned to the House of Representatives, and it was that body which hurled most invective at the veto Presidents. Since the House presumably reflected more nearly the wishes of the people than did the Senate, it was often thought that a veto President was monarchical in thwarting popular will.

Presidents John Adams, Thomas Jefferson, John Quincy Adams, Martin Van Buren, William H. Harrison, Zachary Taylor, and Millard Fillmore did not use the veto power during their incumbencies. This was due in part to their willingness for Congress to hold the initiative in government, to the emphasis being placed on international events, and to the belief of some of the Presidents (Taylor and Fillmore in particular) that the veto should be used only in extreme cases.

In congressional overriding actions, it is not merely party affiliation that determines the outcome. Much depends upon sectional prejudices, upon the political and economic conditions of the country, and upon the image created by the President. That this observation is valid can be seen especially in the early reform movements of the twentieth century. Although much grumbling accompanied many of the presidential vetoes, none was overridden until Tyler's administration, an event that can be explained by the major split between Tyler and the party which put him into power. Under Pierce 5 vetoes were overridden in the resurgence of congressional power in the decade before the Civil War. President Andrew Johnson had 15 of his 29 vetoes overturned by Congress. The reason, of course, was the great disagreement between the President and Congress over the Reconstruction question. Grant had 4 of his vetoes overruled; Hayes, 1; Cleveland (both terms), 7; Benjamin Harrison, 1; Theodore Roosevelt, 1; Taft, 1; Wilson, 6; Coolidge, 4; Hoover, 3; and Franklin Roosevelt, 9. The vetoes of McKinley and Harding in the post-war period remained intact.

It is somewhat paradoxical that most of the major bills which initially fell before a presidential veto have ultimately become law. No one can deny the existence today of a federal internal improvement program, a banking system, land grants to institutions and individuals, aid to farmers, public and private pensions, and broad patterns of government spending on all levels. Yet, by their vetoes of these programs, the various Presidents increased the power and influence of the Executive department and perhaps caused important changes to be made in these proposals before they were finally adopted.

Many persons helped while this book was in preparation. It is my happy priviledge to acknowledge their assistance. Professor Horace Montgomery of the University of Georgia History Department first suggested the idea of running a survey of the vetoes. My gratitude goes to him for all of his valuable suggestions. Mrs. Donna Sheppard of Baltimore read the entire manuscript and gave incisive advice. My friend and colleague Professor Claude C. Sturgill of East Carolina College placed his talents at my service by reading an early draft, as did Mrs. Mary Miller of the Western Kentucky University English Department.

The Research Committee of Western Kentucky granted funds for student help and for travel. To each member I am grateful. Many of my students performed countless tasks in checking sources and in typing. My thanks go to Robert Harrison, Susan Anderson, Ralph Brashear, Donald Craig, and Caroline Page for their valuable assistance.

Finally, I must thank my wife, Pat, and my children, Beverly and Daniel, for allowing me to neglect them so often while this book was being written.

C.J.

History Department
Western Kentucky University

Establishment of a Veto Pattern:
Washington, Madison, Monroe

PRESIDENT Washington's veto on April 5, 1792, of an act for the "apportionment of representation among the several states according to the first enumeration," had ominous overtones. Washington's disapproval sought to counteract a growing sectionalism reflected in the Apportionment Act.

Constitutionally, representation had to be apportioned "among the several states according to their respective numbers" and "the number of representatives shall not exceed one for every 30,000." The Apportionment Act, however, sought to divide the population of the entire country by 30,000 to produce a House of Representatives of 120 members. This method, had it been effected, would have created large, unrepresented fractions in several states. Having selected the 120 members of the House according to the constitutional ratio of one per 30,000, the dominant party, in this case the Federalist, would have devised different ratios to dispose of the fractions left within the states. Those that more nearly approached 30,000 would be given representation, the smaller fractions being left out altogether.[1]

Opponents of the act argued that the number of people in each state respectively must be divided by 30,000 to meet the constitutional requirement. This Apportionment Bill did not apply the same fixed ratio to the fractions in determining how much additional representation each state would have after the constitutional ratio of one to 30,000 had been used. Most of the large fractions were in the New England areas, which would accordingly receive a predominance of representation over the Southern states.[2]

It was also argued by the Southern delegates that the three-fifths compromise would be destroyed by the bill. Slaves accounted for the fractions in the Southern states but their numbers, under the various ratios, were not enough to warrant representation. To show the disparity between the bill and the Constitution, a letter writer to the *National Gazette*, who styled himself "Detector," pointed out that under the proposed legislation, Virginia, for example, would have representation for 456,983 persons, while the

constitutional formula would allow 630,559 people in that state
to be represented.[3] According to "Detector," the New England
states might very well seek to apply different ratios to the fractions in an attempt to destroy representation of three-fifths of
the slaves, for New England as a whole did not contain half as
many slaves as the small state of Delaware, or one seventy-fifth
as many as Virginia. The bill would be just as constitutional,
"Detector" said, if the basis of representation were placed upon a
person's willingness to drink New England rum.[4]

Washington consulted his cabinet on the Apportionment proposal only to find it divided, as was Congress, on sectional lines.
Jefferson opposed the bill because of its varying ratios for dealing
with the fractions. Hamilton was not positive about its constitutionality, but because a majority in Congress supported it, the
Secretary of the Treasury felt it should be approved by Washington.[5] If he accepted the measure, Washington felt all future apportionments for the fractions would cause a fight. If he disapproved it, he would be thought to be favoring one section of
the country against another.

After long deliberation, in which he almost let the alloted
time of ten days elapse, Washington applied the veto for the first
time in American history. He stated that there was no one "proportion or divisor, which applied to the respective numbers of the
states" would yield the representation (120) called for in the bill.
Moreover, the Constitution stated that the number of representatives would not exceed one for 30,000 and that this ratio must
be applied to the separate and respective numbers of the states.
But the bill had allotted to several of the states more than one for
30,000. The Apportionment Bill was, therefore, unconstitutional.[6]

A motion was made in the House to pass the bill, "the President's
objections notwithstanding," but it failed by a vote of 28 to 33.
The *National Gazette* took this vote as proof of the constitutionality
of the President's course. When the bill first passed the House the
vote was 31 to 29, a majority of only two. Upon reconsideration,
however, a majority of five voted against it.[7] Thus, the veto was
vindicated because it helped to stop hasty and ill-timed legislation.

After the failure to repass the first Apportionment Bill, a
committee was appointed to prepare another measure.[8] A discussion
occurred in committee on April 9 between Representative Abraham
Clark from New Jersey, who wanted the ratio set at one representative per 33,000 and Representative Alexander White of Virginia, who desired its retention at one per 30,000. A bill was
passed on April 14, 1792, which allowed one representative for

each 33,000 persons.[9] This increased the number of representatives in the House from 67 to 103.

The President readily signed the second Apportionment Bill because he thought it to be equitable. It increased the number of representatives by 36 in a way that was proportionate to the greatest concentrations of population. It gave the greatest number to New England, but not in the manner which that section had envisioned in the first Apportionment Bill. This veto was apparently only a temporary rupture between Washington and Congress; the President did not use the power again until February, 1797.

Washington's second veto came over a bill to amend an earlier act dealing with the military establishment of the United States. Included in the amending bill was a provision for discharging two companies of light dragoons, appointed to help preserve peace between Indians and the frontier settlers.

In his message to the House on February 28, 1797, President Washington said that if the bill passed, the dragoons would be at that moment legally out of the service, although they were actually to continue in service until the terms of the amending bill became known to them. It would not be lawful, therefore, to pay them during the interval between legal and actual separation unless Congress made further provisions. Washington admitted that the dragoons could be discharged at the pleasure of Congress, but in justice, "they ought to receive their pay, not only to the time of passing the law, but at least to the time of their actual discharge."[10]

Washington's second reason for the veto was that dismissal of the dragoons would be "inconvenient and injurious" to the public, because one of the companies had only recently been used in a "necessary and important" service. Third, many officers and men in the dragoons had not served more than one-third of their enlistments. If they were discharged, a serious deficiency would result in the infantry forces with whom the dragoons periodically served. To discharge them now would not "comport with economy," according to Washington.

The bill was re-read in the House, after which the President's message was made known. James Nicholas of Virginia criticized the President's veto because of its imputation of fraudulent action by the House. The Representative said that Congress intended to give each dragoon officer discharged a $100.00 bonus. A Representative from South Carolina, W. Smith, reminded Nicholas that only the officers, not the men, were to receive the bonus. The

South Carolinian, stating that it would take from six weeks to two months to inform the soldiers of the discharging bill, argued that the Attorney General believed it would be illegal to pay them during the interval. John Williams of New York noted the important recent actions of the dragoons in Georgia and Tennessee and agreed with the President that they were too valuable to discharge. The veto was sustained by a vote of 55 to 26. Afterwards, a new bill was reported with the same provisions as the old one except for the parts to which the President objected.[11]

Washington's second veto was primarily a matter of military expediency rather than for constitutional reasons. Congress had the power to discharge soldiers, but the military background of the President enabled him to see immediately the results of such a bill. He could envision a serious shortage of personnel on the troubled frontier if the bill passed. Congress was attempting to economize, but according to Washington, this was false economy. He applied the veto, therefore, for practical rather than for constitutional reasons.

Washington's two vetoes were in accord with his objective of holding down controversy in the young Republic as much as possible. This is seen by his great care in the case of the Apportionment veto to study and analyze all the reactions that it might have elicited. Even so, some Congressmen objected to the veto, but as Jefferson said, most were relieved that the veto had been used successfully on the first attempt. Washington attempted to be as constitutional as possible in his presidential actions because he felt that this was the best way to hold the Republic together. His first veto reflected clearly his position vis-a-vis the Constitution and his sensitivity about the thoughts of Congress.

In the Dragoon veto, Washington was not so bound to the Constitution nor to Congress as he had been in the case of Apportionment. This was true because his authority as President was now firmly established, the domestic condition of the country was better than it had been in 1792, and he was preparing to leave the presidency. The second veto, therefore, was based on expediency alone, and for it Washington was more severely criticized by some Congressmen, Nicholas of Virginia in particular, than he had been for the Apportionment veto. He was charged with falsely accusing some Congressmen with fraudulent action.

The two vetoes helped Washington set a trend for strong executive leadership in relation to Congress. The real importance of these vetoes was not what they were about or what they said, but simply that they occurred. They set the pattern for future

Presidents who found the power necessary. Finally, Washington established a tone of positive, rather than negative, action in his vetoes. Most Presidents after Washington adhered to these positive principles. Such was the case with James Madison, the next President to find the power necessary.

The presidency of James Madison was a time of growth for the veto power. It was used more often and for reasons more debatable than before. Madison's vetoes were on subjects completely different from those of Washington; thus there is no basis for comparing the vetoes of the two Presidents. Comparisons are possible after Madison's terms in office because he set many precedents used by later chief executives. During his incumbency the veto power first became really noticeable in the country at large, as evidenced by mounting criticisms of its usage by the President.

Madison's vetoes allowed him to maintain an equality of power with Congress and, in some instances, to supersede it. It was during his administration that several pertinent questions about the veto power were first asked. For example, one Congressman suggested that a veto be given to a select committee for study and recommendations. This procedure, according to many, was within the framework of the Constitution. But a majority felt that referral would destroy the efficient administration of the Constitution. This controversy, becoming important for the first time during Madison's presidency, would be debated until the Reconstruction Congress adopted referral without question. Indeed, one measure of power of the Reconstruction Congress was its defeats of vetoes by referrals. One wonders if the practice of referral had been accepted in Madison's, or even in Tyler's administrations, whether or not a major tool of the Reconstruction Congress against Johnson would have been eliminated. If referral had been adopted in the early days of the federal union, it might very well have changed the procedure by which the veto power developed.

Another aspect of Madison's vetoes that showed his relation to the Constitution was his use of the "prescriptive process," that is, the belief that even though a practice is outside the strict boundaries of the Constitution, its usage over a long period establishes its validity. Madison no doubt was able to justify his acceptance of a bank in 1816, though he had disapproved it in the previous year, by a belief in the prescriptive process. He was not willing to apply this test, however, to the question of internal improvements.

Madison's initial vetoes concerned bills which he considered violations of the First Amendment prohibiting the passage of any laws with respect to religious establishments. Congress passed two acts in February, 1811; one for incorporating the Protestant Episcopal Church in Alexandria, Virginia, and the other for the reservation of land in Mississippi territory to a Baptist congregation.

The Episcopal Incorporation bill organized the Episcopal Church in Alexandria and Washington into a religious society. It gave the Church the right to hold property and enacted procedures by which the body would be regulated. All matters in the Church would be decided by a majority vote, over which the minister was to have no control.[12]

Madison stated in his veto message that Congress had exceeded its authority by making no distinction between a civil and a religious function, and that the bill violated in particular the First Amendment to the Constitution. If any rules of the Church were to change in the future, Madison maintained, a law of Congress would be necessary. Moreover, if any of the rules were violated, the offender would be subject to punishment under federal law. Finally, the Incorporation bill enabled the Church to provide for the poor. This would be a precedent for giving religious societies the legal function of carrying out a public and civic duty.[13]

The return of the veto to the House caused a debate on the feasibility of referring it to a select committee, as suggested by a representative from Virginia, Burwell Bassett. He argued that the Constitution necessitates a reconsideration of a vetoed bill, but that it is silent on the procedure to be used. In the absence of detailed constitutional instructions, it would be legal to refer the message to a select committee.[14] The Speaker, Joseph B. Varnum, believed that referral would cause an indefinite postponement of the reconsideration, which would be unconstitutional. Representative Benjamin Pickman, Jr., of Massachusetts, felt that the refusal of two-thirds of the House to reconsider was the same as sustaining the President's veto. This was the course Pickman wished to follow.[15]

Upon a motion by Timothy Pitkin, Jr., of Connecticut, the House proceeded to reconsider. Pitkin claimed that the Constitution did not prohibit Congress from passing laws to incorporate religious societies, thereby enabling them to hold property. The Constitution merely stated that Congress could not establish a national church with mandatory membership for all citizens who wished to hold public office.

Representative Laban Wheaton of Massachusetts continued the attack against the President's veto by asserting that at every session of Congress, chaplains had been appointed and had been paid for their services. If the Incorporation Bill was a violation of the First Amendment, the same was true in the appointment of chaplains. Thus, the President apparently sought to drive religion completely out of the District of Columbia.[16]

Finally, Nathaniel Macon of North Carolina moved that reconsideration be postponed until the members had a better chance to prepare themselves for argument. Many believed that Congress possessed power to regulate the temporal concerns of a religious society, but they wanted time in which to compile specific arguments. Macon's motion was adopted without difficulty. On Saturday, February 23, 1811, the bill was brought before the House. It was read by the clerk and then voted upon. Apparently no one was prepared to argue in favor of the bill, for the vote took place without any important discussion. The reason for this was congressional preoccupation with the bill for rechartering the Bank of the United States. International affairs also occupied much time, so the Episcopal Incorporation Bill was hurriedly dismissed. Newspapers, including the prominent *National Intelligencer*, simply reported how Congress had voted on the Church bill and did not editorialize.[17] By a vote of 74 to 29 the President's veto of the Episcopal Incorporation Bill was sustained.

Less than a week after this veto, Madison returned another bill providing for the relief of certain individuals in Mississippi Territory. Section six of the act alloted five acres of land to the Salem Baptist Church in that territory. Because of that provision, the veto was applied.[18]

In his veto of February 28, 1811, Madison stated that it was illegal for the government to appropriate lands for the use of religious societies. The bill was therefore in violation of the First Amendment and could not be approved. The House called for an immediate reconsideration and vote on this veto, which was sustained 55 to 33.

The significance of these two vetoes is that for the first time Congress openly questioned the President on his veto opinions. Several representatives, such as Pitkin and Wheaton, were setting the stage for charging the President with trying to gain unwarranted power through the use of the veto.

Madison's next veto, concerning the relationship between governmental departments, was in the purely political area. Passed in March, 1812, the bill stated that whenever a district judge was absent from his post for a legitimate reason, a Supreme Court

Justice, allotted to the circuit where the district was located, should perform as head of the district court.[19]

The bill was returned to the House on April 3, 1812, with Madison's objections. He said that if the bill passed, a Supreme Court Justice would be compelled to act in the role of a district judge rather than as a Supreme Court Justice. If the Justice sat as a district judge and if a case were appealed, the Justice would then hear an appeal of his own decision.

No provision was made in the bill to increase the salary of the Supreme Court Justice for the additional work involved, nor were there any provisions to allow reimbursement for additional expenses. Furthermore, the additional services to be performed by the Justice might, because of the distances involved and the resulting taxing of strength, be too much work.

Finally, Madison stated that if the appointments outlined in the bill were "compatible with their original offices," they should be appointed by someone other than the legislature. If the bill passed, it would introduce unsuitable relations between the Judiciary and the chief executive.[20]

The Judiciary veto was reconsidered in the House on April 8, 1812. Representative Thomas Gold from New York spoke in opposition to the President's objections.[21] He cited the continued illness of one of the New York district judges whose infirmity caused that particular court to be behind in 700 cases. He argued that the vetoed bill would have brought much needed relief.[22] Gold also believed that the work and salary of the district judges were incompatible. The salaries were fixed by law but the duties were flexible. The judges' pay was sometimes used up by the expenses incurred while traveling throughout their districts. Therefore, some relief should be offered to the over-worked district judges.[23]

By his veto of the Judiciary Bill Madison sought to preserve the distinct operations of the three departments of government. His chief reason for the veto was that he thought Congress, by the terms of the bill, would have gained unjustified power over the President's authority of appointment. The veto was sustained by a vote of 25 yeas to 70 nays.

Madison used the pocket veto for the first time in American history in November, 1812, against an attempt to change certain rules affecting aliens. Late in June, just after the declaration of war with England, Abner Lacock of Pennsylvania stated in the House that because of hostilities the courts were now prohibited from naturalizing aliens, although many had met the legal requirements.

Lacock felt that the government was pledged to naturalize such people, the war notwithstanding. He introduced a resolution admitting to citizenship any subjects of Great Britain who were residing in the United States prior to June 18, 1812.[24] An amendment was added to this resolution on July 1 by Representative Langdon Cheves of South Carolina. It stated that no alien enemy would be made a citizen if he did not within six months after passage of the act make application for citizenship according to existing law.[25]

President Madison believed that the bill was liable to abuse by aliens who had no real intention of becoming citizens. He suggested changes in the proposal to favor only those aliens entitled to the benefits of citizenship and to prevent the usage of the law for "improper purposes."[26] On November 18, Lacock introduced a new naturalization bill which put the deadline for citizenship at June 1, 1812, instead of June 18. It also changed from six months to nine the period in which an alien enemy must announce his intention of applying for American citizenship. Finally, a proviso was added which said that nothing in the law should be construed as preventing the removal from the United States of alien enemies.[27] In its altered form the bill received the President's signature and became law. This is another illustration of how a presidential veto can substantially alter a law passed by Congress, thus enabling the Chief Executive to participate in the legislative process.

The most controversial of Madison's vetoes occurred on January 30, 1815, when he rejected a congressional proposal to establish a second bank of the United States. As the time slipped away for him to approve or reject, much conjecture arose about Madison's probable action. Many believed with the *New York Herald* that the bank was so necessary to the country's economy that Madison dare not withhold his approval.[28] Madison did dare, though, and the veto became the subject of much controversy.

The act would have created a national bank similar to that instituted by Alexander Hamilton with the exception of the amount of capitalization. Madison agreed that the constitutional basis of a bank had been well established through a prescriptive process of repeated legislative, executive, and judicial recognitions of the bank's value.[29] But he did not believe that the bank could, during a time of war, (the Treaty of Ghent had not yet been ratified, so a state of war still technically existed) accomplish worthwhile economic objectives. To justify its existence such a bank should be able to provide a medium of circulation, aid the Treasury by anticipating revenue, and allow durable loans to the public.[30]

Madison apparently believed that the best way to facilitate the operation of the government's finances was to issue treasury notes, thereby providing a circulating medium. He told Congress that it could either override his veto, or could substitute a bank bill that would better provide for the "exigencies" of the public.[31] Congress adopted the latter course, as is well known, for the following year a second bank was approved by Madison.

The President received harsh criticism for his veto of the bank bill. Senator Rufus King of New York believed that Madison's veto stemmed, not from his objections to the bank proposal, but from his concern for the condition of the country.[32] The President insinuated that the treasury was exhausted, that loans were no longer attainable, and that paper money was the only medium capable of furthering American war objectives.[33] But, thought King, paper money had many attendant evils which could be avoided by a properly regulated bank.[34] The Senator felt it would be logical to issue treasury notes and let them be converted at pleasure into public stock bearing a high interest rate. The stock could be funded by pledging specific taxes to pay the interest. The credit of this type of currency would be superior to that of the highly inflated currency which Madison apparently wanted.

Newspapers critical of Madison's veto included the *Maryland Gazette* published at Annapolis. The *Gazette* bitterly denounced Madison, claiming that a national bank was the only way to save the country from financial ruin.[35] It accused the cabinet members of helping to destroy the bank bill by publishing a conundrum that became popular in some circles:

"Why are his [Madison's] present ministers like the public stock, treasury notes, etc.?"

"Because they are under par."[36]

Madison's 1815 bank veto must be viewed as an example of financial expediency. The times in which the bank was to be established were not normal. No matter how patriotic the bank's directors and stockholders were, they would look first to the benefit of the bank rather than to that of the country.[37] The government might be compelled, therefore, to force the bank to make temporary sacrifices. Madison's reaction to the bank bill marked an interesting change in the reason for using the veto power. Most of the preceding vetoes were based on the Constitution; this one argued financial expediency, and was a positive example of executive-legislative relations.[38] Many of Madison's arguments were used later by President Jackson in his bank veto of 1832.

Relations between Madison and Congress during the next

two years were relatively smooth. The second national bank was put into operation in 1816. One of the provisions of the twenty year charter was that the bank pay $1,500,000 as a yearly bonus to the government in lieu of taxes.

A bill to allocate the bank bonus for internal improvements was passed in late February, 1817. The debate on the bill, introduced into the House by South Carolina's John C. Calhoun, indicated the growing sectionalism in the United States. The Southern delegates opposed the bill on constitutional grounds and because it was "vague, general, and unsatisfactory."[39] On the other hand, Calhoun, going through his "nationalist" period, claimed that the bill would promote national unity rather than discord. He claimed that the bill would be general in application, but he did cite some specific projects which he felt required federal funds. Appropriations were needed "to perfect the communications from Maine to Louisiana," and to connect the Great Lakes with the Hudson River.[40] Speaker Henry Clay from Kentucky joined the debate, stating that internal improvements and domestic manufactures were two of the most important subjects to be considered by Congress. He agreed with Calhoun that the bill would help unify the country.

The bill passed in the Senate by a majority of five (20 to 15) and in the House by a majority of two (86 to 84). The *National Intelligencer* was disturbed by the close vote on the Bonus Bill and reported that "we hope, indeed we are firmly persuaded, it will meet the approbation of a much larger portion of the American people" than it did in Congress. The paper confidently hoped that Madison would approve the bill.[41]

There was enough Jeffersonianism left in Madison, however, to cause him to disapprove the Bonus Bill, and on March 3, 1817, the day before he left office, he returned it to the House where it had originated.

Madison began his veto by saying that he could not reconcile the act with the Constitution. The power by which Congress enacted the bill was not listed in the enumerated powers of Congress, nor did it fall within a just interpretation of the elastic clause.[42] To those who argued that the bill was justified under the Commerce Clause in the Constitution, Madison replied that the clause could not be construed as authorizing the building of roads and canals or for improving navigation. Neither could authority for the bill be inferred from the "common defense and general welfare" clause, because it would make the enumerated powers following it "nugatory and improper." It would give Congress a general power instead of a limited one, subjecting the Constitution and the laws of the states to supersession by laws of Congress. Judicial authority would be disrupted by the bill, because questions of "general welfare are unsusceptible of judicial decision."[43]

Madison was aware of the benefits that would derive from internal improvement projects. But he believed that a constitutional amendment outlining clearly the authority and responsibilities of the federal government in such a program should be approved.

In this opinion he was politically inconsistent. He approved the national bank in 1816, not because it was clearly constitutional, but because experience had shown its value over a number of years. Internal improvements, too, were of relatively long usage, but Madison was not willing to apply his prescriptive process to internal improvements as he was to the bank. Therefore, he demanded a constitutional amendment to legalize programs of internal improvements.

Perhaps one reason Madison vetoed the Bonus Bill was the closeness of the vote as it passed both Houses of Congress. It is possible that Madison wanted to use the veto in this case to elicit a clearer picture of public opinion on the question than the vote in Congress gave him. Certainly it is conceivable that a veto could be used to ascertain public thinking on a given subject. However, this did not materialize in succeeding administrations since future Presidents did not emphasize the prescriptive process to the degree that Madison did. If this conjecture is true, perhaps Madison was trying to lay a foundation upon which internal improvements could be justified through the majoritarian prescriptive process.

The voting in the House on passage of the bill over the President's veto showed 60 representatives to be in the affirmative and 56 in the negative.[44] Although a majority opposed the presidential action, two-thirds were needed, so the veto was sustained. Speaker Clay voted on this occasion—in the affirmative—although the vote was not tied.

This was the first of a succession of internal improvement vetoes during the period before the Civil War. Almost every President after Madison who disapproved an internal improvement bill used much the same interpretation as did the fourth President. John Tyler placed an unusual interpretation on the Commerce Clause in one of his internal improvement vetoes, but for the most part Madison's precedent was closely followed.

By his vetoes, Madison assured his equality, or in some instances (with the Bank veto, and the veto of the Bonus bill) his superiority, over Congress. This was important because it set a trend that would be consummated by Andrew Jackson. Madison's vetoes also established a congressional reaction that assured close scrutiny of presidential rejections. The Bank and Bonus bill disapprovals indicated that henceforth most presidential vetoes would be on issues dividing the political parties. This in turn reflected a growth of sectionalism. Madison elicited respect for the veto power on the part of Congress and the country. He demonstrated that through the veto could be realized the capabilities for strong executive government, which might even be used by a President to dominate the legislative branch.

This latter possibility, however, was not utilized by Madison's immediate successor, James Monroe, who, while in office, vetoed only one bill, which was designed to preserve and repair the Cumberland Road. Congress had appropriated $9,000 for repairing the road and had authorized tolls for maintaining it in the future. Monroe based his veto of May 4, 1822, and a subsequent State Paper embodying his philosophy of internal improvements on many of Madison's premises.

The Cumberland Road Bill, of House origin, caused much speculation as to how President Monroe would treat it. The *National Intelligencer* was optimistic and gave full coverage to the President's revival of appropriations for various projects, notably Dauphine Island and Mobile Point. The paper was pleased over this action and believed it indicated Monroe's favorable inclination toward internal improvements.[45] The paper, in its conjectures on whether or not the President would approve the Cumberland bill, was concerned about the section authorizing tolls.[46]

Although he approved the Cumberland project, Monroe claimed that if Congress appropriated for one road, the same would have to be done for all roads, present and future.[47] This would inaugurate a system of internal improvements not sanctioned by the Constitution. Moreover, by authorizing tolls, the Congress would be encroaching upon the police power of the states. Even if the states desired such an action, it was still unconstitutional because a state could not extend the power of Congress unless specifically given the right by the Constitution.

If the power to establish an internal improvement program existed, said Monroe, it must be specific or incident to a specific power. Proponents of the program claimed that its justification arose from several powers possessed by Congress: to build post offices and post roads; to declare war; to regulate commerce; to pay debts and provide for the common defense and general welfare; to make needful rules and regulations for the territories and property of the United States, and to pass all laws necessary for implementing the enumerated powers. Monroe's judgment was that internal improvements could not be derived from any of these powers, "nor from all of them united." He suggested on this and other occasions a constitutional amendment which would specifically deal with the question of internal improvements.

The theme of the State Paper accompanying the presidential veto was that the Constitution never suspended the functions of state government. For the national government to extend tolls in the states would, therefore, be unconstitutional. The President stated that there were two separate and independent governments established by the Constitution—one for local purposes over each state by the people of the state, and one for national purposes over all the states by the people of the United States.[48] The powers of these two governments must be kept distinct.

Although respecting the consistency of Monroe's expressed opinions, and believing he would have approved the Cumberland Bill but for the toll feature, the *National Intelligencer* defended the erection of tolls by saying that they would be analogous to giving powers to states for collecting tonnage rates on vessels coming into harbors—an activity of long standing.[49] The paper ended its remarks on the Cumberland Bill by arguing that the power of internal improvements was inherent in the federal government and was independent of the will of the several states. It promised to endorse future internal improvement programs and hoped that Monroe's action would not be too detrimental to the system.[50]

The veto was upheld in the House by a vote of 68 to 72. The New England areas were divided on the President's action. New York, anxious to protect her Erie Canal, approved of the veto, as did most of the Southern States.[51] The Western areas, however, sharply criticized the veto. They thought the recent presidential actions inconsistent: first, Monroe stretched the Constitution to acquire Florida, then he interpreted it narrowly on the internal improvements question.[52]

By the time Monroe left office, the use of the veto was fairly well established. It had been used ten times: twice by Washington, seven times by Madison, and once by Monroe. A pattern was now beginning to appear which showed that Presidents would use the power to prevent a situation which they believed inimical to the best interests of the country. No consistency was apparent in the use of the veto, both constitutionalism and various forms of expediency having been cited by Presidents.

The growth of the veto under Madison made the way smoother for the creation of a strong executive department. After the term of John Quincy Adams, who represented the National Republican Party and those favoring governmental appropriations for internal improvements, conditions were ripe for a President to demonstrate the prestige that had been given the veto by James Madison. It took Andrew Jackson, a President who felt he had sufficient popular support, to bring the veto into national prominence.

☆ **II** ☆

Internal Improvement Vetoes:
Andrew Jackson

PRESIDENT Jackson's bank veto has received so much attention that his internal improvement vetoes have been relatively neglected. The most quoted books on the Jacksonian period either omit or deal only briefly with the internal improvement vetoes. The present chapter, then, attempts to place Jackson's internal improvement vetoes in their proper historical perspective.

Jackson generally followed the thinking of Madison and Monroe on internal improvement vetoes. He constantly expressed his approval of internal improvements but, as did his predecessors, felt that Congress did not have constitutional authorization to allocate money for projects which were not national in scope. What was and was not national was continually debated between the President and certain members of Congress. Like Madison and Monroe, Jackson suggested a constitutional amendment to allow a uniform system of national internal improvements.

During his administration, however, Jackson accepted more internal improvement bills than he rejected. Some of those which he approved had no more to do with national affairs than did the Maysville Bill, to which he applied a stinging veto.[1] Indeed, just three days after the Maysville veto, Jackson approved bills which appropriated over $150,000 for surveys and for an extension of the Cumberland Road.[2] Why, then, did he veto the Maysville bill? A brief discussion of its provisions may be useful.

The formal title was an act "authorizing a subscription of stock [$150,000] in the Maysville, Washington, Paris, and Lexington Turnpike Road Company." The company was a Kentucky corporation, authorized by the legislature of that state to build a section of road which would ultimately make a junction with the Cumberland Road at Zanesville, Ohio, and would extend to the Tennessee River at Florence, Alabama.[3] Proponents of the bill therefore thought that it was national in scope since its object was, ostensibly, to help connect two major transportation systems. When Robert Letcher of Kentucky introduced the bill in the House of Representatives, he called it a "minor bill," one that could be

15

passed in a short time. He saw no chance for great controversies to arise from it.[4] The bill, however, was debatable. Representative Thomas F. Foster of Georgia was surprised that Letcher thought it uncontroversial and said that if the Maysville Road could be termed national, any road in the country would likewise qualify.[5] It took three days for the House to pass the bill by a vote of 102 to 86.[6]

In his veto of the Maysville Bill, Jackson sought to justify his actions by arguing on the basis of constitutionality and national expediency, but a personal grudge against Henry Clay probably had much to do with it. The animosity between Jackson and Clay was of long standing; both were from the West and in their contests for popular favor they had become enemies. The estrangement came to a climax after the 1824 election when a supposed "bargain" transpired between Clay and J. Q. Adams, whereby the Kentuckian would support Adams for the presidency in return for appointment as Secretary of State. Between 1824 and 1828 the Jacksonians proved to much of the electorate that popular will was thwarted in 1824 because Jackson was deprived of the presidency although he obtained a majority of the popular vote.

Professor Van Deusen explained the veto as Jackson's effort to ruin the American System formulated by Clay in the framework of the National Republican Party; by the veto he would not only insult the Kentuckian but at the same time he would displease only a small number of voters.[7] This assessment is valid except that the veto was not *just* an attack against the American System, as Jackson repeatedly approved projects which could fit into such a program.

Clay himself did not believe that Jackson was the real author of the Maysville Veto. He said that if he thought the veto really expressed Jackson's internal improvement opinions "because of the unfortunate relations which have existed between us," he would make no comment on the subject.[8] There can be no doubt, however, that Jackson's bitter feeling toward Clay had much to do with the Maysville veto. Because of this, the veto had a negative character missing from most other presidential rejections.

The veto message proper, May 27, 1830, expressed regret over the differences between the Executive and the Legislature on internal improvements. But in a government based upon freedom of opinion, differences were inevitable. A way to eliminate the controversy over this question would be an amendment to "reconcile the diversity." Jackson explained that he had already suggested this in a previous message to Congress and intimated strongly that the lawmakers knew better than to present him with the Maysville proposal.[9] Because of this section of the veto Jackson was charged with acting the autocrat toward his serfs. A President could not, by advance notice, tell Congress upon what subjects it should deliberate. Congress had as much right to interpret the Constitution as had the President and therefore could not be guided by the Executive.[10] This was an opinion that would have interesting repercussions two years later when Jackson vetoed the bill to recharter the national bank.

In his Maysville message to Congress, Jackson said that the public debt must be paid before Congress could indulge in a widespread internal improvements program. The improvement bills already passed and those proposed exceeded the ability of the Treasury Department to liquidate national debts. If all the improvement bills that Congress wanted were passed, said he, the payments on the national debt would either have to be postponed or additional taxes would be necessary. Though United States taxes were lower than those in other parts of the world, Jackson felt that the American people would justly protest increased taxes for "irregular, improvident, and unequal appropriations of the public funds."[11] It was reasonable to expect that the federal government would aid internal improvements at a future date, but for the present such schemes must be deferred. From the standpoint of fiscal expediency, therefore, the Maysville bill was illogical and ill-conceived and should not become law.

Jackson drew heavily upon Madison and Monroe's opinions in the Maysville message. Madison had objected to bills which conferred only local benefits and had argued that the consent of the state in which the improvements were to be placed did not give Congress sufficient authority to provide for them. Furthermore, said Madison, internal improvements could not be justified by any of the existing powers in the Constitution; only an amendment would make them legal.

Secretary of State Van Buren, who had been instrumental in writing the Maysville rejection, began to fear that the veto would cause such a general reaction against internal improvements that items as necessary as lighthouses, fortifications, and armaments would be neglected.[12] He believed a way must be found to show the public the proper areas for governmental appropriations. He therefore began to correspond with the aged James Madison about the latter's reasons for his veto of the Bonus Bill in 1817.

Jackson claimed in the Maysville message that Madison had conceded that Congress's right to appropriate should be kept distinct from Congress's power to effect the measures for which the money was asked.[13] These conclusions were derived from Madison's implication in the 1817 veto that Congress, in providing for the national defense, was able to appropriate money to carry out the "great and most important measures of Government. . . ."[14] This was true even though Madison had denied elsewhere in his message that the national defense and general welfare clause could be used to justify a general program of internal improvements.

If Jackson's interpretation of Madison's veto were correct, Van Buren's fears were unfounded, for this would mean that Congress's power to make general appropriations was not limited although Congress had no power under the Constitution to carry into effect those programs for which money was appropriated. The power of appropriations and the power to execute them, according to Jackson's thinking, were separate and distinct. Thus the Maysville veto should not be construed as a denial to appropriate for national defense and general welfare. He believed that Madison's veto justified this line of reasoning.

When Madison read the Maysville veto, he protested immediately that Jackson had placed an improper interpretation on his 1817 disapproval. By that message, Madison denied to Congress not only the power of carrying out internal improvements but appropriating for them as well.[15] This was his general opinion in 1817, and nothing had happened in the meantime to make Madison change his mind.

Van Buren continued his efforts to interpret the Maysville veto flexibly enough to allow appropriations for necessities. In a letter from Madison, Van Buren was told that appropriations for light-houses and harbors should depend on how local or how general they were and that each work must be decided on its own merits.[16] Madison concluded by asserting that internal improvements were unconstitutional "but that, they are highly important when properly selected. . . ."[17] 'Van Buren could, therefore, get no comfort from the former President.

Jackson also referred to James Monroe's veto of the Cumberland bill to bolster his arguments for the Maysville rejection. Monroe had claimed that Congress had an unlimited power to raise money but only a discretionary power over its distribution. Any appropriations must be for national security, and only then on projects of national, rather than local, significance.[18] The history of the Cumberland Road, said Jackson, was sufficient proof of the ineffectiveness of internal improvements at their present stage. Some Congresses had appropriated money for the road, others had refused. Such a fluctuation of opinion needed to be stabilized by an amendment to the Constitution.[19] The Cumberland Road had received a total of $1,668,000 before Jackson came to power. It is interesting to note that during the remainder of Jackson's presidency after the Maysville veto, the Cumberland Road received $3,728,000.[20] Thus the President aided the inconsistency which he so fervently attacked.

Aside from using the Constitution as a base for his veto, Jackson also developed the theme that federal appropriations for the Maysville Road were inexpedient. The bill was purely local in nature, since the road was located exclusively in one state and ran only sixty miles. Even within the state local, not general, privileges were conferred. Jackson was, of course, bitterly attacked for this stand. Clay constantly referred to an earlier appropriation approved by Jackson for a stream known as Conneaut Creek. Although claiming to know something about American geography, Clay confessed that he had never heard of this stream until a bill was passed for its improvement. Investigating, he found that the creek rose in one corner of Pennsylvania and discharged into Lake Erie in a corner of Ohio. The full extent of the improvement was seven miles. Clay and his followers wanted to know, then, if Conneaut Creek was more national than the Maysville Road.[21]

According to engineering reports, in a month's time the Maysville Road was traversed by 9,400 persons, 12,800 horses, and 1,570 carts and wagons. This travel, plus its use for carrying the mail between the Atlantic and the West, assured beyond doubt the nationality of the Maysville Road,[22] but Jackson disagreed.

People who favored internal improvements, Jackson's veto continued, would not be embarrassed by an amendment which authorized the program. Lacking such an amendment and provided that the federal government could ultimately go into the internal improvement business, Jackson thought it should be done by distributing surplus money among the several states according to population. If distribution were questionable, Jackson believed that another constitutional amendment should be considered.[23]

His distribution proposal was readily attacked on the grounds that inequities would be an immediate result. At this time the West was most in need of help but if aid were to come solely on the basis of population, it would indeed be scanty. For every $34,000 received by New York under Jackson's suggestion, Missouri and Illinois would each receive $1,000 and Indiana would get $3,000. Such a scheme, then, would not only enable the larger states to "relegate to insignificance" the smaller states, but it would be unconstitutional as well because it would thrust the federal government into the field of state taxation as a collector of state revenue.[24] The Constitution prescribed that states lay and collect their own revenues.

It was not to be expected that the House of Representatives, to which the veto was returned, would unanimously approve the President's views. The members sat silently while the veto was read, and afterwards a "hurried and anxious" debate arose[25] in which, instead of debating the bill, the representatives merely discussed whether it should be reconsidered immediately or postponed. Although the main question before the House was postponement, the Speaker had difficulty in keeping the members from discussing the veto itself.

Generally speaking, the debate in the House on the Maysville veto revolved around the President himself. Members either condemned or eulogized Jackson, depending upon party affiliation and upon the section of the country they represented. There were no finely drawn interpretations of the Constitution in their comments.

Representative Henry Daniel of Kentucky opened the House remarks by saying that the veto marked the first time in history that the head of a nation had imposed his authority to stop extravagance.[26] Jackson had been elected, maintained Daniel, on the principles of reform and economy; therefore, he acted correctly in vetoing the Maysville Bill. Daniel thought that too many internal improvements would lead to logrolling tactics and to the creation of a large bureaucracy. The best course to follow, said the Representative, was to "suspend" the Maysville issue and let the people decide it at a subsequent election.

The next speaker, Henry Stanbery of Ohio, a state greatly in favor of internal improvements, was not nearly so kind in his comments. He lashed out at Jackson for the latter's claim that improvement bills already approved by Congress would overtax the Treasury. Jackson used this argument to prove that Congress was extravagant. Stanbery said that the bills in question had not yet been passed but, merely being listed as reported in the House or Senate, represented only committee opinion. The unpassed bills gave to Congress an appearance of extravagance which did not exist.[27] Jackson used the bills unfairly to substantiate his veto, according to Stanbery. This line of attack was corroborated by the *National Intelligencer*, which remarked that the unpassed bills gave no proper ground for a veto. Indeed, just after the Maysville rejection, the President signed one of those bills he had used in his argument against internal improvements.[28]

Stanbery further said that the veto was "artfully contrived" to disgrace the entire system of internal improvements. It was a "low, electioneering document," in which the hand of the "great magician," Van Buren, was visible in every line.[29] The Ohio Representative was supported in this opinion by the *Intelligencer*, which stated that Stanbery had perhaps erred in courtesy but not in fact.[30] Jackson was an open-minded person who never had occasion before to indulge in such low-handed actions. It was not he, then, but Van Buren who was the real author of the veto.

Even if extravagance did mark the House, said Stanbery, the Congress was not at fault since most of the appropriations had been requested by executive officers. Appropriations for Indian removal were cited as evidence. In closing, Stanbery ranted against opponents of internal improvements: "Sir, let them commence their denunciation—I fear no bravo, unless he carries the assassin's knife. Against every other species of attack I am prepared to defend myself."[31]

Future President James K. Polk from Tennessee spoke next, denouncing Stanbery for his "vindictive" remarks against Jackson. Polk's comments on this occasion give a fairly accurate indication of how he would treat internal improvements when he himself became President. He asserted that the broad powers claimed for internal improvements did not originate until the administration of John Quincy Adams.[32] If such a system could grow to dangerous proportions in a short time, it would be immeasurable after several years. The President could not ignore "the constant collisions, the heart-burnings, the combinations, and the certain corruption to which they [internal improvements] would tend, both in and out of Congress."[33]

Polk contended that Jackson's statesmanship grew immensely by the veto, for if the President had approved the bill which gave full scope to internal improvements, he would have created a "powerful branch of executive patronage and influence."[34] Lesser men than Jackson would have succumbed to the idea, said Polk.

The Tennessean also defended the veto power itself. He presented a brief history of the veto and said that the Constitution had generally been the base for its employment. This did not mean, however, that expediency could not be used, and he cited Washington's rejection of the Dragoon bill as an example. The veto had never been viewed with alarm, said Polk; on the contrary, it was a "necessary and wholesome" check by the Executive on the Legislature.[35]

Countering Polk, opponents of the Maysville Veto stated that it was the use rather than the existence of the veto that concerned them. The veto power should rarely be used for mere expediency.[36] There was more potential danger in an unrestricted veto power than in the ordinary course of congressional business. The President should use the majority by which a bill passed as a guideline. He should have less excuse for rejecting a bill with a large majority than one whose majority was small. Unfortunately, said the opposition, Jackson thought otherwise.[37] The only hope for internal improvements was for Jackson to change his mind or for Congress to override his vetoes. Neither possibility seemed likely.

Citizens of the West reacted quickly to the Maysville veto. Kentucky Senator George M. Bibb, who had voted against the bill, became the victim of public displeasure. At Maysville Bibb's effigy was placed in a coffin and "interred with great solemnity and profound silence in the middle of the Turnpike."[38]

Representative of Western opinion in Congress was Joseph Vance of Ohio, who said that the West must "stand or fall" on the issue of internal improvements. He defended Stanbery's remarks against the veto, declaring that Jackson had deceived people by earlier intimations that he favored an internal improvement system. The South, said Vance, had received during the past year (1829) more disbursements of the federal government than the entire region of the West. As soon as the wealth in the West deriving from emigration was exhausted, every dollar would be drained from that region unless internal improvements were implemented.

Vance's speech was in direct conflict with the opinions of some Southern editors at this time. The *Alabama Journal*, soon to become the leading Whig paper in that state, claimed that Northern and Western states deliberately sought to raise the tariff and delay payments on the public debt so they could use the surplus revenue for internal improvements. Not a cent of the surplus had been spent in the Southern states, said the *Journal*. Alabama alone had paid $3,000,000 into the national treasury since her entry into the Union in 1819 and had received nothing in return.[39] The paper praised the Maysville Veto, saying it would halt the ruinous economic policies of the North and allow the national debt to be paid. No longer would it be necessary for the South to subsidize Northern and Western internal improvement schemes.

Congressional oratory on the veto was concluded by John Bell of Tennessee who, in defending Jackson, was called to order for accusing Stanbery of assuming the manner of a blackguard and for various remarks on Jackson's voting record on internal improvements while a member of Congress.[40] William Kennon, Sr., of

Ohio, concluded that not a single opinion would be changed by all the argument, so he called the previous question. The result was 96 to 90 in favor of overriding Jackson's veto. The necessary two-thirds not being attained, the veto was upheld.[41]

The *National Intelligencer,* in an examination of the veto, believed the message was directed toward a higher tribunal than Congress. It was a declaration to the country at large that Jackson was now making war, not only on internal improvements, but on the tariff and the bank as well.[42] If federal protection of manufacturers were withdrawn, there could be no great excess of revenue. Without the excess there could be no internal improvements. So Jackson's veto was striking at the tariff quite as much as at internal improvements. This was a clear indication, said the *Intelligencer,* that Jackson wanted to destroy what he considered to be the monied interests in the country, interests which included the national bank. By indicating that he would use the veto to prevent the passage of any legislation which did not have his personal approval, Jackson destroyed all semblance of harmony between Congress and the President. The continuation of this attitude, said the opposition, would be distinguished enough from previous presidential administrations to "mark this as an era in the history of the country."[43]

The veto met with approval throughout large portions of the country. The Alabama legislature overwhelmingly passed a resolution in favor of the "firm and patriotic course pursued by Andrew Jackson . . . in opposition to the passage of the Maysville Road Bill. . . ."[44] The *National Gazette* criticized the "nullifying politicians" in South Carolina, who would not accept the veto because they wanted too much "to divide the spoils of the South."[45] A Pennsylvania letter writer, claiming to represent much of the thinking in that state, doubted that any good would come from internal improvements. A farewell dinner for the ambassador to Russia, John Randolph, at Hampton Roads, Virginia, turned into a round of toasts in favor of Jackson: "The rejection of the Maysville Road Bill—it falls upon the ear like the music of other days."[46] In Maryland the Legislature passed a set of resolutions that approved not only the Maysville veto but everything else Jackson had done. In New Hampshire similar resolutions were passed.[47]

The President's course was apparently vindicated as indicated by majority opinion in the country. The Maysville veto was thought to be representative of Jackson's future attitude on similar legislation. This was not always a valid appraisal because Jackson approved many bills that were just as debatable as the Maysville Bill. The President did invoke the language of Maysville in some of his subsequent internal improvement vetoes, but the whole question was so mercurial that no reliable definition of what was national and what was local could be given. The Maysville issue also indicated the extent in 1830 to which sectionalism had grown in the United States. For example, an analysis of the 1817 Bonus Bill shows that approximately 14 per cent of Southern congressmen favored it. The Maysville Bill, however, received less than 1 per cent of Southern support. Conversely, the Northern states accounted for 29.4 percent of the support for the Bonus Bill and roughly 30 percent for the Maysville Bill.[48] Clearly, then, internal improvements were primarily supported by the Western areas. Aligning with the West were the Northern and Eastern states, who were interested primarily in a national bank and protective tariffs. The three objectives, of course, complemented each other.

The agricultural South, however, could see potential danger if such a system were carried to its ultimate conclusion. Southern opposition to internal improvements was almost solid in 1830 because the South felt it was being called upon to contribute money to the national treasury but was getting nothing in return. When Jackson vetoed the Maysville Bill he stopped, according to Southern opinion, a dangerous trend. But to the North and the West, Jackson's veto was purely a retrogressive step.

A second internal improvement veto was handed down by Jackson on May 31, 1830, but the furor of Maysville caused it to be overlooked. The bill authorized a subscription of stock in the Washington Turnpike Road Company. It was designed to improve a road between Frederick and Rockville, Maryland, a distance of approximately 30 miles. Returning the bill to the Senate, Jackson referred that body to the provisions of the Maysville veto. The *National Intelligencer* regretted the veto, which would halt the development of the upper part of Maryland. The Senate sustained the veto by a vote of 21 to 17.

Jackson next pocketed two internal improvement bills at the close of the stormy first session of the Twenty-first Congress. He announced his intention to "retain" the bills for "further consideration." The first bill appropriated funds for building "lighthouses, light-boats, beacons, and monuments, placing buoys, and for improving harbors and directing surveys." The second authorized federal help to the Louisville and Portland Canal Company to construct a way for boats to bypass the falls of the Ohio.

The President's retention of these bills posed an intriguing question. By his action was Jackson rejecting the bills outright, or would it be constitutional for him at any time during the remainder of his presidency to sign them? And if he did, would they become law? There was no precedent for the course Jackson took on this occasion, and the *National Intelligencer* at first believed it to be a breach of the Constitution.[49]

A few days later the paper mellowed in its interpretation of the President's retention policy and admitted its probable constitutionality. On June 4 an elaborate essay was published on the veto clause. In summary it said that if a President signs a bill, there is no need to return it to the house of origin. Thus, the words "return" and "returned" should be considered in connection with a President's rejection of a bill. The essay quoted the veto clause: "If any bill shall not be returned (that is, with his objections) within ten days . . . it shall be a law in like manner as if he had." The paper wanted to know "as if he had done what?" Returned it? No! "As if he had signed it. It is the signing of a bill that consummates it."[50]

To understand the veto clause, one must read the first and last sentences together and assume that all in between is parenthetical, continued the paper. If this is done, "the adjournment of Congress, before a bill is returned by the President, has the effect simply of enlarging his authority," thereby giving him the power of rejection without considering the right of Congress to review his actions. The fate of the two bills was in the hands of the President who, as long as he had not returned them, had not actually rejected them. Until the next session the bills were "inchoate" laws. The question of whether or not they would be put into operation would probably be answered in the next session of Congress.

The retention of the bills was ample proof to Jackson's enemies that the President was striving to create a monarchy. They seized this opportunity to recommend again that some restrictions be placed on the veto power, arguing that Jackson's retention policy conformed with the ancient usage of the British executive in rejecting bills. The phrase used by the King on such occasions was: *Le Roi s'avisera* (The King will consider the matter). It was, therefore, a mild method of expressing disapproval.[51] The threat of a veto, said the *Intelligencer*, would cause Congress to go on the defensive; before any legislation was considered, the question of "what will the President say" would have to be asked. If American government fell into that condition, a calamitous state of affairs would exist. It would have the effect of changing the republican character of the government into an elective monarchy.[52]

Since the bills were not subsequently approved by Jackson, they must be viewed as ordinary pocket vetoes. He gave his reasons for disapproval at the opening of the second session of the Twenty-first Congress. The light-house bill was unnecessary since it was already the practice of the government to render navigation safe and easy. The bill called for an additional fifty-one light-house keepers, a number which Jackson thought excessive. Moreover, the light-house bill was vague in that it did not make specific appropriations. The President feared that the general nature of the bill would reduce it to one which made appropriations for purely local purposes. If it had provided appropriations for specific projects, said Jackson, the bill probably would have been approved.[53]

Governmental subscription to the Louisville and Portland Canal Company would impair the relations between state and general governments. The power that would accrue to the company from bills of subscription, Jackson said, would be dangerous "to the liberties of the people." He closed his comments on the bill by stating that the interests of the nation would be better served by "avoiding all indirect modes of [internal improvements].[54]

The pocket veto was used in the remainder of Jackson's internal improvement rejections. In his annual message to Congress of December, 1832, Jackson explained why he had kept a bill "for the improvement of certain harbors and the navigation of certain rivers." He claimed this situation was essentially the same as Maysville; therefore he could not approve the bill without denying the precepts he used in the Maysville veto.[55]

His final internal improvement veto was given in his sixth annual message to Congress on December 1, 1834. He vetoed a bill for the improvement of navigation on the Wabash River. Here, he did attempt to define more clearly his idea of what constituted a national internal improvement. Congressional expenditures should be confined to areas on waterways below ports of entry or places of delivery established by law.[56] But this interpretation would not work because Congress would continually be establishing "paper ports" to circumvent presidential requirements. In his Wabash message Jackson reiterated his former arguments that bills of this nature would destroy the line that must be held between the state and federal governments and that an amendment was essential to further an internal improvement program.

A study of Andrew Jackson's conception of internal improvements is in many ways a key to understanding his presidency. If one word would express this concept, it would be "inconsistency." Perhaps it was the very inconsistency in Jackson's administrations that made them of lasting value to American history. Jackson was a pragmatic President, one ruled by experimentation instead of by a well thought out political philosophy. Thus the term

"Jacksonian democracy," of which the internal improvement vetoes were the first example,[57] is difficult to define.

Through his internal improvement vetoes, Jackson attained a power that had been denied all previous Presidents. Never before nor for a long time afterward did a President present his opinions to the public, challenging the electorate to do something about it if it disapproved. Jackson's veto of the Maysville Bill was based in large part upon what had been said before on the subject, but in subsequent internal improvement vetoes his stand became one of unabashed boldness. The general acceptance of the Maysville veto enabled Jackson to play the intermediary between the people and a Congress bent on unequal distribution of the public treasure. His was the responsibility for judging the character of internal improvement bills, a responsibility which had been given him by the people. It was he, therefore, who set the standards of what was and what was not national. This power of choice made Jackson the strongest President up to that time.

His doctrine of retention, seen in the 1830 Light-house and the Louisville and Portland Canal vetoes, was completely new in American history. Apparently, Jackson was the only President to pronounce this doctrine of retention of bills because it does not appear in subsequent presidential vetoes. The nearest thing to it, though not a good example, was Lincoln's 1864 action on the Wade-Davis bill. In 1929, as will be noted, a Supreme Court decision was given on the subject.

Jackson also set a precedent by using pocket vetoes to disapprove internal improvement legislation. There were six internal improvement vetoes in all, four of which were pocketed. He always explained his reasons for the vetoes in his annual messages, which were directed not so much to Congress as to the people.

In conclusion, Jackson's internal improvement vetoes established a pattern that was freely used by future Presidents. Tyler, Polk, Pierce, and Buchanan had occasion during their incumbencies to quote the Old General on the role of the federal government in regard to internal improvements. Jackson did not, of course, settle the question. On the contrary, he only perpetuated the conflict between the Executive and a large part of Congress, a conflict which reflected the growth of sectionalism in the United States.

☆ III ☆

The Bank Veto: Andrew Jackson

EXECUTIVE disapproval of the Bank Rechartering Bill of 1832 remains the most celebrated veto in American history. It marked the climax of the presidential-legislative dispute which had been steadily developing since 1830. It showed the courage of Jackson in handing out a rejection whose consequences could not be foreseen. It also appeared to introduce a startling interpretation of the Constitution which could have momentous consequences if carried to its ultimate conclusions. Finally, it assured Jackson of re-election in 1832, although the Jacksonians could not be certain that this would result.

The major secondary sources on the Jackson period use the bank war as the focal point of their work. They go into detail on the background, the veto, and the subsequent deposit of government money in the "pet" banks.[1] There is then no reason for the present chapter to consider anything beyond the salient points of the veto itself and the immediate congressional reactions.

Bank President Nicholas Biddle and Senators Henry Clay and Daniel Webster attempted to recharter the institution in 1832, a presidential election year. They felt that if Jackson approved the measure he would lose support in the South, much of which opposed the bank; if he vetoed it, he would alienate the Northeastern manufacturing areas. Thus, no matter which course he took, thought the proponents of the bank, Jackson would damage his chances for re-election. The Recharter Bill was introduced in the Senate in March, 1832. The bill stipulated that the charter was to be continued for fifteen years from March 3, 1836. The bank could hold no property (except bank buildings and mortgaged property) for longer than five years, and no more than two branches would be located in any one state. The bank would pay a bonus of $2,000,000 a year to the government during the fifteen-year period. After March 3,1836, Congress could prevent the bank from issuing or keeping in circulation bills of less than $20.00. The bank's cashier would report annually all the names of the stockholders to the Secretary of the Treasury. The treasury of any state, on request, would be given the names of stockholders within the state for taxation purposes.[2]

The bill passed the Senate 28 to 20. The vote indicated the sectionalism of the country. The South and the Southwest opposed the bill; Kentucky, Illinois, and Missouri divided their votes, while the rest of the West voted for the measure. New England and the Middle Atlantic states, with the exception of New York and New Jersey, favored it.[3] It passed the House of Representatives 107-85, although not until after many members tried to kill it by continual motions of postponement.[4] When the President returned the bill to the Senate on July 10, 1832, it was reported that he had spent all July 4 preparing his veto message, and Jackson himself declared that Independence Day was a fitting occasion to determine the question of the bank.[5]

The President began this famous veto by conceding that although a national bank was convenient, some of its powers were not authorized by the Constitution and therefore it was dangerous to the liberties of the people. Jackson had urged in the past that the wrongs of the bank be eliminated, but the bill before him "had not incorporated those suggestions."[6]

Jackson claimed that the bank had acquired a monopoly of domestic exchanges. By elevating stock beyond par value, millions of dollars had fallen into the hands of a few individuals. In effect, this constituted a gratuity which had gone to both domestic and foreign stockholders. If the bank were rechartered, its stock would be increased another 25 percent, thus increasing the gratuities.[7] This "bounty" to both citizen and foreigner would have to be exacted from the American taxpaying public. Jackson believed that "if we must have such a corporation, why shouldn't the government sell out the whole stock" and give all American citizens the full market value of bank privileges.[8]

The recharter did not permit competition in buying stock. Many people had petitioned to buy but had been refused. Some had also indicated that to buy stock they would support a charter more favorable to the government than the present one. But the proposition had been ignored by the directors of the bank. It therefore appeared, said the President, that the present stockholders felt they had a "prescriptive right not only to the favor but to the bounty of the government." The President believed that if monopolies were to be given, they must not be exclusively for foreigners or small classes of American citizens. The masses must be allowed to share in the bounties of government.[9]

Proponents of the Recharter Bill argued that unless Jackson approved it, distress would result by the recall of loans. Jackson, however, felt that enough time existed for such recall. If the bank's management had been sound, said he, no hardships would result. There would be distress only if management had been poor; thus, distress would be the fault of the bank and would furnish an additional reason for destroying it.[10]

Jackson asserted that the restrictions on the bank in the Recharter Bill were ineffective, and that the old evils would be continued. For example, section four of the bill gave the state banks privileges withheld from private citizens. If a state bank, in payment of a debt to the national bank, wished to use notes from a bank other than its own, this would be a legitimate action. But if a private citizen wished to do the same, he would have to take a discount at the national bank or get his notes cashed by the initial issuer of his notes before paying his debt to the national institution. This was a boon to the state banks and "though not unjust in itself" it did not "measure out equal justice to the high and the low, the rich and the poor."[11] Section four was apparently an effort to "unite the state and the national banks and make their purpose separate from the purpose of the people."

Jackson set himself firmly against foreign influence in the bank. Under the Recharter Bill foreign stockholders would not be reported to state treasurers for taxation. Residents of states, however, would pay a tax on their stocks. In some states the tax was as high as one percent of its value. Thus, foreign stockholders would make one percent more profit from the bank than would a resident stockholder. Moreover, according to the terms of the annual bank dividend, the value of the stock to the foreigner would be from 10 to 15 percent higher than for the American citizen.[12]

The Eastern stockholders were in collusion with foreigners, according to Jackson. This combination caused great harm to the Western area of the United States. Although little stock was held in the West the Western debt to the bank was huge, about six million dollars in specie being drawn from the area in the previous two years. The Western debt was obviously "a debt to the Eastern and foreign stockholders."[13] The interest on the Western debt was drained off into the East and to foreign countries, especially England. The Recharter Bill offered no relief to the Western states; they could find no "adequate compensation for this perpetual burden on their industry and drain of their currency." Because of these inequalities, the bank was unworthy and should not be rechartered.

If passed, the Recharter Bill would place the United States in the same relationship to foreign countries in regard to the bank that the West had with the East. Since foreign stockholders were not taxed, the tendency was for stock to leave the country. This, in effect, made the United States a debtor to foreign countries. From two to five million dollars in specie left the country yearly in payments of bank dividends to foreign stockholders,[14] and if the Recharter Bill passed, additional amounts would be necessary to satisfy foreign appetites for American money.

It was true, Jackson admitted, that foreigners were excluded from membership on the Board of Directors, but this was a disadvantage. Since one-third of the stock was owned by foreigners, that amount would not be represented in bank elections. Control of the bank would "necessarily fall into the hands of a few citizen stockholders," creating a temptation to "designing men to secure . . . control in their own hands by monopolizing the remaining stock." There was a danger that a President of the bank and its directors could elect themselves indefinitely and thus manage the bank free from control or responsibility. The concentration of such power in the hands of a few might cause irreparable damage to the country's economy, as well as to its political structure, for the bank would have the ability to influence men in high places. Such a condition would "endanger the purity of our elections in times of peace and our independence during times of war.[15]

Jackson closed this part of his message by stating that if there must be a bank, it should be purely American. The stockholders should be American citizens who would support the country in times of danger. Abundant capital was available for a completely American bank as witnessed by recent attempts of several people to buy stock. Jackson conjectured that enough capital existed in America for the subscription of a $200,000,000 bank. Not only should foreign residents be prevented from participating in an American bank, but resident aliens should be treated likewise.[16]

The next section of the veto contained a most interesting opinion of the American Constitution, one that led many to believe the President's drive toward dictatorship was all but complete. The primary thesis was that "mere precedent" was a dangerous source of authority. This argument was used to counteract the claim of the pro-bank people that precedent and Supreme Court decisions had settled the constitutionality of the bank. Jackson believed that even if precedent were used as a justification for the bank, there would be as much argument against the bank as for it. In 1791 Congress had established a bank; in 1811 Congress had rejected a bank proposal; in 1815 President Madison vetoed a bank bill; and in 1816 Congress approved the present bank. As for the states, Jackson claimed they had consistently opposed a national bank by a ratio of four to one. Thus there was no precedent which, "if its authority were admitted, ought to weigh in favor" of the bank.[17]

After dealing with the question of precedents, Jackson disclaimed the authority of the Supreme Court as the final arbiter of the constitutionality of the national bank.[18] He did this to weaken the argument of those who maintained that since the Court had recognized the validity of the bank in 1819 it was constitutional. Jackson said the Court could not control the co-ordinate authorities of the American government. The Congress, the President, and the Court must "each for itself" be guided by its own opinions of the Constitution.[19] Public officers should support the Constitution as they understand it, not as that document was understood by others.

The President felt that "it is as much the duty of the House of Representatives, of the Senate, and of the President to decide upon the constitutionality of any bill or resolution which may be presented to them for passage or approval as it is of the Supreme Judges when it may be brought before them for judicial decision." The opinion of the judges had no more authority over Congress that that body did over the Court, "and on that point the President is independent of both." Jackson wrote that the authority of the Court must not control the Congress or the Executive when they acted in their legislative capacities. Past judicial interpretation must not be the guiding factor for Congress in its determination of legislation, or for the President when he considers that legislation.[20] If such judicial interpretation were permitted to weigh congressional and executive decisions on bills and resolutions, the Supreme Court would, in effect, acquire a legislative function outside the realm of the Constitution.

Jackson thus was trying to destroy the threat of a judicial veto upon executive approval in the same way many members of Congress wanted to avoid an executive veto on legislation. By the influence of past decisions and by threat of disapproval, the Court could acquire power over legislation that it was never meant to have. This was the very same argument that congressmen used in their fight against Jackson's threat to use the veto on legislation. To Jackson, it was improper for judicial precedent and influence to weigh upon the President or Congress in their consideration of bills. It was proper, however, for the President to influence bills being discussed in Congress. Of course many congressmen disagreed with this feeling, believing that the President's threat of veto should not sway congressional opinions.

Jackson based his interpretations on the grounds that legislative authority belonged to Congress and the Executive and was in no way connected with the Supreme Court. But this interpretation gave to Jackson an appearance of inconsistency and despotism. He was not necessarily claiming by this doctrine that he could choose the laws he would enforce; he had begun that before the bank veto.[21] His chief thesis in the doctrine was that the Court should not influence legislation before it was passed and approved by Congress and the President respectively.

Jackson referred specifically to the 1819 Supreme Court decision in *McCulloch vs Maryland,* and said that the Court did not decide by that action "that all the features of the bank are compatible with the Constitution." The Court had stated only that Congress possessed the power to create a national bank, that institution being an appropriate means for carrying into effect the enumerated powers of Congress. But the Court made clear, said Jackson, that it would not "inquire into the degree of necessity" of the bank, for so to do would cause the Court to tread on legislative grounds. The Court decision, then, made it the exclusive prerogative of Congress and the President to decide whether the particular features of a national bank were necessary and proper for effecting public functions. The institution of a bank, therefore, was legal, but the provisions of the present charter were unconstitutional.[22] Jackson listed a number of examples to prove his point.

First, section twenty-one of the original charter prohibited future Congresses from instituting other banks. The Recharter Bill continued this provision. Jackson felt it improper for one Congress "to barter away the rights and powers of succeeding Congresses." If Congress had the power to establish one bank, it could establish others. One Congress must not "limit the discretion of their successors." The restrictions of this provision, plus the grant of a monopoly to the bank, made the Recharter Bill unconstitutional.[23]

Jackson also believed the Recharter Bill was an attempt to amend the Constitution through an act of legislation. The Constitution states that Congress shall have exclusive right of legislation over the District of Columbia. But the Recharter Bill continued the provision of the original charter which restricted the control of Congress over banks in the capital area. For example, Congress could not increase above $6,000,000 the capital ceilings of any District of Columbia bank. This restriction on all future Congresses gave an unwarranted monopoly to bankers in the District. Congress had the power to grant monopolies in two areas only: those of patents and copyrights. To grant exclusive privileges in other areas was unconstitutional.[24]

Jackson claimed that the Constitution allowed the federal government to acquire state lands only for forts, magazines, arsenals, and dockyards. Yet, with the government being a part owner of the national bank, state lands would be taken for purposes which were unconstitutional. The bank's purpose was not public, said Jackson, but private. Apparently ignoring economic changes, Jackson pointed out that the old bank had been established at a capital of $11,000,000. The present Recharter Bill asked for a capitalization of $35,000,000. This amount was $24,000,000 more than necessary for the bank to perform public functions. The increase was therefore not for public purposes, but for private.[25] The mere fact that the bank was to pay to the government an annual bonus of $2,000,000 was a "confession" that its powers were greater than necessary. The bonus was a payment for the "exclusive privileges and benefits" of the bank.

To those who argued that the bank would be a useful means of carrying out the constitutional powers of coining money and regulating it, Jackson retorted that only Congress had that responsibility, and could not delegate it to other authorities. If the bank was rechartered, Congress would lose its power over the currency for a number of years, a period in which the Constitution would be a "dead letter."[26]

Jackson also claimed that the bank was supposedly a part of the executive branch of government, and that its constitutionality must be judged upon this basis. But the President had not been given the opportunity heretofore to say whether or not he wanted such a bank. "Whatever interest or influence," Jackson maintained, "whether public or private, has given birth to this act, it cannot be found either in the wishes or necessities of the executive department. . . ."[27] He was sharply criticized by those who said that the Secretary of the Treasury, who would be the cabinet member most affected by this opinion, was bound by the law of Congress which originated the office. For Jackson to claim that cabinet officers were exclusively under the President's jurisdiction was unconstitutional and evidence of his attempts to usurp power.[28]

In the closing section of this long and tedious veto, Jackson stated that most of the troubles that had faced the country in the past had been caused by legislative deviation from the legitimate aims of government. Many rich people, wanting more than their fair share, were not happy with equal protection under the government. Implying that he identified the bank with tariff, internal improvements, and other parts of Clay's American System, Jackson claimed the American scene was becoming one of "section against section, interest against interest, and man against man." His final sentence was a plea that the time had arrived "to review our principles and revive that spirit of compromise which distinguished the sages of the Revolution and the Fathers of our Union."[29]

Senatorial comment on the bank veto was voluminous, covering 75 pages of *Gales and Seaton's Register*. Senators Daniel Webster of Massachusetts, Thomas Ewing of Ohio, John Clayton of Delaware, and Henry Clay of Kentucky led the fight in the Senate against the veto. Hugh L. White of Tennessee and Thomas Hart Benton from Missouri defended the President's actions. The Senators addressed themselves to each of the major parts of Jackson's message.

The critics lashed out at Jackson for his statement that the stockholders had acquired an economic monopoly. Webster said there was no foundation for Jackson's remark that the stocks operated as a gratuity to their holders, since the stockholders had not obtained the charter gratuitously, but by a considerable investment of money. The Recharter Bill was not motivated by a desire to give additional bounties to stockholders, but to promote public interests. According to Webster, it would be impossible to charter a bank that did not give profits to its stockholders. When Jackson spoke of a stockholder's monopoly and stated that all monopolies are granted at the expense of the public, he was talking from mere assumption and not from a factual basis.[30]

Senator White refuted Webster by claiming that the foreign stockholders and the few American citizens who were stockholders created a danger to the American government, especially in times of war. The bank should be the mainstay of government during a conflict. Yet there was nothing in the charter which compelled the bank to make loans to the government. White alluded to the War of 1812, showing how New Englanders, with whom the war had been unpopular, had tied up the economy in a time of distress. Since New Englanders now had control of the bank, one might expect them to operate it according to their own financial concerns, even if this meant disregarding the needs of the government. Moreover, the bank's potential power was so great that it could conceivably acquire an influence stronger than the government itself. Such an eventuality was to be studiously avoided.[31]

Webster, in opposition to White, commented at length upon the disadvantages the bank would suffer by having to close operations within a three year period. The debt to the bank was $30,000,000 and he maintained that three years were not long enough to liquidate this amount. Moreover, the circulating medium would be withdrawn if the bank expired. Thus there existed the unusual situation of having to call in millions of dollars of debts and at the same time withdraw the circulating medium.[32]

This argument was attacked by White, who said that the bank charter had almost four years to go and an additional two years in which to collect its debts. This doubled the amount of time that Webster claimed was available for collection of debts. If the contracts made by the bank were legitimate, there was no cause for concern in collecting money owed to it. White, concerned that the bank had allowed debts to become so numerous in fifteen years, asked what the state of things would be at the end of thirty-five years. He felt that the debts could not be regarded as a reason for continuing the bank's charter.[33]

Senator Ewing did not agree. The time for closing the bank, he said, depended on many variables such as the number of loans in existence and the pressure of business throughout the country. Jackson's veto assumed that only the wealthy owed money to the bank. This was not true, said Ewing, because many Western farmers depended on the bank for economic favors, primarily in the form of loans.[34]

The Senators also criticized at length Jackson's reference to foreign stockholders. Webster held as untenable Jackson's claim that states could not tax the foreign stockholder. He said the stock was no more valuable to the foreigner than to the citizen except that capital was more abundant in Europe; thus foreigners had greater opportunity to invest in national bank stock than Americans. The foreigner was not exempt from taxation on the stocks; his own government saw to that. The veto, then, was most injurious to the American image abroad. It manifested a jealousy and a disposition of disrespect regarding the property of foreigners "invited hither by our own laws."[35]

The influence of the foreigners was negligible, Webster said, because they could never be directors nor have a voice in the selection of directors. Their money was controlled by managers who were appointed by the President, the Senate, and the American stockholders. Webster felt that "so far as there is dependence, or influence, either way, it is to the disadvantage of the foreign stockholder."[36] The national bank had operated for twenty-six of the forty-three years that the American government had been in existence. During this time, foreigners had held stock in the bank and there had never been any "danger to liberty," any "introduction of foreign influence," or "any accumulation of irresponsible power in a few hands."[37] To those who argued that foreign stockholders presented a special danger in war time,

Webster said the bank had always been advantageous during conflicts. Through the bank, the federal government could control the funds of those stockholders who might be enemy subjects, thereby preventing the money from being used against the United States.[38]

Senator White said that while it was true that the foreigner had no voice in the selection of directors, he could still exert influence in the regulation of exchanges between the bank and his country in a manner favorable to the bank. Increasing the profits for the foreign stockholder would injure the American citizen. The Baring family of England, for example, owned over a million stocks, and White could not see how this amount of ownership would fail to influence the policies of the bank. He repeated Jackson's argument that since the states could not tax the branches of the bank, the profit to the foreigner would be unduly increased.[39]

Clay, speaking of this aspect of the veto, followed closely the line of argument established by Webster. The mere fact that so many foreigners bought stock in the national bank proved the institution's stability. Clay refuted White's reference to the potential dangers of foreigners holding stock during a time of war. The Kentuckian maintained that some of the distresses experienced by the United States during the war of 1812 could have been avoided if a national bank had been operating. He made no reference, however, to Madison's veto of the bank in 1815.[40]

Senators Webster and Ewing also attacked that part of the veto which claimed that the bank did not distribute its favors to the rich and poor alike. Webster maintained that any privileges resulting from the recharter were incidental to the efficient operation of the bank. The Massachusetts Senator turned the tables on Jackson, by saying that the veto, rather than the Recharter Bill, was designed as a class measure. The veto sought to influence the poor against the rich because it "wantonly attacks whole classes of people, for the purpose of turning against them the prejudices and resentments of the classes." It was Webster's opinion that if the veto was sustained, the Constitution would not last to its fiftieth year.[41] Ewing agreed with Webster that the veto would sap the prosperity of the people, create a host of banks with fictitious capital, and make necessary legislative aid to a distraught public.[42]

The President was attacked for his insistence that the West was damaged by the bank. The interest rate on loans in the West, said Webster, was two percent lower than the actual value of money in that region. The bank veto would, therefore, adversely affect the West. It would "depreciate the value of western property;" it would lower the prices of land, crops, and labor; it would repress enterprise and embarrass business and occupations. The West was wealthy in land, products, and enterprise. All of its great potential would be damaged, if not destroyed, by the President's action.[43]

Senator Ewing continued Webster's argument, averring that the New England areas could do without a national bank, but the Western areas could not. The residents of Ohio, Kentucky, Indiana, Illinois, and Missouri had gained what wealth they had through small savings, industry, and enterprise. The very wilderness in which these people lived precluded the accumulation of large amounts of capital. The bank was necessary, therefore, to sustain the Western farmers.[44]

Ewing rejected White's thesis that no hardship would come to the West by closing the bank. White argued that state bank notes could be substituted for national bank notes and that these would sustain the Western farmers. Ewing noted, however, the dependence of state institutions upon the national bank, and said the destruction of the national bank would lessen the financial stability of the state banks. The notes of the state banks would have to be used to pay states' debts to the national bank. Thus, the states would lose specie and could not help the Western areas.

Clayton agreed with Webster and Ewing on the effect of the bank's withdrawal from the West. He stated his opinion that the bank's demise would cause distress, not only in the West, but throughout the entire country. That capital of the bank belonging to foreigners, $8,500,000, would be drawn away to European countries. Another $7,000,000 would go to the United States government, not to be loaned again, but to be used according to the whims of the President. Without national bank notes, the farmers would have to take discounted state notes for their produce. The use of state bank notes would inevitably lead to the depreciation of paper money, thus levying an unintentional tax on all people using merchandise. The consequences, said Clayton, would be devastating to the country's economy.[45]

But the words of Webster, Ewing, Clayton, and Clay seemed to be refuted by the reaction from the West. On the whole, said the *National Intelligencer*, the veto was met with approval in that region. Those who sincerely approved of the veto were precisely the ones who could not be damaged by the change in currency which would result from the destruction of the bank. Those in the West who did need banks seemed to be intrigued by Jackson's idea of a bank without property, debts, or credits, with the

President at its head. This would at least offer the West something new.[46]

It was to be expected that the Senators would dwell at length upon Jackson's interpretation of the Constitution expressed within the veto. Webster said that the President's constitutional reasoning was extraordinary, past events having shown without a doubt that the bank was constitutional. Many members who had voted against the bank in 1811 did so on grounds of expediency rather than constitutionality. It could not be stated with certainty, as Jackson claimed, that a majority of Congress in 1811 thought the bank unconstitutional. Furthermore, in 1815 Congress had not decided against a bank, although this was implied by Jackson. The bank bill in 1815 had passed the House of Representatives by the wide margin of 120 to 39. Thus, the 1815 bank bill provided a precedent for the constitutionality of the bank.[47]

Legislative precedents, said Webster, had been the law of the land for almost forty years, but the President rejected all precedents except those suitable to his own purposes. Jackson's interpretation that each department had the right to judge the Constitution was inconsistent with good government. Free government required that the final constitutional decisions rest with the Judiciary, but Jackson was, apparently, trying to change that concept.[48]

When a bill passed Congress and was approved by the President, Webster continued, neither the President nor his successors had the power to pass constitutional judgment on it. The President, therefore, had no right to nullify one bill and enforce another according to his pleasures. This was the policy that Jackson seemed to adopt. By doing this, Jackson thought he could lay aside the law of 1816 which had chartered the national bank and the Supreme Court decision which had sustained it.

Webster did not mention Jackson's qualifying statements in this section of the veto. Jackson had stated that the Court had no constitutional authority over Congress or the President when *they were acting in their legislative capacities*.[49] Also, Jackson had not denied the validity of the Supreme Court's decision that a national bank was constitutional. The institution itself was legitimate, but the form that it took depended upon Congress and the President. Jackson did not think the form of the bank as presented in the Recharter Bill was constitutional. He took care in his veto to show that the Court, in *McCulloch vs Maryland*, had expressed its desire not to tread on legislative grounds.

Webster believed that it was the constitutional power of Congress to pass a bill without executive interference. Jackson, however, felt that the President possessed an important legislative power and therefore could review bills before they were sent to him. This thesis was defended by Senator White, who said it had never been unusual for a President to see proposed legislation in draft form and to make recommendations upon it. In determining constitutional questions, the President was not bound by any influence of past judicial decisions on simliar subjects. Moreover, said White, a court decision was not necessarily the ultimate word on a given subject. It was possible for both Congress and the Supreme Court to err in determining the constitutionality of a measure. Unless the President checked the error, serious consequences could result.[50] If the Constitution did not give Congress the right to a certain power (and Jackson believed it did not in the Recharter bill), a prior court decision could not change its unconstitutional basis. Jackson was, therefore, checking the errors that had been made in 1816 and 1819. In doing so, he was at variance with James Madison's prescriptive process. Jackson's view meant, in effect, that if something were unconstitutional at one time, it would be unconstitutional at another unless in the meantime the Constitution had been changed to make it legal. Madison had argued, of course, that even if something were outside the realm of the Constitution, its usage over a long period of time made it legal.[51]

Jackson's doctrine brought forth tremendous cries of protest. Senator Clayton exclaimed angrily that when the Senate had wished to find presidential reasons for removals from offices, that body had been told to mind its own affairs. The Senate should now tell the President the same thing on the bank question.[52] Clay accused Jackson of wishing to practice executive initiative in legislation similar to the Old Regime of France. The veto, in Clay's opinion, created an executive nullification process that was just as deplorable as the nullifiers in South Carolina. Clay expressed his concern over the growth of a presidential dictatorship.[53]

Commenting on the President's assertion that the Recharter Bill was unconstitutional, Webster said that in the veto Jackson himself showed an insincerity toward the Constitution. Section 21 of the bill, prohibiting future Congresses from chartering other banks while the present one existed, was legitimate according to Webster. If the President were right in his observation that one Congress could not legislate for future Congresses, the lawmakers would be deprived of their right of contract: each Congress could bind its successors to the same extent that it could bind itself.[54] Moreover, Jackson's suggested bank, to be attached to the Treasury Department, might be declared invalid by a future President using the same reasoning with which Jackson was trying to destroy the national bank.[55]

Clay corroborated many of Webster's statements, and said that it was the President rather than Congress who was acting unconstitutionally. Jackson violated the Constitution by his excessive use of the veto, a device which he used so much that Congress was on the defensive, ignoring some bills because the Legislature feared presidential disapproval. A veto should be used only to "check the precipitancy" of Congress against the President, maintained Clay. In reality the veto power was a feature of monarchial governments, but even in England, where the "royal prerogative" was absolute, the veto had not been used for over a century. In France and in several states, Kentucky being an example, a majority of the Legislature could destroy an executive veto. The same rule should also apply in the national government, thought Clay, for one man's opinion ought not to be superior to the collective will of the lawmakers.[56]

At the conclusion of Clay's remarks Benton gained the floor, but because of a previous order to recess, he had to relinquish it after a short time. The next day, July 13, Benton was the first speaker on the bank veto. He joined White in a defense of the presidential message. He accused the supporters of the bill, especially Clay, of being discourteous, "indecorous, and disrespectful to the Chief Magistrate."[57]

Clay defended himself at once against these remarks. He said he could not, at this period of his life, allow Benton to teach him the rules and practices of politeness. Even if he could, he would not "know to which of the opposite opinions, he [Benton] at different periods has entertained of the President," he [Clay] ought to conform.[58] (Here, Clay alluded to the time when Jackson and Benton were enemies. Benton answered that it was true the two had fought, but he hoped they had fought as men. When the contest was over, so was the enmity, and Jackson and Benton had been fast friends ever since.)

The Chair, occupied by Senator Littleton Tazewell, interrupted Clay and said the debate between Clay and Benton could no longer be endured; Clay must take his seat. When Clay wanted to explain his position, Tazewell peremptorily told him that no further explanations would be heard; that he was out of order in the language he had used toward Benton. Clay countered by charging the Missouri Senator with intemperate language. Tazewell said he had not occupied the Chair when the debate arose, so he could make no ruling on Benton's performance. George M. Poindexter of Mississippi had been presiding when Benton first made his remarks. Poindexter arose to explain but was cut short by Benton, who said that he had, in fact, been out of order, and wished to apologize to the Senate. Clay then remarked that he would also offer an apology to the Senate, but "for the Senator from Missouri I have none." Poindexter again tried to explain the nature of Benton's remarks, only to have his voice drowned out in a call of Question! Question!"[59]

The vote taken on the President's veto was 22 to 19. The necessary two-thirds majority to override the veto not being obtained, the President's action was upheld. Thus, the long and bitter congressional fight over the veto was brought to a close.

The *National Intelligencer*, the chief critic of Jackson's policies, felt with Clay, Webster, and other supporters of the bank that the veto would harm Jackson's chances for re-election. It applauded the distribution of thousands of copies of the veto message, hoping to prove to the country how hopelessly ignorant Jackson was of financial and constitutional matters. It reported mass meetings throughout the country which occurred in opposition to Jackson's move. A Pennsylvania meeting, for example, resolved that Jackson had demonstrated utter contempt for that state's support of him in the 1828 campaign. Jackson should be more grateful than to destroy the state's means of obtaining necessary capital.[60] The paper believed that these protests were indicative of how the vote would go in the 1832 presidential election. As late as August 13 the editor wrote that the bank veto made it highly improbable that Jackson would be re-elected.[61] The paper erred completely, however, for Jackson was re-elected by a very comfortable majority.[62] He took his margin of victory to mean that the people wanted him to destroy the bank. After his second inauguration, he began to distribute federal money into the "pet" banks throughout the country, a scheme that provided another interesting and important chapter in the bank war.

It is difficult to draw concrete conclusions about Jackson's bank veto. He tried to use the Constitution as a basis for the veto, but he usually invoked it as an excuse rather than a reason, since he interpreted the Constitution to fit his own conclusions about the functions of government. On the surface it appears that Jackson, or his writers at least, was a great expositor of the Constitution. Internally, though, the major reason for his veto was that of political expediency; the Constitution was used as a mask.

The bank, along with the tariff and internal improvements, was a part of the American System, and against this program Jackson had steadfastly set himself. The President felt that the bank, as it was proposed in 1832, would foster sectionalism in addition to favoring a few stockholders to the exclusion of the masses. This aggrandizement of the few against the many was comparable to the local *versus* national argument seen in the Maysville issue. The bank, therefore, must be national and not for just a small group of people.[63]

The bank veto cannot be regarded as a positive example of executive action. It left no room for compromise between the President and Congress. It closed the executive door, so to speak, on further attempts at rechartering a national bank as long as Jackson was President, something that none of the other vetoes, including the Maysville rejection of 1830, had done. Jackson once more regarded himself as having the ultimate responsibility to say whether or not the national bank would continue its operations. In carrying out that responsibility, it was convenient to charge that the bank was unconstitutional, monopolistic, and dangerous to the liberties of the people. He used this argument though it brought into question his abilities in dealing with financial and constitutional matters. But to the people at large, and especially to those in the low economic groups who voted for the first time in 1832, Jackson's word was infallible. Largely because of this veto, Jackson was re-elected for another four years.

☆ IV ☆

Miscellaneous Vetoes: Andrew Jackson

THE most controversial of President Jackson's vetoes have now been considered. Five vetoes in the miscellaneous category, although not as well known as those on internal improvements and the Recharter Bill, contain some provocative material. Three of these vetoes dealt with financial affairs; the other two with the relationship between the President and Congress.

The first was a pocket veto on a Senate bill "for the final settlement of claims of States for interests on advances to the United States" in the War of 1812. Its object was to pay interest to those states which had advanced money and supplies to the militia during the war.[1] Ezekial Chambers of Maryland was the sponsor of this legislation.

Chambers felt that interest should be allowed on the advances in state money and supplies as if they had been made completely in money instead of material. Maryland, for example, had sold some of its six percent stock to enable it to provide for the militia. This was essentially the same as borrowing the money at six percent, and that should be the interest paid to Maryland by the federal government.[2] Georgia's Senator John Forsyth was interested in the bill too. He said that his state had furnished material to an army contractor during the war and had never collected either the principal of the debt or the interest from the national government. He felt that Georgia should qualify for remuneration under the Chambers bill.[3]

The types of allowable claims against the government were argued throughout the congressional session. It was difficult to determine whether to claim the interest only on debts whose principals were already paid, or on all debts to the states regardless of the status of the principal amounts. The Senate passed the bill on January 5, 1832. It was discussed in the House until July 14 and was finally presented to the President essentially in the same form prescribed earlier by Chambers. Since it was within the ten day period before Congress adjourned, President Jackson pocketed

45

it. He gave his reasons in his annual message to Congress on December 6, 1832.

In his short veto message the President admitted that he had not studied the bill closely because it had been presented to him during the last four days of the congressional session "when other matters weighed heavily." The allowance of interest outlined in the bill was at variance, said Jackson, with established practices. For one thing, the bill made no specific appropriations for the states claiming interest against the federal government. It was, therefore, incomplete.

In the past, Jackson said, the United States had always paid the principal amounts to the states without respect to interest. Periodic deductions in the principals had lessened the interest that would ultimately be paid. The bill before him though sought to change this practice by not allowing amounts of declining interest over a space of years.

Jackson claimed that a law passed on August 3, 1790, and another of February 12, 1793, paid the revolutionary debts to the states by periodic deductions of the principal amounts, saving the government much money in paying the interest.[4] Chamber's bill extended the practice of allowing interest upon accounts with the government, thus requiring larger payments from the Treasury Department. No good reason existed for the change, so Jackson, although admitting that he was not too familiar with the bill, thought it best to kill it. There was little congressional comment on the veto. By this time, of course, many people considered a veto from Jackson as mere commonplace and refused to comment. Discussion on the veto ended when it was reported that another bill dealing with state interest claims would be introduced.

This veto can be viewed as an example of Jackson's inconsistency. The principles espoused by Jackson were predominantly nationalistic, seeking to prevent the states from taking advantage of the federal government. In other vetoes, the one on land, for example, he claimed that the rights of certain states must be protected against federal encroachments. It is impossible, then, to tell whether Jackson was a nationalist or a states-rightist, for at different times in his career he leaned both ways. At least, he was upholding a principle of established procedure in the Interest Claim veto, something quite different from his other rejections, many of which had resulted from personal bias. This veto was, therefore, a positive action coming from President Jackson. Much the same can be claimed for the next veto—also a pocket veto. It dealt with the proceeds of land sales and was introduced into the Senate by Henry Clay.

Many people, including the President, had talked previously about distributing among the states the proceeds from the sales of public lands. It will be recalled that Jackson's feelings along these lines were included in his Maysville veto of 1830. Differences of opinion existed, though, on methods of distribution. Jackson thought money should be allocated according to the population in each of the states. He had been criticized for this view because it would enable states already self-sufficient to get most of the federal money while states actually needing it would go without.

Section one of Clay's bill provided that after December 31, 1832, Ohio, Indiana, Illinois, Alabama, Missouri, Mississippi, and Louisiana would receive an additional 12½ percent from the sales of public land. These states were to receive the increase only from those lands sold within their borders after the above mentioned date. The money was to be spent on internal improvements and education projects to be supervised by the state Legislatures.[5] This was the section which disturbed Jackson most and he dwelled upon it throughout the veto

He began his message, given to Congress on December 4, 1833, with a history of the cession of Western lands to the federal government. He mentioned that Maryland, New York, Virginia, North Carolina, and Georgia, when ceding their Western properties, had stipulated that the lands be for the common benefit of the American people.[6] The proceeds from their sale, therefore, had been placed in the treasury and were used, among other things, to liquidate the national debt. The states had benefitted from this policy because it reduced their responsibility for payment of the national debt. Although the debt was now virtually extinguished, the government was still obligated under the original compacts to dispose of the lands in an equitable manner.[7] The practice of the government in the past had not been to separate the land sales funds from the rest of the treasury. If Clay's bill passed, the 12½ percent, or roughly $3,000,000, would be separated from ordinary revenues.

In addition to the 12½ percent increase, the states named in Clay's bill would also receive the ordinary apportionments according to the ratio of general distribution. Jackson believed that this condition would violate constitutional pledges that "nothing in this Constitution shall be so construed as to prejudice any claims of the United States or of any particular State."[8] The cessions of the Western lands were older than the Constitution and they must be honored. Clay's bill would abrogate the conditions by which some states entered the Union (that is, that by doing so and by ceding their Western holdings, the land would be forever

used for the common benefit of all the people). According to
Jackson, the Constitution did not give Congress the right to
abrogate compacts, only the responsibility to carry them into
effect.[9] Ironically, this opinion caused Jackson to be in agreement
for once with his old antagonist, John Marshall, who had given a
similar judgment concerning state legislatures in the 1819 case of
Trustees of Dartmouth College vs Woodward.

A most interesting part of the veto dealt with a repetition of
Jackson's earlier statements on internal improvements. If Clay's
bill were to become law, Jackson maintained, it would be an in-
fraction of the Maysville veto; that is, it would apply federal
funds to purely local projects. Jackson found irresistible the statement that he could "not be mistaken in supposing" that the Maysville veto "has received the unequivocal sanction of the American
people."[10] Jackson lectured the Senate on a point that had been
utilized earlier by James Monroe in his veto of the Cumberland
Road bill in 1822. If federal money could not be allowed for local
internal improvements, it could not be legalized by passing the
responsibility for implementing these improvements to the states.
The attempt by Congress to enact such an implementation in the
form of tolls in 1822 had provided the major reason for Monroe's
veto of the Cumberland bill. Jackson felt that if such a relation
ever existed between federal and state governments, the federal
government might as well pay the salaries of the state officials.
He concluded this "sectionalistic" part of the veto by claiming,
as had Monroe, that it was unwise and unsafe to abridge the power
of local assemblies in their taxing responsibilities. Clay's bill would
do this, in Jackson's opinion.[11]

Clay's bill was not only unjust and unconstitutional, believed
Jackson; it was financially inexpedient as well. Its object was not
to return to the people a surplus from the sale of land, but to
create a surplus for distribution among certain states. The bill
proposed to take at least $3,000,000 from the general treasury, an
amount which could be increased by a future Congress. Thus
there was a danger that by this bill the states would become entirely dependent on the federal government. The extra money
allocated to the states in Clay's bill would have to be collected
from other sources. This meant that the old states would continue
receiving the same amount of funds, but they would have to
pay larger amounts than before to make up the $3,000,000 de-
ficiency in revenue created by Clay's bill. The bill would represent a loss to the old states in a ratio of 8 to 7. For every $7.00
received by the old states under Clay's distribution, the people of
those states would have to pay $8.00 to the federal government.[12]

This was a scheme of inequitable distribution, according to Jackson, one that set the old states against the new ones. The bill could not be approved by the President, then, for the sectionalism that would result would be untenable.

In the final passages of the veto, Jackson pointed out that the true interest of the new states was in the development of their land. They needed to reduce the price of land as quickly as possible to attract settlers. Long range development on the state's own initiative would be superior to receiving special favors from the government. Clay's bill would ruin the development that had already taken place in the Western states and would make impossible any further development.[13]

Senator Clay reacted angrily to the veto. He said that the bill was for a limited time only, five years, and even if it lent itself to the dangers which the President supposed, the time was too short for it to cause irretrievable damage. The fact, however, that the bill was limited to five years provided one of the reasons why Jackson vetoed it. The President felt that a permanent system for dealing with the land problem should be developed and that Clay's bill would only add difficulties to an already complex question.[14] Clay expressed bitterness over the President's retention of the bill because of the shortness of the congressional session. Withholding the bill was unconstitutional, said Clay, and disrespectful of the Senate. He wondered how Jackson, who claimed that he did not have enough time to consider the bill fully because it was presented to him on the last day of the session, found time to study all the less important bills during the closing hours of Congress. All Presidents were pressed on the last day, Clay admitted, but Jackson knew that this bill was coming because he had mentioned the distribution problem several times before.[15] He closed his speech by calling Jackson's rejection of his land bill "arbitrary and unconstitutional."

Senator Benton, who defended Jackson, moved to take up the vetoed bill. Poindexter, however, pointed out that such a reconsideration would be illegal because the Congress that "had cognizance of the bill" had gone out of existence. It would not be proper for a Congress to reconsider a bill that had been pocketed at the conclusion of a previous Congress. Debate ended with a promise from Clay that he would soon introduce another bill to deal with the proceeds from the sale of public lands.[16]

Jackson's veto of the land bill was a case of two offensives meeting. On the one hand, Clay was determined to have internal improvements and he sought to use the land bill to that end. On the other hand, Jackson was equally determined to prevent Clay's kind of internal improvements. The President very quickly saw through the facade that Clay was erecting. Jackson wanted the states to use the public lands as a means of long range development. Clay was interested in quicker development through internal improvements.

On the whole, Jackson's veto of the land bill was a positive reaction. Perhaps in the section on internal improvements he allowed himself to indulge in anti-Clay sentiments, and in so doing he created the paradox of a positive action on a premise that could be considered negative. His constitutional arguments in the veto were tenable because of the care with which he treated the history of the cessions of Western lands to the United States, and his constant emphasis upon the requirement that the lands be used for the common benefit of all citizens. His argument concerning the financial unsoundness of Clay's bill was sensible too because the bill would have created a deficit of at least $3,000,000 —one that could grow in succeeding years. Finally, Jackson forced Congress to think through, once again, the whole question regarding the disposal of the public lands. Largely because of this a distribution bill was passed in 1836 which received Jackson's sanction.

The Whigs were so distressed by Jackson's use of vetoes that a resolution was introduced in the Senate on February 20, 1835, to curb the veto power. Senator Joseph Kent from Maryland wanted a constitutional amendment allowing a simple majority instead of a two-thirds congressional vote to override a veto. His thesis was that the Founders of the Constitution intended the veto to be defensive in nature, that is, to be used only as a protective device against Congress. Jackson had used it, however, to such an extent that it tended to unify the legislative and executive branches of government. The Founders would never have sanctioned the course that Jackson had followed.[17]

The most important branch of government, continued Kent, was the legislative, since it reflected the wishes of the people better than any other body; thus, the lawmaking power must be retained by the people's representatives. Indeed, this was one reason for the American Revolution, whose generation proclaimed that the British Parliament could not control the colonies; only duly authorized representatives could do that. Revolutionary sentiment in this respect caused the Constitution to vest lawmaking power in the Senate and the House of Representatives. No President could justifiably interfere with the creation of laws except to protect himself against legislative encroachments. Kent invoked the opinions of Jefferson, who had counselled Washington on the first bank, that if a majority of Congress favored a particular procedure, "the weight of that body ought to sway the President's actions."[18] Madison had expressed his thoughts in a similar fashion, and even Hamilton had argued that the "superior weight and influence" of the legislative body satisfactorily assured that a presidential "negative would be employed with great caution."[19]

It was inevitable that Kent would compare Jackson with the King of England, since that practice was so much in the vogue. The King had a deep personal interest in the English government, which had been passed to him through generations. His veto was supposedly absolute and ostensibly he would be compelled to use the power quite often to maintain tradition. Yet, the King of England had not vetoed a bill in over a century. On the other hand, Jackson's tenure of office was only four years; he had no traditions to uphold, no hereditary titles to maintain; he would soon become an ordinary citizen again; and yet he used the veto repeatedly.[20]

Kent's amendment would have made the President an advisor on bills rather than a judge. The Executive, he said, could aid Congress in shedding new light on legislative proposals. The more often a bill was examined, the less were the chances for error. The President, then, should act only in a recommending capacity, without the ability to thwart the will of Congress by a veto that required two-thirds to override it. There was more danger in executive supremacy than in legislative aggrandizement, said Kent, and he gave numerous historical references to prove his point. He asked: "Was it Pericles or the Areopagus that subverted government in Athens? Was it Caesar or the Senate that destroyed the liberty of Rome? Was it Cromwell or the Parliament that destroyed democratic government in England?"[21] These incidents indicated that it was the inevitable tendency in every country throughout history for the Executive to try to gain unwarranted power. The same course was being followed in America by President Jackson, and for the sake of governmental stability, the Congress had a solemn duty to pronounce its disfavor.

He accused the President of distributing his vetoes among the various sections to get the most political good from them. The veto of the public land bill pleased certain states, the internal improvement vetoes gratified the South, the bank veto satisfied still other sections of the country. Thus, the veto was used to win a majority for the President in each of the sections, "but neither would be entirely satisfied with what so much pleased the other." Through subterfuge and a lust for power, then, the President had used the veto. The Executive had always been the "bane of liberty," said Kent, so the people must curtail the veto or prepare for subjugation.[22]

Senator Clay complimented Kent at the conclusion of the latter's resolution. The Kentuckian agreed wholeheartedly with the sentiments expressed therein, but the lateness of the congressional session would not allow the subject to be considered with the determination that it deserved. Clay moved to lay the resolution on the table and to call it up again at a more propitious moment. The motion carried.[23]

Undaunted by this resolution and by other similar expressions, Jackson continued to employ the veto whenever he felt the occasion called for it. Indeed, the next veto occurred just days after Kent's resolution. A short one, it dealt with the power relationship between the executive and legislative branches. The veto was returned to the Senate on March 3, 1835, rejecting an act to "compromise the claims . . . under the treaty with the King of the two Sicilies, concluded on October 14, 1832." The treaty made with the King of the Two Sicilies provided that he would pay indemnities to American merchants whose vessels had been destroyed by the Sicilies in 1809, 1811, and 1812.[24] The claims were not fulfilled rapidly, and in December, 1834, certain claimants indicated that they would take an immediate settlement at reduced rates. A bill to that effect was passed by Congress early in the following year.

Jackson stated that the act was inconsistent with the powers of the Constitution. It was founded on the assumption that Congress could give power of negotiation to the Executive. The debt owed by the King of the Two Sicilies was the private vested property of the American claimants. Neither the Executive nor the Legislature could interfere with those claims without the consent of the claimants. If the claimants assented to have their rights with the Two Sicilies further negotiated, it would come within the realm of the executive department. Congress could not constitutionally abridge, stipulate, or increase the negotiating power of the President. Foreign policy belonged to his branch of the government and could not be initiated by Congress.[25] Upon its return to the Senate, the veto message was simply read and laid on the table.

The next veto, June 9, 1836, was similar to the one just discussed in that it dealt with power relationships between the Executive and the Legislature. The act, "to appoint a day for the annual meeting of Congress," was also returned to the Senate. The President did not doubt Congress's authority to set a day to convene, but the last part of the act stipulated that the second

Monday in May after the start of the first session would become
the date of adjournment for this and all future Congresses.[26]
This provision of the bill was not in accord with the Constitution,
Jackson said. He quoted Article 1, Section 5, which stated that
"neither House, during the session of Congress, shall, without the
consent of the other, adjourn for more than three days . . ."[27]
Also, Article 2, Section 3 of the Constitution states that ". . . in
case of disagreement between them [the houses of Congress]
with respect to the time of adjournment he [the President] may
adjourn them to such time as he shall think proper."[28] The Constitution, then, did not intend for one Congress to act upon the
adjournment date of succeeding Congresses. In providing rules
for adjournment, the Constitution had placed the question beyond
the realm of legislative inquiry, because to fix a date for adjournment of all future Congresses would take away the power of the
President to settle anticipated disagreements on adjournment dates.
The bill was, therefore, outside the Constitution and could not be
approved.

When the bill was reconsidered in the Senate, Senators Clay,
Webster, Calhoun, Clayton, and Robert Goldsborough from
Maryland favored passing it despite the President's objections.
Goldsborough claimed that the section of the bill found most objectionable by Jackson referred only to the temporary adjournment of Congress pending an adjournment of the session. Jackson's
critics agreed that one Congress could not set the adjournment date
of another, arguing that if Jackson had read the bill with more care,
he would have found that it said that future Congresses could
adjourn at any other time than that stipulated in the bill if only
both houses agreed to the change.[29] Reconsideration was delayed
until June 27, when the bill received a vote of 16 to 23.

Of all the bills that he rejected during his terms as President,
Jackson's grounds for vetoing the two bills just discussed were the
most constitutionally sound. The Constitution clearly outlines that
the President is responsible for all negotiations with foreign countries. By the bill of compromise with the Two Sicilies, however,
Congress attempted to state conditions upon which the President
would handle foreign relations. Jackson correctly informed Congress that foreign relations were in his sphere of authority and not
Congress's.

In the veto on the congressional sessions, Jackson correctly used
the Constitution to prove his points. It is true that some Senators
accused the President of misreading the bill, but he thought it was
aimed at limiting his powers and he could not give it his approval.
That these vetoes did not lend themselves to finely drawn con-

stitutional interpretations was apparent from the lack of congressional comment on them.

President Jackson's final veto came just fifteen minutes before he left office in 1837. It occurred so late in his presidency that the veto was not returned to the Senate where it originated, but deposited with the Department of State. It was on an act "designating and limiting the funds receivable for the revenues of the United States" and stipulated that deposit banks and the Secretary of the Treasury accept notes of all specie paying banks in payment of duties or for public lands.[30]

The *National Intelligencer* was pleased with the bill but feared for its success with the President, since if the bill became law, it would nullify Jackson's Specie Circular of July 11, 1836, an order that made it mandatory for public lands to be bought in specie.[31] Jackson admitted that the bill was too complex for him to readily comprehend, so he attached a report from the Attorney General, whose opinion was that sufficient laws already existed which declared what type of money should be used for certain debts. If this bill passed, funds receivable for the public lands would have to be taken in notes of any specie paying bank. It would therefore, become a subject of "discussion and controversy," and would "probably remain involved in much perplexity and doubt until it shall have been settled by judicial decision."[32] Acting on the advice of the Attorney General, then, President Jackson withheld his signature. Since the veto was never sent to Congress, but deposited with the State Department, it was never reconsidered. Thus, Jackson left the presidential office in the same stormy way as he had entered it eight years before.

The funds receivable veto was the most exceptional example of the veto power, in the opinion of the *National Intelligencer*. The bill had passed both houses by more than two-thirds majorities, indicating that the Specie Circular, "so much, so universally, and so justly complained of," was not popular with Congress. The President knew that if he returned the bill with an ordinary veto, Congress would have overridden it. But Jackson acted in the "least responsible manner" by preventing Congress from re-examining the bill. He could not allow his Specie Circular to be destroyed, which surely would have resulted if an ordinary veto had been applied.[33] Since this veto was used to maintain one of Jackson's own executive orders and not necessarily to uphold a political or constitutional principle, it was the most negative of all the miscellaneous vetoes. As such it was a departure from the other vetoes in this category.

Jackson did not make the same public appeal with his miscellaneous vetoes, with the possible exception of the land rejection, as he did with those on internal improvements and the bank. They were highly interpretive questions and since Jackson spoke a more forthright language than Clay, Webster, and their Whig followers, the public rallied behind the Old General. Had it not been for the overwhelming public approval of Jackson's vetoes, his use of the power would probably have been more restrained. His vetoes were prophetic of the "positive state" that Clinton Rossiter talks about in *The American Presidency*, that is, that the government "regulates, stimulates, and operates in every part of the American economy and society. . . ."[34] This popular basis for his vetoes seemed to anticipate such twentieth century concepts as "democratic totalitarianism," and the "enforcement of freedom." The Jacksonian revolution, in which the veto played a leading role, emanated from the people, shifting, as Professor Rossiter points out, "the basis of our government from aristocracy to democracy without destroying its essential republicanism."[35] One reason Henry Clay and his Whig followers were so frustrated during the Jackson period was that they "could never rid themselves of the assumption that executive power is inherently antipopular."[36]

Jackson used the veto power, too, as Edward S. Corwin points out in *The President: Office and Powers*, to hold Congress to a strict interpretation of the Constitution, while by this same process he magnified executive power.[37] His vetoes enhanced the spread of "popular sovereignty" because Jackson was always able to identify himself as "the choice of the people,"[38] and the defender of the "liberties of the people." These concepts still have a most important meaning in the twentieth century, having affected the presidency ever since Jackson emphasized them during his terms in office. Since his vetoes were used to delineate such concepts, it may not be amiss to claim that they enabled Jackson to anticipate twentieth-century America.

John Tyler and the Whig Party, 1841-1842

WHIGGERY suffered a minority status through the Jackson period, gaining political strength during the Van Buren administration largely because of economic failures throughout the country and Van Buren's apparent reluctance to do anything about them. As a reform party in 1840, the Whigs conducted a memorable campaign for General William Henry Harrison. With his election the Whigs were estatic. The corruption of Jacksonianism would be abolished, and a progressive era would be forthcoming in which the tariff, the bank, and internal improvements would play leading parts. So great was Whig enthusiasm that the Southern members quickly forgave their Western and Northern brethren for not nominating Henry Clay. This forgiveness was due, in part, because John Tyler, a Virginian, was made vice-president. The ticket of "Tippecanoe and Tyler too" overwhelmed the Democratic opponents.

In his campaign, Harrison promised judiciousness in his use of the veto power. This was taken by the Whigs as an assurance that the Legislature would regain supremacy in government. Clay, seeking to control the Whig legislative program, suggested so many changes to Harrison that the President was obliged to tell Clay that he, and not the Kentuckian, had been elected President. The Whigs in general, however, settled back contentedly, ready now to reap the benefits of what they believed to be a worthy program. Harrison, however, aged and infirm, died a month after inauguration. His demise brought John Tyler into office as the tenth President of the United States.

The Whigs, while lamenting the passing of Harrison, still felt that their interests were in good hands. Tyler was of "good Virginia blood," a true Whig of the old-fashioned Republican school. This put him in the same company with Washington, Jefferson, and Madison, said the Whig papers. Of course, there was a "locofoco" rumor going around that Tyler was anti-bank, but the Whigs attributed this to the poor sportsmanship of the Democratic party. Tyler and his cabinet were honest people who had acted up to this point in a "patriotic" manner toward the fiscal question;

no good reason existed, therefore, to fear that Tyler would disapprove a national bank.[1] Tyler may have said a short time before that he doubted the constitutionality of a bank, but he doubted not its financial expediency. If the majority of Congress wanted a bank, Tyler would, as he said, react in the light of the "everglorious example" of the "Father of the great Republican school."[2] Such a statement could only mean, said the Whig press, that "like Washington, Madison, and Marshall, Tyler would favor a United States Bank!"[3]

A bill to create a bank similar to the one destroyed by Jackson was thus introduced in the Senate on June 21. Its title was "An act to incorporate the subscribers to the Fiscal Bank of the United States." The most debatable feature of the bill was connected with the establishment of branch banks. Senators William Rives of Virginia, William Preston from South Carolina, Rufus Choate of Massachusetts, Richard Bayard of Delaware, Samuel S. Phelps from Vermont, and Thomas Ewing of Ohio thought that before branches of the bank were established in the states, the consent of the state governments concerned should be obtained.[4] Clay, James F. Simmons of Rhode Island, and Jabez Huntingdon from Connecticut believed, though, that if the Constitution gave power to establish a national bank without the consent of the states, approval was not necessary to create branches.[5]

The debate on the branching question gave the Democrats an opportunity to report that disharmony existed in the ranks of the Whig party, and that a rift was developing between President Tyler and his cabinet. The *Jonesborough Whig* (Tenn.) gave no credence to these reports, and said they were "locofoco" inspired.[6] The bill was reluctantly modified by Clay on July 27 so that a state's permission would have to be obtained to establish branches of the bank. Assent of a state, however, would be assumed if its legislature did not, during its first session after the passage of the bank bill, give either its approval or disapproval to a branch within its borders.[7] The Senate acted favorably on the bill on July 28 by a vote of 26 to 23, and it was approved in the House on August 6. To the surprise of many Whig leaders, it was returned to the Senate on August 16, 1841, with President Tyler's objections.

Congressional power to establish a national bank to operate *per se* over the union, Tyler said, had not been definitely decided.[8] He claimed that he had never concealed his opinions about the unconstitutional nature of the bank, proclaiming them in the Virginia Legislature, in the United States Senate, and in speeches and reports extending over a 25 year period. Congressmen should not be surprised, therefore, at the action he took.[9] His general opinion was the same as Jackson's: the bank was unnecessary in executing governmental powers to "collect, safely keep, and disburse the public revenue, and incidentally to regulate the commerce and exchanges."[10]

The heart of the veto dwelled upon the branching provision of the bank bill. If a state assented to a branch, it could never be withdrawn except by Congress. Furthermore, if a state's dissent was not expressly given, its assent was implied. Many state elections had already taken place without any knowledge by the people of the branching question. Some states might want to take a vote on the question, but the time required for this might be longer than the first session of the state Legislature after the passage of the bank bill. Thus, the branching provision used the "language of the master to the vassal," because any delay, postponement, or incapacity of the state Legislature to answer in a specified time produced an implied assent "which is ever after irrevocable."[11]

Innumerable possibilities existed, too, for showing the irrationality of the branching provision. The popular branch of a state government might express itself unanimously against a branch of the bank, but its decision might be defeated by a tie vote in the state senate.[12] Both houses of a state Legislature might resolve against a branch bank, yet the governor might use his veto to destroy the resolution, thereby giving permission for a branch to be established. The branching provision, then, asserted that Congress had the power to establish branches in a state not only without its assent, but against its dissent. As a result of this provision, the entire bill was opposed to the philosophy of state rights, so Tyler could not approve it.

A disturbance broke out in the Senate galleries at the end of the reading of the veto message. Some spectators applauded; others hissed their displeasure at the veto. Several Senators requested that the galleries be cleared at once, but Benton loudly demanded that the Sergeant-at-Arms take the hissers into custody. He felt indignant that the American President was insulted by such behavior, since the villains were "bank ruffians" who, by depredating the veto message were, in effect, insulting the American government.[13] Senator Rives thought that perhaps Benton was mistaken, since he seemed to be the only one who had heard the hisses. Benton insisted that he had heard aright and demanded again that the culprits be brought before the bar of the Senate. Senator Preston said that he had not heard the disturbance himself, but if the Senator from Missouri had, or even thought he had, then an investigation should be held. Finally, Senator Robert Walker of Mississippi announced that one of the offenders had been arrested by the Sergeant-at-

Arms, and was penitent, contrite, and sorrowful for his deed. This pleased Benton, who said that because the offender was no longer acting contemptuously, he (Benton) would no longer demand his arrest.[14]

After the Benton interlude, Senator Clay suggested that the veto message be laid on the table and printed before reconsideration, its importance demanding that each Senator know well the issues that were to be discussed. Senator William Rufus King of Alabama thought the Senate was constitutionally obligated to take up reconsideration before any other business. Clay countered by referring to the Bank veto of 1832, saying that it was not considered until three days after it was received in the Senate. Finally, the reconsideration was postponed until noon the following day.[15]

On August 17, 1841, at noon, Benton moved to reconsider the vetoed bank bill. Senator Willie P. Mangum of North Carolina counter-moved that reconsideration be further postponed until noon the following day. Benton, of course, objected to Mangum's suggestion, and stated that the Constitution clearly outlined that vetoed bills be reconsidered as soon as they were printed in the congressional journals. Clay argued that the Constitution did not specify a time limit in which to reconsider a returned bill. On the vote that followed, the reconsideration was postponed 29 to 21.[16] The next day at noon, John Berrien from Georgia moved another postponement. This motion displeased more than just Democrats because the galleries and lobbies were packed to capacity by people who came in anticipation of an interesting debate. Calhoun objected to Berrien's motion, saying that enough time had elapsed and that the Senate was being disrespectful to the President by continual postponement. The South Carolinian accused Berrien of personal motives in the postponement motion. Berrien denied the charge and said that not enough time had passed for all to fully comprehend the issues. Berrien's motion carried again by the vote of 29 to 21.[17] The continual motions for postponement by the Whig members was a political maneuver to gain support. They knew the vote would be against them when the bill was reconsidered, but still they persisted in the hope that they could change some of the Senators' minds. Finally, on August 19, 1841, reconsideration of Tyler's bank veto took place. The result was a vote of 25 to 24.

The Democrats, of course, reacted joyously to the veto and its approval in the Senate, while the Whigs protested loudly that they had been betrayed. The veto message was "quite Democratic throughout—aye, *Jacksonian* and *Van Burenish* and will be altogether acceptable to that portion of the Locofoco party, who are opposed to a Bank."[18] Tyler had attended the 1839 convention as a friend of Henry Clay's and had given the impression that he was for a national bank. There was now no doubt that Tyler was a traitor to the party that put him in power. He would be denounced by the Whigs and by his cabinet.[19] The veto was the result of a coalition between Tyler and the Locofocos, said the Whigs. Since Tyler knew of the Whig principle of one term for Presidents, he hoped that by courting the Locofoco elements, he could capture the presidency for a second time.[20] The *National Intelligencer* was more charitable in its comments on the veto than many of the other Whig papers. It was, to be sure, disappointed with the President's reaction, but it conceded to Tyler honesty of motivation. The freedom of conscience, it said, was more valuable to the Whig party than political issues, and the paper was confident that Tyler would approve a bank with but a few changes from its present form.[21]

Early in September anti-Tyler meetings were held by the Whigs. A Jonesborough, Tennessee, meeting resolved that the "pure gospel light of Virginia Abstractions, which shines through the Veto Message of President Tyler, is not sufficient to illumine our minds."[22] At similar meetings in Nashville and Murfreesboro, Tyler was hanged in effigy. The *Baltimore Patriot* believed that Tyler should not have allowed himself to be the vice-presidential candidate in 1840 if he had thought so differently on the bank question from his Whig compatriots. The *Raleigh Register* reported that by the bank veto, Tyler had thwarted the will of 19 of the 26 states, and had disobeyed the dying injunction of his illustrious predecessor. The *Knoxville Post* said that the veto power was the strongest monarchial feature of the Constitution and presented a grave danger to the American government. The *Nashville Banner* spoke more in sorrow than in anger, because the veto was an "unmatched and unpardonable defection." The *New York Express* had not expected such locofocoism from a professing Whig, while the *Philadelphia Chronicle*, stating that the veto was an anomaly in the Constitution, forecast that Tyler's political days were numbered. The *Lynchburg Virginian* felt that the Whigs had been elected in 1840 because they would defer to popular will; Tyler had miserably betrayed that promise. The *Louisville Journal* called the veto the "most astounding and atrocious act of perfidy that ever occurred in any government in the civilized world," and agreed with the *National Intelligencer* that the veto could very well destroy the Whig party.[23]

While the Whig journals seethed with expletives over the veto and the Democratic ones acted smugly, Clay was calling Tyler a turncoat, a dishonest states rightist, a dictator, and a narrow-minded politician.[24] On the day of the veto, a Whig caucus met to determine upon another bank bill, one that would meet the President's approval. Accordingly, a revised bill was introduced into the House of Representatives by John Sergeant from Pennsylvania.

The new bill, creating a "fiscal corporation" instead of a "fiscal bank," was to be capitalized at $21,000,000, with the option of extending to $35,000,000. The bank proposal vetoed by Tyler had a capital of $30,000,000 which could be expanded to $50,000,000. The former bill provided branches for discount and deposit, but the new bill called for "agencies" to handle these activities. The dealings of the corporation were to be confined to buying and selling "bills of exchange," including those drawn in one state and paid in another. There was to be no time limit on these bills.[25] The changes thus incorporated, it was hoped by the Whigs, would cause Tyler to give his sanction to a bank bill. The bill passed the House 125 to 94 and the Senate 27 to 22. It was sent to the President on September 3 and was returned by him to the House on September 9.

His second bank veto expressed regret that he was again compelled to differ with Congress on the question of the bank. He could not, however, reconcile the bank with his constitutional principles. As in the first veto, he said that Congress did not have the power to create a bank that would operate *per se*, that is, over the whole union. Moreover, the branching provision of the first bill was in reality continued under the second. By its power to deal in "bills of exchange" which had an unlimited time to run, and drawn in one state and payable in another, the bank could operate in "mere local discounts" under the name of "bills of exchange."[26] This could lead to a system of discounts which would operate as much against the states as did the branching provision of the first bill.

Tyler, in this message, gave his philosophy concerning the use of the veto. This was done in an attempt to assuage Whig hostility toward his actions and to prevent an open split in the party. He said that the veto was a conservative instrument which ought never to be used except in "a case eminently involving the public interest or one in which the oath of the President, acting under his convictions, . . . imperiously requires its exercise. In such a case he has no alternative.[27] If a President should hesitate to use the veto to protect and preserve the Constitution, he would be guilty of moral turpitude. Mere regard for the will of a majority must not be the guiding factor in a President's use of the veto. Only the Constitution and what in the President's judgment was good government should be the determining motives. In most instances, however, he said that upholding the Constitution was the same as reflecting the popular will. He thus expected public approval of his bank rejections.[28]

The returned bill was reconsidered in the House on September 10. Representative John Minor Botts of Virginia spoke for an hour, scurrilously denouncing President Tyler. Although he had predicted the veto, Botts was at a loss to explain Tyler's reasoning. The President had objected to a national bank *per se*, but Botts, although admitting that he was no lawyer, snidely remarked that he did learn a little Latin in school and remembered that *per se* meant "by itself." He wanted to know, therefore, what national bank was there that was not a national bank "by itself?"[29] Tyler said in the message that the veto power should be used cautiously. Botts agreed with him on this point and wished the President would act according to his own premises. Tyler also objected because Congress could not charter another bank for 20 years after this one went into operation. Botts presumed, then, that if Congress chartered half a dozen banks, Tyler's objections would be removed. Botts went on to give a history of Tyler's past activities, showing that Tyler had objected to Madison's veto of the bank in 1815 and to Jackson's veto in 1832. In the latter case, Tyler had even accused President Jackson of having "evil advisors" around him. Must the same now be said of President Tyler?[30]

Finally, Isaac D. Jones of Maryland arose to "invoke a ray of sunshine" into the debates. He asked what was the constitutional duty of the House on the returned Fiscal Corporation bill. Was it to inquire whether the President had the right of the veto power? Was it to determine whether the style of the message was within the proper rules of rhetoric? Whether he ought or not to have quoted Latin? Whether his motives were patriotic or corrupt? If any of these points, collectively or singly, were to be considered by the House, said Jones, the proper course to take would be a resolution of impeachment. But, as a "practical utilitarian," he felt that the only question to be considered was whether the bill would or would not pass, despite the President's objections, and he urged his colleagues to proceed with this most important responsibility. After Jones' speech, Roger L. Gamble of Georgia moved the previous question. Upon its being seconded, several motions were made to adjourn, but they were all either rejected or withdrawn and the vote was taken. Tyler's veto was upheld 103 to 80.[31]

Typical of Whig papers strongly protesting against the second veto was the *Jonesborough Whig*, which called Tyler "the long-eared Virginia Ass." The paper reported the raucous behavior of the congressmen in discussing the returned bill and predicted that Tyler's cabinet would soon abandon him.[32] A week later the paper confirmed this prediction by reporting the resignations of Crittenden, Bell, Badger, and Ewing. The latter had tried to make the second bill acceptable to Tyler but failing, had chosen to quit his office.[33] The *National Intelligencer* maintained its moderate stand on the second bank veto. Again, it stated respect for the President's opinions, and hopefully forecast that the Congress would treat him likewise. The paper chastised some of the more "excitable" Whig papers by saying that they were aiding the opposition, whose aim was to split the Whig party.[34]

But the split was already too far advanced for the *National Intelligencer* to do anything about it. In the first week of October a Whig caucus met and read Tyler out of the party. John P. Kennedy of Maryland presented a message to the American people in which he said that Tyler had shown his true colors in the second veto. What the President actually wanted was a sub-treasury system; thus, the President had voluntarily separated himself from the Whig party, which could no longer be responsible for his actions.[35]

The *Alabama Journal* was more circumspect in its criticisms of Tyler than the *Jonesborough Whig*. It presented a sober, well reasoned exposition on the veto power, in which its major thesis was that by using the veto, a President destroyed the republican requirement of the greatest good for the greatest number. The whole people, said the *Journal*, was theoretically present in Congress when bills were passed. Thus, a President's veto could never be directed merely against Congress, but against the entire population of the country. The *Journal*'s opponent, the *Montgomery Advertiser*, said that even if the *Journal*'s argument were admitted, there was still the distinct possibility of "corruption" on the part of "the people." This being so, the President's veto was a useful governmental tool. In refutation, the *Journal* surmised that it was better to risk corruption from Congress than from the President, because the "whole is less easily corrupted than the part."[36]

By November, 1841, the cleavage in the Whig party was complete, causing despair among the Whig journalists, who attributed the weaknesses of the party in the fall elections to the "base treachery" of President Tyler. Southern Whigs were faced with the dilemma of choosing between Clay, "representing the old principles," and Tyler, "the States rights opponent of Clay's nationalism."[37] Many found a solution to their problem by a courtship with the Democratic party. Whiggery was at a low tide in

1841, making it probable that the Democrats would capture the next presidential election.

Whiggery suffered again because of the tariff question, which arose in the summer of 1842. On June 30 of that year, the compromise tariff act of 1833 was due to expire.[38] Unless some action was taken before that date, the custom duties would either be frozen at 20 percent, or, depending upon one's interpretation of the law, there would be no duties at all.[39] Clay and his Whig followers took the law to mean that there would be no duties after June 30, and they hoped to show Tyler that such a calamitous condition could be corrected only by a return to protective tariffs. To prepare for the fight, Clay introduced in February a resolution for an amendment to allow a simple majority to override presidential vetoes. This was done, of course, to lessen the possibilities that his tariff proposals would be destroyed by Tyler. In presenting the resolution, Clay repeated the Whig arguments that had been used ever since Jackson's administrations. He argued that the will of the majority was being destroyed by Tyler's use of the veto; that in 1840 with Harrison's election, the people had indicated their favor of a national bank and other Whig measures; and defended in a Jacksonian way the popular majority concept of American government.[40]

Refuting Clay's resolution, among others, was Senator Calhoun, who said that not even the President is elected by a popular majority. In the Electoral College each state's senator is added onto the ratio of population, with the result that 7,125,000 voters could defeat a majority of over 8,500,000.[41] Even in the constitutional convention, said Calhoun, 250,000 could have rejected the document, thus ruining the desires of 3,500,000 people.[42] Furthermore, the Supreme Court judges were by no means put into office according to the will of popular majority, Calhoun claimed, and no one would seriously question that body's right to judge legislation.

The veto power of the President, therefore, was essential to good government. Without the President's right to judge legislation for himself, there would be no division in the American government. The veto enabled the President to receive support from majorities representing various interests by forcing 18 of the 26 states represented in the Senate, and a vote in the House representing over 10,500,000 people, to destroy the rejection.[43] Thus, the American government was based on a proposition quite different from mere popular majority. In making each branch of government different from the other, the Founding Fathers had planned for concurrent majorities to "ensure the broadest support of the Government's measures."[44] The veto, then, was a "wise pre-caution" to prevent the tendency of falling under the control of a dominant interest acting by a mere numerical majority.[45] Clay's resolution was a symptom of that tendency. So forceful was Cal-houn's reply to Clay's resolution that after it was ended, the Senators of both parties gathered to congratulate him. Clay's resolution was lost after Calhoun's performance.

As it turned out, Clay's resolution and Calhoun's reply were the valedictories of the two Senators. Both resigned shortly afterward: Clay on March 31, 1842, and Calhoun a few months later. Clay resigned, he said, for purposes of rest and relaxation. Calhoun said that the people of the United States would determine how long he would remain in retirement. Everyone knew, however, as one of Calhoun's biographers put it, that both men retired to await "the call" to the American presidency.[46] Without the two who had so much to do with it, the tariff became the most discussed con-gressional issue in mid-summer, 1842.

As previously stated, the compromise tariff of 1833 was due to expire on June 30, 1842, with the result that duties would be set at 20 percent. The Whigs wanted a higher tariff than that, but if they attempted it, they would run afoul of Tyler on a provision of a land bill that had been passed in 1841. Echoing Jackson, Tyler had insisted in 1841 that if the tariff went above the 20 percent level, distribution to the states would have to be halted. Tyler, like Jackson, had been quick to note that an artificial connection was made by the Whigs between the tariff and internal improvements and he feared that efforts would be made deliberately to raise the tariff, thus extending such a system under the guise of distribution. Knowing full well the President's feelings on the mat-ter, the Whigs, nevertheless passed a bill in 1842 that postponed the reduction of the tariff for one month, but provided that dis-tribution could not be stopped for two months, no matter how high the tariff rose.[47] It was inconceivable that Tyler could do anything but veto the bill on the "little tariff."

The President conceded that the compromise tariff of 1833 had not been perfect, but at the time of its passage it had been the only available solution, and it had worked satisfactorily for nine years. Perhaps the duties now needed to be raised because of the depleted condition of the Treasury Department, but to do so would violate both the tariff of 1833 and the land law of September, 1841. The latter law had been quite clear in its stipula-tion that if the tariff rose above 20 percent, distribution to the states would cease. If higher duties were required to build up the treasury, a continuance of distribution would again lower the funds, and a "vicious circle" would be begun. He noticed that the act was meant to be temporary, but he felt this would only clear the way for permanent measures of a similar nature. If it were not the intent of Congress for this arrangement to be permanent, why postpone the reduction in the tariff at all? If Congress were sincere, the members would be willing to let the laws that were already in existence operate.[48]

Condemnations of Tyler fairly leaped from the editorials of the *Jonesborough Whig*: "The corrupt fool and knave who pretends to act as President of the United States, has vetoed the Provisional Tariff bill, recently passed by large majorities in both houses of Congress." The paper's solution for "Tylerism" was for "an overgrown Whig ruffian" to choke him to death. "Or he ought to be shot down in his tracks, as he walks along. We by no means, would encourage mobs, or murder, but one villain had better suffer even death, than that a whole nation should be famished to death."[49] Because of the veto, custom houses were in doubt as to whether or not a revenue law existed. This produced a lamentable situation, said the *Whig*, and all because of the "stupid ASS who disgraces the Presidential Chair."[50] Tyler, like Jackson, regarded himself as the Government. This might do, in the opinion of the *Whig*, if Tyler had either the sense or popularity of Jackson. He did not, however, and this fact only compounded the troubles of the country. Even the *National Intelligencer* began to lose its patience after the tariff veto. Nothing could have been more unexpected "than that this extreme power should be exercised by the Executive." The paper, nevertheless, hoped that the Whigs would not be too much provoked by the "exultations and taunts" of their enemies.[51]

Bitter debate occurred in the House, to which the veto was returned on June 29. All congressmen agreed that a financial crisis faced the country, but they differed in their opinions over its nature and who caused it. Most simply indulged in either praise or condemnation of the President, without offering any real solutions.

Representative W. Cost Johnson of Maryland suggested that the best solution to the distribution problem, one that should please both the President and the Whigs, was for the federal government to assume the debts of the states. Revenues that would come from a "properly adjusted tariff" and from the proceeds of the public lands sales should be used to pay the debts of the states. Such an action, deemed visionary by most of Johnson's colleagues, should "invigorate every department of life in the United States."[52]

Representative George Proffitt of Indiana wanted to put the

issue to the people of the country. The Whigs were making the veto unpopular by deliberately forcing upon the President bills which he could not approve. There had never been a republic in all history that did not have the veto power, said Proffitt, and since the Whigs were attacking it to such an extent, the proper course was for the people to decide. John B. Weller from Ohio denied Whig reports that the veto came from an agreement between Tyler and various elements of the Democratic party. In a caustic speech, Weller told the Whigs, amid laughter in the House, that the people would drive them into the retirement from which they ought never to have come. "A new set of books will be opened," he proclaimed, in which the Whigs would not find their names. He said that the Whigs had accepted Harrison and Tyler in 1840 in the same way that many people accepted bank notes—not knowing their full value. The Whigs were now attempting to pass them off for more than they were worth, "and . . . are caught in their own trap."[53]

Referring specifically to the tariff, Weller said that everyone had fought for their special interests and had threatened to kill the entire bill if they were not catered to. Joseph L. Tillinghast of Rhode Island, said Weller, had even demanded the protection of pins. This brought great laughter from the rest of the House. Tillinghast, however, rose solemnly and said that no pin manufacturers existed in Rhode Island; that the point in question was over his presentation, as a member of the committee on manufactures, a petition from New York for the protection of pins. This caused still more merriment and added to the discomfort of the hapless Tillinghast.

While debate on the veto continued in the House, the Senate was quite busy discussing it as well. Senator Levi Woodbury of New Hampshire introduced two bills on July 1 which would, in his opinion, solve the financial crisis. He first suggested continuing the law which prohibited duties from exceeding 20 percent. This proposal did not, he said, violate the constitutional requirement that bills of revenue originate only in the House, because his bill sought to put into effect what was already in existence.[54] Furthermore, the bill he sponsored would omit any mention of distributing the proceeds of land sales and should, therefore, receive presidential sanction.

The other bill that he proposed was on home valuation, which would impose charges in addition to duties on goods arriving in this country. All goods coming from beyond the Cape of Good Hope would have 20 percent added to their original value, while goods coming from this side of the Cape of Good Hope would have an additional 15 percent added onto their value. These procedures would constitute a fair method of home valuation for imported goods.[55] Other Senators disagreed with Woodbury's plans: George Evans of Maine said that no matter what Woodbury's objective, the effect would still be to bring in revenue to the Treasury Department. The Constitution clearly stated that only the House could originate bills of revenue; thus, Woodbury's proposals were unconstitutional. Senator Robert J. Walker of Mississippi agreed with Evans, and together they helped defeat Woodbury's proposals. The question of home valuation was looked upon as a subtle way of increasing the tariff despite the President's veto.[56]

Meanwhile, in the House the debate was still raging on Tyler's veto of the "little tariff." Charges and countercharges were being hurled indiscriminately by both Whigs and Democrats. Robert L. Caruthers of Tennessee again brought up the charge of collusion between Tyler and the Democrats, only to be chastised by Robert Barnwell Rhett of South Carolina. Rhett claimed that the President was not the only governmental official with a veto, pointing out how one person could defeat bills upon which there were close votes.[57] Indiana's Joseph L. White called the veto a message of "pointless reasoning, pointless satire, reckless assertions, and unblushing effrontery,"[58] while William Payne of Alabama defended the right of a President to use the veto, saying that the Constitution gave power to a President to veto a bill, not because of constitutionalism or expediency, but on the grounds of mere disapproval.

Eventually the representatives exhausted all of their adjectives, so they were able to take a vote on the bill. Nathaniel Pendleton of Ohio moved the previous question on July 4, 1842, allowing a vote on the question of whether the bill would pass despite the President's objections. The result was a vote of 42 to 144. With the necessary two-thirds far from being obtained, the tariff veto was sustained.

Another tariff bill was immediately introduced by the House Whigs. It was quite similar to the one that had just been vetoed, except that it was permanent rather than temporary. President Tyler returned the second Whig tariff bill to the House on August 9, 1842.

Many of the President's objections to the second tariff bill were the same as in the first. He did, however, point out in the second tariff veto that by combining two factors so opposed as distribution and the tariff, the fate of each was made dependent on the other. The tariff was variable while the public lands were of a permanent nature. To combine something that was flexible (tariff) with something inflexible (public lands) would ultimately produce great harm to the country. Permanency and stability were the chief desires of the manufacturing classes, but these would be sacrificed if the tariff and distribution were combined.[59]

Former President John Quincy Adams, now a representative from Massachusetts, rose upon the return of the veto and solemnly announced that civil war existed between the President and Congress. All the wrongs of the country would have been corrected by Tyler's signature on the second tariff, but his recalcitrant nature had once again ruled over orderliness, said Adams. He moved that the reconsideration of the second tariff go to a select committee of 13 for study and recommendations.[60]

Adams' suggestion immediately drew fire from several representatives; Foster of Georgia said that such a course would be unconstitutional because Congress as a whole must reconsider returned bills. Caleb Cushing of Massachusetts agreed, and pointed out that the question was really on re-passage of the bill instead of reconsideration. Concurring in this opinion was Virginia's Henry A. Wise, who said that if the veto went to a select committee of thirteen, seven members could thwart the will of the entire House of Representatives. It was obvious, said Wise, that the design of those who wanted reference was to delay to the last day of the session without taking any action on the returned tariff bill.[61] Millard Fillmore of New York believed that the representatives were overstating the case. The committee could have no final decision on the vetoed bill; all it could do was study it and make recommendations to the whole House.

Christopher Morgan of New York then moved the previous question on Adams' motion. This brought a protest from New Hampshire representative Charles G. Atherton, who said the previous question should pertain to a reconsideration of the vetoed bill. He was overruled, however, and Adams' motion was approved by a vote of 108-84. Those selected to the committee were: John Q. Adams, Massachusetts; John M. Botts and Thomas W. Gilmer, Virginia; James Cooper, William W. Irwin, and C. J. Ingersoll, Pennsylvania; James Roosevelt and Francis Granger, New York; Jeremiah Morrow, Ohio; Truman Smith, Connecticut; James A. Pearce, Maryland; Kenneth Rayner, North Carolina; and Thomas J. Campbell, Tennessee. It was easy to discern what the majority report of the committee would be since all the members except Ingersoll and Roosevelt belonged to the Whig party.

Immediately upon selection of the committee, Proffitt moved to take up the vetoed bill. When Fillmore asked that he wait for

the report of the select committee, Proffitt angrily declared that
the committee decision would have no bearing on his vote, and
should not on any other vote. The committee was, therefore,
simply a time wasting device. His motion to bypass the committee
and immediately reconsider the bill was defeated 82 to 104.[62]
Another disturbance was precipitated when one of the committee
members, Irwin, asked to be excused because of his belief that
reference of the veto to a committee was unconstitutional. In the
midst of giving his speech, Irwin was called to order for irrelevancy.
Wise defended Irwin by saying that the representative could not
legally be forced to do something which, in his opinion, was outside the Constitution. The Chair then called Wise to order on the
grounds that Irwin's request was not debatable. When Wise tried
to protest, his voice was drowned out by cries of "Order! Order!"
As he sat down, the congressional reporter heard him mumble
incoherently: "tyrannical decision. I despise such . . .; Sir, it is
contemptible. . . ."[63] Irwin was finally replaced on the committee
by Henry S. Lane, a Whig from Indiana.

As the imbroglio raged in the House, newspapers were having
their say. "ANOTHER VETO," cried the editor of the *Alabama
Journal*. The country was in a miserable condition, the paper believed, because the Whigs passed laws according to the Constitution,
only to have them destroyed by an overbearing President.[64] The
mortified *Jonesborough Whig* headed its article with the title:
"VETO THE FOURTH." It said that the "rogue and royalist"
John Tyler "had furnished the country with another veto. If
any country felt the damning influence of the imperial veto, these
United States have."[65] The *Journal* reported that the "quiet" sub-
missions with which the vetoes were being received by the American people were exciting much surprise in monarchial Europe. An
article from the *London Times* was summarized which said that a
power was nearing destruction when it was deliberately used to
destroy the will of the public.[66] The *National Intelligencer*, now
bereft of its moderate reactions to the first three of Tyler's vetoes,
demonstrated "unfeigned" pain. Remorsefully, it accused Tyler of
"arrogating powers" over the country's legislation.[67]

The Democratic papers were, of course, happy over Tyler's
continued use of the veto. The *Jacksonville* (Alabama) *Republican*,
writing in refutation of its chief competitor, the *Wetumpka Argus*,
reported facetiously that a few Wetumpka (Alabama) Whigs
had a case of the "Botts" (referring to the Virginia critic of Tyler).
The *Republican* gleefully recommended as a cure for this malady
a "few grains of common sense." Some Whigs, though, would
never recover before they were "buried under a bank of Clay."[68]

The paper went on to defend Tyler against lingering "Clayism" in the Congress. The Kentuckian was called the "maginficant brag player," who had been voted down so often by the people that he and his followers were now ready for desperate measures.[69]

The House acted again on the veto on August 16, when it heard the majority report of the select committee. In summary, the report said that Tyler had ruined the will of the people who had put in power in 1840 both a Whig President and a Whig Congress. The spirit of the Constitution made the President dependent on Congress; but Tyler was reversing this, and in so doing, he was acting unconstitutionally. Tyler was most inconsistent in his vetoes, the report said, because in the past he had favored a connection of the tariff and distribution, the latter to be used for internal improvements. If the proceeds of the public land went into the ordinary expenses of the government (as Jackson, and now Tyler, had wanted), instead of being set aside for internal improvements, the funds would be lost forever to the benefit of the people. Impeachment would probably be tried, but the discord between Tyler and Congress was reflective of general discord throughout the country, so any impeachment attempts would be abortive. The report closed by suggesting an amendment to the Constitution making it possible for a majority to override a veto. The majority report was signed by Adams, Botts, Cooper, Rayner, Campbell, Truman Smith, Granger, Morrow, Pearce, and Lane.[70] The majority report was complimented by the *National Intelligencer*, which said it was a paper that would not only "challenge universal attention," but would also become the "text-book for the whole army of Whigs all over the Union." The report would provide instruction to all the young Whigs and a confirmation of principle to the old.[71]

After the majority report, Gilmer, departing from his committee colleagues, entered a protest and a counter report. He said the House had handled the veto in an extraordinary manner, since a returned bill should be reconsidered, not referred. The President had only a qualified veto. If it were absolute, there would be no such thing as reconsideration of returned bills. The Virginian expressed the opinion that if a returned bill could be referred to a select committee, Congress could also refuse to reconsider it. There was no need to pass laws abridging the power of the presidential veto, because if it were weakened or destroyed, the absolute veto of the Supreme Court would then be utilized. If Tyler had abused the veto power, the proper course was to impeach him.[72]

Another minority report was presented by the two Democratic members of the committee, Ingersoll and Roosevelt. They stated that each house of Congress had an absolute negative on the other, while the Supreme Court also possessed a veto power. But the President merely had the power to cause Congress to reconsider legislation; thus, there were several governmental agencies with more power than the President. If the House had followed the Constitution, it would immediately have reconsidered the returned tariff bill. Instead, valuable time was lost in quibbling over the issue. The two congressmen believed that the fight between Tyler and Congress would ultimately be settled by the Supreme Court when that body adjudicated the tariff question. If the Supreme Court failed to settle the problem, the "charitable ballot-box" was always at hand, and the people would surely hold the House responsible for the wasted efforts of this legislative session.[73]

When all of the reports were finished, Wise moved a reconsideration of the returned tariff bill. Fillmore countered by claiming that other, long neglected bills needed to be considered. Wise refused to withdraw his motion, and it was defeated 104 to 99. Finally, Johnson of Maryland gained the floor and said the tariff bill had been designed to afford protection to manufacturers for the next 25 years. The committee reports, in his opinion, had not changed a single vote on the issue, so Congress must reconsider. His motion for reconsideration carried 123 to 77.[74] A vote was then taken on the second tariff bill, and the result was 126 to 76.

Even after the vote of reconsideration, the congressmen were reluctant to drop the subject. Gilmer's minority report was criticized by Rayner, who said that it had been too harsh toward Congress and too favorable toward the President. Wise mentioned the question of impeachment that had been brought out in the majority report, and he challenged Botts to initiate impeachment proceedings. Botts intimated that he would do so at the next congressional session.[75] Several other congressmen indulged in last minute speeches, both for and against the tariff veto. Debate began dwindling after several resolutions to introduce another tariff bill were offered.

President Tyler's rejection of the bank and tariff bills represented the height of the veto power during the period covered by this book, because they destroyed the very foundation of the Whig political program. They were all the more unbearable to the Whigs, who had finally won their long awaited victory in 1840. To have the victory taken from them, first by the death of Harrison and then by the intransigence of Tyler, was enough to make any Whig bemoan his fate. The Whigs were, they felt, victims of a giant doublecross which ruined their cherished hopes of a national bank and a high protective tariff. They were forced to go on the defensive at a time when they, by right of the

victory in 1840, should have been initiating governmental programs and enjoying a golden age of Whiggery. These hopes came
to naught, however, so no wonder the Whigs became so bitter.

But they were incorrect in their conjectures that Tyler would,
as a matter of course, support a national bank. As his biographer,
Oliver P. Chitwood, points out, the Whig victory in 1840 could
not be taken as a mandate from the electorate to create a national
bank.[76] The narrowness of the Whig victory that year in the
popular column, and the fact that many Whigs were in agreement
with the Democrats against the bank, provide proof of this observation.[77] Especially on the question of the first bank the Whigs
had no right, based on past events, to expect that Tyler would
approve it. On the second bank, there was some question that
Tyler had approved it in draft form and then had deviously
changed his mind; this charge, however, has never been sub-
stantiated.[78] Another charge frequently brought against Tyler
was that he had secretly agreed with the Democrats to destroy the
Whig political program in return for the Democratic nomination
in 1844. This cannot be proven because if it had been true, Tyler
would have openly supported the Democratic party instead of
trying to maintain an affiliation with the Whigs.[79] If his reasons
for the vetoes were not ulterior, then, what were his motives?

Tyler had long possessed a reputation as an advocate of states
rights. An honorable man, his statement in the first bank veto that
he had always proclaimed his opinions that a national bank was unconstitutional cannot seriously be doubted. When the bank bills
were presented to him, he felt that Congress was acting in a national
capacity when it was constitutionally legal for Congress to charter
a bank only in the District of Columbia. A national banking institution violated his philosophy of states rights, so he could not
approve the bills. Thus, he was the first President to reject a bank
purely on constitutional grounds. Madison vetoed the bank in 1815
because of financial expediency, and Jackson, although attempting
to use the Constitution as his reason in 1832, was not convincing.

In vetoing the tariff, Tyler believed, as had Jackson, that the
Whigs were deliberately connecting the tariff with distribution
as a means of providing federal internal improvements, a program
that neither Jackson nor Tyler would allow. The higher the tariff,
the greater the distribution; the greater the distribution, the larger
the federal appropriations for internal improvements; the larger the
federal appropriations, the dimmer the indispensable line between
federal and state governments. If there was to be a tariff, then, it
must not go above the revenue level of 20 percent, or distribution

would cease. The Whigs could have whichever bill they wanted, but they could not have both.

Because he upheld political principles of long standing, Tyler's vetoes of the bank and the tariff should be viewed as positive reactions. No where in these vetoes did he seem to be motivated by personal antagonisms; on the contrary, he attempted, at least in the second bank veto, to smooth relations between himself and the Whigs by giving in detail his philosophy of the veto power. This effort failed, though, and the executive-legislative rift continued.

James Madison probably would have approved the Whig programs that Tyler rejected. The fourth President's belief in the weight of Congress and in the prescriptive process would have caused him to give his assent, even if he were not convinced of the constitutionality of the measures. Madison's beliefs in these respects had held true on most questions except those on internal improvements. Tyler, therefore, drew more upon the practices of Jackson for his bank and tariff vetoes than he did from Madison.

Tyler's use of the veto can be compared to Jackson's; neither President ever feared to employ the veto, regardless of consequences. It is also clear that both Presidents had states rightist inclinations; here again they may be compared in their use of the veto. Similarities end, though, when one studies the objectives of their vetoes. Jackson often used the veto as a political device to gain favor in the various sections and as a method of enhancing the power of the executive department. These objectives seemed to Tyler to be secondary to his real purpose of safeguarding states rights. Moreover, Tyler's reaction to legislation could be more readily predicted than Jackson's. This is demonstrated by the fact that Jackson quite often approved bills similar to ones that he vetoed, indicating that a personal motive was frequently involved in his disapprovals. The same cannot be claimed for Tyler's vetoes on the bank and the tariff. There were negative aspects in some of Tyler's later vetoes, but for the most part, he acted in a positive manner.

☆ VI ☆

John Tyler and the Defense
of State Rights, 1842-1845

THE Twenty-seventh Congress was perhaps the most bitter assembly in American history. The majority party witnessed the disintegration of its cherished political program of many years' standing. The bank and the tariff, at the very center of its plans, were killed by Tyler. While these were being destroyed, the Whigs worked feverishly to enact laws that would in turn control the President. One such law to repeal the sixth section of the 1841 Land law was passed near the end of the second session. This section had stipulated that when the tariff rose above 20 percent, distribution to the states would cease. It will be remembered that the violation of this provision in the two Whig tariff bills was the reason for Tyler's vetoes of them. The Repeal bill was designed to circumvent Tyler's requirement on the tariff relating to distribution.

The bill was introduced on August 25, 1842, just days before the second session was to end, and its presentation to the House caused another bitter debate among the members. Representative Meredith P. Gentry of Tennessee introduced the bill for the committee on public lands. He was immediately challenged by Jacob Thompson of Mississippi, who said the committee had no right to originate the bill, that no order or petition had referred it to the committee. The Mississippi representative was joined by Wise, who asked if there had been a quorum in committee when it was decided to report the bill to the whole membership.[1]

It developed that Thompson, a staunch opponent of Whiggery, had left the committee after his failure to win postponement of the bill for 24 hours. The Mississippian said, moreover, that the committee was meeting while the House was in session, a procedure in violation of House rules. Gentry rejoined that Thompson had known that the Repeal bill was to be decided upon in the committee and had left the committee deliberately so that it would have no quorum. The remainder had decided that one man should not obstruct their work, so the bill had been reported out by the votes of four men.

Wise fought House acceptance of the committee-reported bill. He did so because there had been no quorum in committee when it was decided to report the bill and because the House was sitting while the committee was deliberating. His efforts were overruled, however, by a 91 to 77 vote to take the bill from committee.[2]

The next motion, from Truman Smith of Connecticut, sought to limit all debate on the Repeal Bill to one hour. This was adopted 106 to 80. Thomas D. Arnold of Tennessee spoke in behalf of the bill, pronouncing himself in favor of protection. He doubted that the President would approve the bill, saying that the manner pursued by Tyler so far would make government simpler just by having Congress register his edicts.[3] Wise was indignant at Arnold's outburst. He said that the bill had been reported most irregularly to the House and then a gag rule had been imposed upon its discussion by the Smith motion. The Virginian was not able to overturn the sentiment for the bill, however, and it was passed by a vote of 104 to 86.[4]

President Tyler disposed of the Repeal bill by a pocket veto. In a message signed December 14, 1842, he simply stated that Congress should refer to his earlier veto messages to ascertain his reasons for rejecting the bill.[5] This was his first use of the pocket veto, and it was positive proof to his enemies that his conversion to Jacksonism was complete. If Tyler had approved the bill, he would have repudiated the principles upon which he based his politics. His opponents accused him of personal motivation in the veto, but there is little evidence to show that this was true. Tyler saw the bill as an indirect way of imposing Clay's program of internal improvements and high protective tariffs, which in turn would destroy the division between state and federal government. His political temperament and his reputation as a state-rightist therefore dictated disapproval of the Repeal bill. It was a positive reaction on Tyler's part, one that could have been accurately predicted by studying his record.

Accompanying the pocket veto of the Repeal Bill was another on "an act regulating the taking of testimony in cases of contested elections." This bill was connected with the Apportionment Act of June 22, 1842, and became the source of abusive discussions over federal-state relations. The Apportionment Act had stipulated that every state populous enough to be entitled to more than one representative must be divided by the Legislature into districts "composed of contiguous territory." The effect of the bill had been to destroy the General Ticket system in several states. The Democratic party in the South, especially, had protested this legislative "mandamus."[6]

Since it appeared likely that the Democratic party would capture Congress in the fall elections of 1842, the Whigs took the precautionary measure of seeing that the provisions of the Apportionment Act would be carried out by proposing the Contested Elections Bill. According to its terms, either House could set up a commission to study contested elections to the Twenty-eighth and succeeding Congresses. Moreover, Justices of the Peace in the states would be given vast powers of subpoena whenever an election was contested. The Clerk of the House would be empowered to omit from the rolls any person who had not been elected to the Congress from a district according to the Apportionment Act.[7]

The proposed law immediately became the subject of dissension among those who thought the Constitution had been violated by the Apportionment Act and was being further misused by the Contested Elections Bill. William M. Gwin of Mississippi spoke to the House against allowing the federal government to control elections; since the states had always made their own rules in that respect, he felt that these should not be changed. He recommended that the Apportionment Act not go into effect until after the elections to the Twenty-eighth Congress.[8]

Another discussion on the bill revolved around the method of punishing offenders. Many representatives followed Fillmore's lead in trying to impose severe penalties for infractions. The New Yorker said that without enforcement provisions, there would be no way to judge a contested election. In times of great political excitement, party feelings would induce witnesses to absent themselves, to withhold their testimony, and even to refuse to testify altogether. These possibilities offered strong inducements to writing strict enforcement procedures into the bill.[9]

But who would punish the offenders? The federal government or the state government? Justices of the Peace, said the Democratic members, were state officials and as such could not rightfully be subjected to federal regulations as stipulated in the bill. One section of the bill provided penitentiary terms for violation, but some states had no penitentiaries. It was, therefore, suggested that punishment be left up to the states involved. Fillmore countered that this would ruin the uniformity of the bill.[10] Finally, after several days of argument, the bill passed with most of the Whig supported measures in it, that is, increased power to Justices of the Peace, investment of authority over the Congressional rolls in the Clerk of the House, and the requirement that representatives be elected by the district system. By a vote of 99 to 82 the bill was approved in the House.[11]

In the Senate, the bill's opponents called it the "disenfranchise-ment" bill. Levi Woodbury felt that it was unjust for the federal government to force districting upon the states. The Contested Elections Bill was designed chiefly, in his opinion, to punish the states that did not district. New Hampshire, his home state, did not district, and now it was to be treated shamefully by the Con-gress. The bill gave the Clerk of the House too much power in deciding whom to put on the rolls. It also sought to compel Justices of the Peace, who were state authorities, to carry out federal man-dates.[12] Woodbury's arguments were ineffective, and on August 29 the bill was reported favorably out of the Senate and sent to the President.

Tyler explained his reasons for withholding the bill in his mes-sage of December 14, 1842. He called attention to the fact that the seventeenth joint rule of the Houses, which stated that legislation would not be forwarded to the President on the last day of the session, had been violated. Congress had agreed to adjourn at 2 p.m. on August 31 and the President did not receive the Contested Elections bill until 1:30 p.m. that day. He had tried to read it and comprehend its 27 sections, but continual interruptions made im-possible any understanding; therefore, he thought it best to keep the bill.[13]

Tyler said that he would remain uncommitted toward any future action on the bill should Congress choose to send it to him again. He did point out, however, his belief that each House possessed unqualified power to decide for itself upon the elections and qualifications of its own members.[14] This view indicated that the President might approve a similar bill if presented to him in the future, since his states-rights principles probably would have pro-vided the justification. Although he agreed in principle with the Contested Elections bill, Tyler's veto was indicative of the con-tinuing lack of cooperation between the President and the majority of the Whig party. The Whigs wanted to ensure obedience to the Apportionment Act, but Tyler was not impressed with its necessity. He believed the Apportionment Act was sufficient, at least for the time being, and that no urgent protection of it was required.

The *National Intelligencer* expressed the fears of the Whig party when it said that Tyler's veto of the Contested Elections bill would enable the Locofocos to make the Apportionment Act un-enforceable. There was evidence that the Locofocos, as a result of their congressional victories, intended to abrogate the provisions of the bill because it destroyed the General Ticket system in so many Democratically dominated states. The Whigs believed that the Democrats, if they felt the Apportionment Act wrong, should repeal it rather than refuse to execute it.[15] Tyler was simply aiding the Democratic radicals by withholding his approval of the Contested Elections Bill. Whig fears caused by the pocket veto were apparently unfounded, for the Apportionment Act was employed by the states in subsequent congressional elections.

The next dispute between the President and Congress occurred at the close of the third session of the Twenty-seventh Congress, which seemed to be a calmer and more deliberative body than the first two, since no bills conducive to controversy were debated. One reason for the absence of violent discussion in the third session seemed to be that the lawmakers, weary of being abused by Tyler, now indulged in debates of substance. The only bill sent to Tyler from the third session which he did not approve was a joint resolution directing certain awards to the Cherokee Indians.

The resolution had its origin in the House of Representatives. It sought to reimburse Cherokees who had paid their own expenses to relocate in the West in 1835. An arrangement had been made so that an Indian, if he so desired, could go alone to the West. Before departure he was given a certificate by an Indian agent which would entitle the Indian to $53.00 once he reached the Western terminal. A number of the certificates had remained unpaid for one reason or another, mostly because of difficulty in identifying the Indians who went West unattended, so the resolution was designed to settle the matter once and for all.

Many feared, as did Indiana Senator Albert S. White,[16] that the resolution would create an opportunity for fraud because it would enable unscrupulous individuals to redeem certificates for other than legitimate purposes. Moreover, only $130,000 remained of the original appropriations, while the claims amounted to $450,000. Because of this disparity, some felt the claims resolution to be illogical.

President Tyler kept the resolution and explained his reasons for doing so in a message to Congress on December 18, 1843. He said that the balance of funds under the original treaty with the Cherokees was insufficient to meet all the claims asked for in the joint resolution. For Congress to pay the entire amount of the remaining funds to those who immediately presented certificates would injure those who might be unaware of the resolution. It would prevent a "ratable distribution of the funds among those equally entitled to benefits called for in the resolution."[17]

Tyler also maintained that the fund had been appropriated for a specific purpose; therefore, it belonged to the Cherokee Indians. The authority of the United States government to direct the application of the fund to particular claims was "more than questionable."[18] Here, Tyler took the same line that Monroe and Jackson had used before; that is, the Congress may have unlimited power to raise money, but only discretionary power over its distribution.

Finally, Tyler argued with the mode of payment called for in the joint resolution. He agreed with Senator White that a mere presentation of certificates was not a valid way of determining payment. The correct system of disbursing government money required that payments from any department be made on requisition and countersigned by the proper auditor and comptroller.[19] Because of the monetary irregularities which would result from the resolution, because it was doubtful whether or not Congress had the power to direct payments in the first place, and because it would require additional appropriations to be just to all claimants, Tyler kept the joint resolution on the Cherokee claims. In doing this, he held to the Jacksonian method of limited congressional authority over disbursements of money and to the principle that the executive department was the proper governmental agency to deal in treaties with foreign countries and Indian tribes. Although this veto did not deal specifically with a state, it had overtones of states-rights principles in that it prevented Congress from extending its authority.

For several months after the Cherokee veto, executive-congressional relations were relatively cordial. All of the legislation of the first session of the Twenty-tighth Congress was approved until June of 1844. In that month, Congress passed an internal improvement bill which appropriated $340,000 for the improvement of Eastern harbors. Called the "Eastern Harbor bill," it was returned to the House of Representatives on June 11, 1844, with Tyler's objections.

The President began by generalizing that internal improvements at federal expense would tend to take away the power of the states. Furthermore, the Commerce Clause could not be used to justify internal improvements; according to Tyler, to employ the clause for "mere convenience" would open doors to unrestrained authority by Congress.

Tyler's interpretation of the Commerce Clause in this veto was extraordinary. He said that its plain and obvious meaning was "that Congress may adapt rules . . . prescribing the terms and conditions on which the citizens of the United States may carry on commercial operations with foreign states . . ., and on which the citizens . . . of foreign states . . . may prosecute trade with the United States." The right of Congress to regulate commerce among the several states, therefore, included only the trade that the states might have with foreign countries. In arriving at this conclusion, Tyler misquoted the Commerce Clause which prescribes that Congress "regulate commerce with foreign Nations, and among the several States, and with the Indian tribes."[20] Tyler omitted the conjunction "and" after the first comma, which made it read that Congress could ". . . regulate commerce with foreign Nations, among the several states. . . ." Here, Tyler's purpose was in opposition to Jackson's in his veto of the Land bill in 1833, in which Jackson used positive means to defend a negative end.[21] Tyler, in safeguarding his long-time principle of state rights, was positive in most of his operations. But his twisting of the Commerce Clause in the veto of the Eastern Harbor Bill imposed upon it a negative character that was missing from all his other vetoes.[22] He therefore used negative means to attain a positive end.

Tyler's interpretation of the Commerce Clause in the Eastern Harbor veto was much more astounding than Jackson's conclusions toward executive authority in the Bank veto of 1832. If Tyler's views had been carried to their ultimate limits, Congress would have possessed no power at all to deal with commerce except that carried on between the states and foreign countries. He certainly went beyond Jackson in this veto by trying to limit the power of Congress to a strict interpretation of the Constitution.

Tyler returned to a more reasoned exposition on internal improvements after the section on the Commerce Clause. He showed, for example, how the bill would harm certain economic interests. In the bill $20,000 had been appropriated for the improvement of Richmond harbor, an improvement which would increase all the property values in Richmond. The increased value of property in Richmond, however, would in turn damage the town of Petersburg, some 20 miles away, because its trade would be diverted to Richmond. Also, the improvement of the James River up to Richmond and Appomattox might "by inviting the trade to those two towns" ruin the economic life of Norfolk.[23] These possibilities provided good reasons for vetoing the bill, said Tyler, because discrimination would result if it were approved.

At the same time he vetoed the Eastern Harbor Bill, Tyler signed one for the improvement of the Mississippi River. Lest he be thought inconsistent in the matter, he explained that the Mississippi was different from all other water courses in the country because it was interstate. By common assent, he claimed, the Mississippi belonged to all the country; it was a great avenue of commerce for the United States. As such, it must be provided for by the federal government.[24] He regarded the Mississippi and the Great Lakes as inland seas and argued that this identity entitled them to federally supported improvements.[25]

The debate in the House that was engendered by the veto did not revolve around the President's reasons, but over the method of reconsideration. According to John Q. Adams, when the veto was read on June 11, a member moved to postpone the whole subject until the following day. Immediately after this the previous question was moved and seconded. The Chair, in the absence of the speaker, ruled that the question being voted upon was the one of postponement. The Speaker, J. W. Jones of Virginia, returned and decided that the main question was on the reconsideration of the vetoed bill, which cut off the motion for postponement of the veto. The vote on the previous question was 104 to 84 and the Speaker ruled that the veto was thus sustained.[26]

Adams and his Whig followers protested that actual reconsideration had not taken place, and hinted that the Speaker's actions had aided Tyler's undemocratic use of the veto power. The Speaker, of course, defended himself by saying that all constitutional requirements had been met. He was supported in this opinion by Thomas H. Bayley from Virginia, who said that the very act of voting implied reconsideration of the returned bill by every member of the House.[27] Bayley used this occasion to defend the veto power against the attacks made upon it by Adams and other Whigs. Bayley said that the veto was one of the most democratic features of the Constitution: "It enacted nothing; it inflicted no measure on the country," it did nothing more than enable the President to "halt" Congress when it "began running in the wrong direction."[28]

Bayley was followed by another Virginian, George C. Dromgoole, who accused Adams of confusing "discussion" with "consideration." He looked upon the debate before the House as an abstract question rising from the Constitution. If the opinion of the Speaker was overturned by a House vote, and the veto was reconsidered again, it would lead to endlessly absurd reconsiderations of votes. Shortly after Dromgoole's oration, the previous question was called, and the result was in favor of the Speaker's decision, 97 to 85.[29] The Whigs used these proceedings to pronounce their displeasure with the "railroading" tactics of the Democratic party.

The press, like Congress, made few comments on the veto. The *National Intelligencer*, as was expected, disapproved of Tyler's actions and said that he was using the veto power to defy the will of the people as expressed by their representatives in Congress.[30] The *Baltimore Sun* simply reported the veto along with the congressional comment on the method of reconsideration, and did not editorialize.[31] The *Richmond Enquirer*, edited by Thomas Ritchie, praised Tyler's veto of the Eastern Harbor Bill, stating that Tyler had "interpolated" the Constitution to save it from violation. Internal improvements had already bankrupted half the states in the Union and they would do the same thing to the federal government if indulged in too much. Tyler should be thanked for enrolling "his name with Madison, Monroe, and Jackson in saving the Constitution."

The *Enquirer's* only regret was that so many Democrats had supported the bill. It was awkward, said the editor, for a Democrat to follow John Quincy Adams, "whose study of the Constitution seems to have been directed toward destroying it."[32] The paper's statement can probably be attributed to the growing Democratic support of internal improvements in such key states as Pennsylvania, New York, and Ohio. A check of the *Congressional Globe* reveals a slight trend among Democrats to compromise their constitutional qualms about internal improvements. This trend, which would grow to major proportions during the Pierce administration, was caused by expanding commerce, which in turn required improved transportation systems.

Another indication of the growing sentiment against presidential restriction of Congress in regard to the country's commercial and transportation facilities occurred in February, 1845, when a veto was overridden for the first time in American history. The situation was ironical, for the vetoed bill related to the President's authority to order the construction of revenue cutters and steamers which could be used, at the discretion of the President, as dispatch vessels.

The bill was introduced into the Senate on January 6, 1845, by Jabez Huntingdon from Connecticut. It prohibited the building of revenue vessels or steam cutters by order of the Executive, unless appropriations for such construction had been previously made by Congress.[33] This, in effect, would take away the President's power over maritime activities in the same way that the President had taken away the power of Congress over internal improvements. It was to be expected that Tyler would reject the bill.

Tyler began the veto message with an assertion that the public interest would be damaged by the Revenue Cutter Bill. He said that two boats had already been contracted: one for the coast of Georgia and the other for Mobile Bay. The contractors, one from Richmond and the other from Pittsburgh, had gone to considerable expense in procuring materials and sites for construction.[34] Tyler was confident that the Senate did not deliberately mean to violate the sanctity of contracts entered into by the United States government; therefore, Tyler's chief reason for rejecting the Revenue Cutter Bill was his desire to protect existing contracts.[35]

When the veto was reconsidered in the Senate on March 3, 1845, the day Tyler left office, Huntingdon called it a "philosophical" veto, presumably because of Tyler's arguments about the sanctity of contracts.[36] He was joined by Crittenden, who said there was no good reason for Tyler's rejection of the bill. In an anti-climactic fashion, the Senate killed the veto by a vote of 41 to1, the dissenting vote being cast by Walter T. Colquitt from Georgia. When the vote was completed in the Senate, the veto was immediately sent to the House of Representatives.

The debate in the House was more lively than in the Senate. Speaking for the veto Bayley said that he could prove in five minutes that the bill ought not to become law.[37] He said that if the bill passed, it would repudiate rightful contracts, causing much injury to be inflicted upon innocent parties unless the House expressed itself against the Senate[38]

Bayley did not impress his colleagues, however, for when the roll was called, most were in favor of the Revenue Cutter Bill. When the voting was about half completed, Bayley announced that the hour was past midnight, and that the second session of the Twenty-eighth Congress was legally out of existence.[39] He was shouted down by cries of "Order!" A few minutes later, James E. Belser of Alabama stopped the calling of the roll again and said that it was unconstitutional for the House to transact business after the session had legally ended. Considerable confusion and uproar followed,[40] amid exhortations to the clerk to "go on, go on."[41] When the voting was completed, Tyler's veto had suffered a 127 to 30 defeat in the House.[42] Thus, Congress had the last word in its long and bitter struggle with President Tyler.

The most obvious aspect of John Tyler's vetoes was his consistency in defending state rights concepts. He usually stayed within the realm of reasoned arguments except in the Eastern Harbor veto where, as we have seen, he carried his interpretation of the Commerce Clause to an unwarranted conclusion. Tyler was the first President to use consistently the Constitution to uphold state rights principles. Madison, Monroe, and Jackson, in the vetoes in which they argued state rights, usually did so on grounds of expediency of one form or another.

Tyler's vetoes affected some institutional relationships. For example, he proved the great importance of the veto as a tool by which the President can control Congress. The tendency of strong executive government, begun in Jackson's time, was all but completed under Tyler. It was mainly Tyler's vetoes which enabled him to attain power as President, whereas Jackson's vetoes, though powerful, were not the only devices he used to develop strong executive leadership. Thus Tyler should be viewed as the President who carried the veto to its fullest extent in the period before the Civil War. By his vetoes, Tyler helped to produce the poorest executive-legislative relationship up to that period in American history, and he helped to weaken the Whig party, thereby aiding the Democratic victory in 1844. A counterpart to Tyler's control of Congress through the veto would be the congressional reaction against President Johnson in the Reconstruction era.

Tyler's administration can be viewed as an adjunct to several practices begun during Jackson's incumbency. Tyler provided form for much of the malleable material of Jacksonian democracy. Jackson was a pioneer in formulating some of his principles on the bank and internal improvements, while Tyler took these principles and added constitutionalism to them. Later, James K. Polk adopted both the principles of expediency used by Jackson and the constitutionalism of Tyler and provided what may be called the nineteenth century fulfillment of Jacksonian democracy.

James K. Polk and Jacksonian Democracy
1846-1847

JAMES K. POLK is aptly titled "Young Hickory," because in his congressional career he was a devoted follower of Jackson. His presidency demonstrated a strong respect for the governmental precepts established in the Jackson period, and his vetoes were a mixture of Jacksonianism and Tylerism. This is not to claim that Polk was merely a "carbon copy" of Jackson; only to say that in his three vetoes he more nearly reflected the spirit of Jackson than any other president included in this study. This was definitely shown, with a few exceptions that will be noted, by Polk's reactions to internal improvements at federal expense. It will be remembered that Polk hotly defended Jackson and the veto power in the Maysville issue.[1] He continued to fight against internal improvements during the interval between 1830 and his election to the presidency in 1844. There could have been little doubt, then, about how Polk would react to an internal improvements bill which reached him relatively early in his administration.

The bill, of House origin, made appropriations for the improvement of certain harbors and rivers, allocating $1,378,450 for more than 40 internal improvement projects.[2] Many of the improvements were to be in the West. For example, $80,000 was appropriated to improve the Ohio River above the falls, $240,000 for improvement below the falls, and $80,000 for the harbor at St. Louis.[3] The bill brought together many interests of the country, which held in common a desire to improve transportation facilities to cope with an expanding commerce. It is significant that this bill was passed by a Democratic Congress—in the House by a comfortable majority (19) and in the Senate by over a two-thirds majority. This indicated that the trend among some Democrats, which began during the Tyler administration, was resulting in a looser interpretation of internal improvements.

Polk's veto message, August 3, 1846, stayed close to the mood established by Jackson in dealing with internal improvements: no specific authority existed to give Congress power of internal improvements, and there was nothing incidental to an expressed power which could justify the program. It would be much wiser and safer to obtain an amendment allowing internal improvements than to pass laws of dubious validity.[4] If the bill in question passed, it would repudiate all previous internal improvement vetoes and would begin a system limited only "by the ever-varying discretion of successive Congresses and successive executives."[5] Furthermore, it would consolidate the power of the federal government while diminishing that of the states. The few would be benefited at the expense of the many, engendering sectional feelings and prejudices which, in turn, would "disturb the harmony of the Union."[6]

Moreover, many of the improvements called for in the bill were purely local in nature. Some places, even creek mouths, designated in the bill as "harbors," had nothing to do with foreign or interstate commerce. Nor were they places of refuge or shelter for the United States navy or commercial marine.[7] These provisions of the bill, said Polk, proved the ineffectiveness of Jackson's definition of proper expenditures in his Wabash veto of 1834.[8] It was too easy for Congress to establish "paper ports" allowing expenditure of money for improvement below them. The bill was a classic example of the advantage that proponents of internal improvements tried to take of Jackson's definition. This was the one point in the veto where Polk disagreed with Jackson's feelings toward internal improvements, since the Wabash veto provided a loophole that Polk now hastened to correct.

In addition to stating constitutional reasons against the bill, Polk argued that it would be inexpedient. The United States was at war with Mexico, and federal money was needed to win it. This was especially true since few of the improvements in the bill were of pressing necessity. If the bill passed, it would create a huge public debt which could probably be liquidated only by further taxation. Finally, the bill would begin an unwholesome relationship between the federal government and the states, one that would grow to great proportions in succeeding years.[9]

In the House, where the bill was reconsidered on August 4, Representative Stephen A. Douglas of Illinois pointed out that the appropriations for St. Louis would have forced the waters of the Mississippi to run along a wharf on the right bank instead of allowing them to run in their natural channel near the left bank. This would aid the inhabitants of St. Louis considerably, said Douglas, but it would not improve the safety and facility of navigation on the river.[10] This was the sort of extravagant localism, he intimated, that caused Polk to veto the bill.

Douglas' remarks were challenged by Michigan Representative Robert McClelland, who said that the sum for St. Louis had been estimated and approved by the War Department. He and his associates could not understand why the President, who had presumably approved the St. Louis project when presented to him by the Secretary of War, would now use it as a reason for vetoing the Internal Improvements Bill.

Douglas replied that the veto did not reject appropriations for harbors that were to be used for foreign or interstate commerce. In this respect, he did not subscribe to the distinctions that some people made between Congress' power over foreign commerce and interstate commerce, since the power of Congress to regulate both types of commerce was given in the same constitutional clause. Douglas presumably was attacking here the interpretation that Tyler had placed upon the Commerce Clause in the Eastern Harbor veto of 1844.[11] Douglas also rejected Jackson's thesis in the Wabash veto that improvements could be made below a port of entry. If Congress had the right to improve a harbor at all, said Douglas, it could do it either below or above ports of entry. He found illogical, too, the distinction that some made between fresh and salt water, as well as amounts of ebb and flow, as criteria upon which to base improvements. He claimed that these distinctions came from England, where all waters were navigable by law if not by fact. This not being the case in the United States, Douglas said, only navigable waters of fact should be provided for by the federal government. He concluded his speech by recommending that the Committee on Commerce study the veto, remove the President's objections, and reintroduce the bill.[12]

David Wilmot of Pennsylvania defended Polk's veto by saying that the Internal Improvement Bill was passed by a combination of interests. Sectional and local concerns had united to give the bill enough votes; therefore, it was an example of colossal logrolling. The veto was Jacksonian in character, and because of the similarity to Jackson's actions, the country would approve it. The veto power, said Wilmot, was a great conservative feature of the Constitution and every Democratic President who had ever used it had been completely supported by the American people. The same would be true with Polk's veto of the Internal Improvement Bill.[13]

Pennsylvania Representative Richard Brodhead stated that he was in favor of internal improvements, but on this occasion he would vote to sustain Polk's veto, because many Westerners had voted against the tariff[14] which had recently been passed. Brodhead said the Westerners could not expect to get improvements in rivers and harbors if they struck down the very revenue (tariff) which would provide such improvements. The veto was, therefore, a just "retribution" against the West for its stand against the tariff.

Jacob Brinkerhoff of Ohio mentioned the tariff too, and said that if its passage had been delayed just one week, Polk would have signed the Internal Improvement Bill, having been forced to this action to get his tariff proposals enacted.[15]

The last word on Polk's veto was given by Tyler's old defender, Bayley, who claimed that the inequities resulting from systems of internal improvements were contrary to the spirit of the Constitution.[16] Some had criticized Polk because he had not told Congress that a veto was forthcoming on the Internal Improvement Bill. Bayley observed, though, that if Polk had given such a warning, he would have been accused of dictating to Congress.[17] After Bayley's speech was completed, a vote was taken on the returned bill. The result was 96 to 91; Polk's first veto was sustained.

Newspapers representing the Whig party were, of course, unhappy over the veto. The *National Intelligencer* spoke out in despair and agreed with Brikerhoff that Polk probably retained the Internal Improvement Bill until the Walker tariff was safely passed. The paper said that the American government could not recapture its republican character until "one man power" was destroyed. We did not have a democratic government, the paper asserted, but a "quadrennial elective" despotism.[18] The veto stopped many works of national importance, said the *Intelligencer*, while the continuing growth of commerce and transportation in the country made internal improvements inevitable. Presidents might stop them temporarily, but they were bound to come.[19]

The *Jonesboro Whig*, which had been a bitter foe of Tyler, now turned its editorial guns on Polk. The Internal Improvement Bill, said the paper, was passed by large majorities in both houses of Congress only to be defeated by the "grandson of old Ezekiel Polk," a Tory in the American Revolution. The paper took the political allegiance of his grandfather to mean that Polk would not give his best to the development of the country.[20] The paper noted that many Democrats had voted for the bill and said that its defeat would be felt by both the Whig and Democratic parties. Because of the veto, the internal commerce of the country was unprotected, harbors were left to decay, millions of dollars in property were put in peril, "in order that party schemes may be pursued without interruption, and personal selfishness may be satiated without hindrance or stint."[21] The *Whig* thus amply demonstrated that it had not lost its fervor for politics, or its sense of drama.

The *Baltimore Sun*, which appeared to take a more independent position on most issues than the other papers mentioned in this narrative, merely reported the veto in its columns. It did betray its feelings, though, by mentioning that among the items in the vetoed bill was $20,000 for the improvement of Baltimore harbor, and $20,000 for Havre de Grace, thus hinting at its displeasure.[22]

The *Richmond Enquirer* supported and eulogized Polk for crushing "the nest-egg of extravagance" known as internal improvements.[23] He had acted in accordance with the republican principles of the Jeffersonian standard[24] in killing a bill, the passage of which would have turned the federative government "into an evil consolidation." Polk would not have been true to his principles if he had not vetoed the Internal Improvement Bill.[25]

The Whigs, said the *Enquirer*, should not criticize the President for the veto. Instead, they should turn their attacks on the Founding Fathers, who had the wise foresight to include it in the Constitution. The value of the veto was evidenced by the dwindling of the majority when the bill was reconsidered. Upon initial passage in the House, the majority was 19, but upon reconsideration, the majority was only 5.[26] This showed the importance of the "sober second thought" which was encouraged by the veto power. The *Enquirer*, along with other Democratic journals, regretted the fact that the bill had been passed by "the Union of a few Democrats and the whole Whig party,"[27] but comforted itself because a "Democratic President killed it, carrying out the wishes of a majority of the Democratic party."[28] As long as Polk was President, "internal improvements will never rear their ugly heads."[29]

The *Jacksonville* (Alabama) *Republican* took this occasion to write an essay on the power and the relation of the Whigs to Polk's veto. It had been the misfortune of the Whigs, said the paper, to retain so many colonial tendencies that they could not "sympathize with the great mass of American people." The veto power received its character from the person who exercised it, said the *Republican*, and if the Whigs could not discern the difference between use of the veto and "one man power," they could never understand the American people. Since the adoption of the Constitution, Congress had passed more than 6,000 acts, but Polk's rejection of the Internal Improvement Bill was only the thirty-second veto. Therefore, the "shallow notion" that the qualified veto was dangerous to national liberty must be done away with. The veto had "no permanent force save as it reflect[ed] the popular will."[30]

Polk's next veto came less than a week after the Internal Improvement rejection. It was on a congressional proposal known as the French Spoliation Bill, which sought to pay $5,000,000 in land scrip to liquidate mercantile claims against the government growing out of the French disputes prior to 1800. These claims had not been included in the general settlement with the French during Jackson's administration. The claims, long a source of contention, had been introduced into the Senate on numerous occasions and had been reported favorably by several House committees, but had never passed the House until now. Of the 25 reports made by Congress on the claims over a period of several years, 22 urged payment.[31] The Whigs, for the most part, championed the cause of the claimants, while the Democrats opposed it.

The *Richmond Enquirer* led the opposition to the claims. It printed a long article, signed by "Quaestor," in an effort to prove that not one dollar in the bill was due. The claims were supposedly transferred to the American government by French-American agreements of 1799 and 1800 in which France, according to proponents of the claims, repudiated all indemnities caused by the naval warfare between the two countries during 1797-1798. By so doing the American government assumed them. But the American negotiators in 1799, said the *Enquirer*, wanted to leave the claims open, so they inserted an article in the original agreement to negotiate them later at a more convenient time. The American Senate, desiring to make clear the abrogation of all prior agreements with the French as stipulated in a treaty of July 7, 1798, feared that this article in the 1799 treaty would recognize the existence of earlier treaties. Consequently, the Senate would not ratify the 1799 agreement until this article on the claims was expunged. The French acceded to this demand and said that they thereby renounced all indemnities.[32] Advocates of the French Spoliation claims, therefore, believed that the American government had assumed the French claims in return for French recognition that the 1799 agreement abolished all former treaties between the two countries.

The claimants and their supporters in Congress also used the French-American convention of 1800 to justify their demands. Here, the French, ignoring the 1798 treaty, argued that if the American government wanted to be relieved of the burdens of the former treaties, it should assume the indemnities resulting from naval war. However, the American negotiators would not yield to this demand, stating that the United States had abrogated all former treaties by the 1798 agreement. Hence, the federal government could not abandon in 1800 what had already been abandoned in 1798. The United States had rejected the claims and the former treaties well before the agreements of 1799 and 1800 upon which the claimants based their case.[33]

President Polk's veto message to the Senate on August 8, 1846, agreed with the *Enquirer's* interpretation. The remoteness of the period to which the claims belonged, along with the complicated nature of their origins, made it difficult for the President to come to an immediate decision on the bill. No greater necessity existed now than in the past for settling the claims. The treasury had often been affluent enough to pay them if they were just, and Polk cited the treasury surpluses of 1808 and 1836 to prove his point. The claims had been periodically brought to the attention of Congress for over half a century and nothing had been done. Therefore, he could not believe that the American government would have reneged so long on the claims if they were valid.[34]

The war with Mexico was another reason why Polk could not approve the French Spoliation Bill. There was no surplus in the treasury at the moment, and a public debt of several million dollars existed. He realized that the payments were to be made in land scrip, but he said the effect on the treasury would be the same as if they were paid in money. To relinquish control over vast areas of land would be to lose a large source of revenue; moreover, most of the holders of the scrip would be non-residents who could demand exorbitant prices from people who actually wanted to settle the land. It was also possible that the scrip holders would keep the lands in question off the market, "thus retarding the prosperity and growth of the states where they are located."[35]

In conclusion, he said that the claims really amounted to more than $5,000,000, yet the claimants were willing to settle for far less than the actual indemnities. If the claims were just, there was no reason to repudiate part of them. He regretted the conclusions to which he had been forced in the veto of the French Spoliation Bill: "In interposing my objections to its becoming a law I am fully sensible that it should be an extreme case which would make it the duty of the executive to withhold his approval of any bill passed by Congress upon the ground of its inexpediency alone. Such a case I consider this to be."[36]

In the Senate where the bill was reconsidered on August 10, Senator Clayton said that this was the first veto in American history based solely upon grounds of expediency.[37] He was, of course, overlooking Washington's veto of the Dragoon Bill in 1797.[38] In the Senator's opinion, the veto opened a new chapter in executive history, because it gave the President power over claims against the government that the Founding Fathers never meant for him to possess. Polk's judgment that the claims, if just, would have been paid in good times, would be ridiculed in any court of the land, said Clayton. The President was inconsistent in his reasoning, according to the Delaware Senator, for in one part of the veto Polk said that the claims were extravagant and could not be justified; in another part, he said the true claims exceeded five millions and the government should not seek to pay less than their actual worth. Polk also argued that the claims would hinder the settlement of new states. Clayton countered that the exact opposite would be the result.[39]

Clayton was supported in his opinions by Webster, who said that the veto was an alarming new extension of executive government that was countenanced neither by precedent nor by the Constitution.[40] Huntingdon closed the debate by asserting that if the President could veto bills like the one on French Spoliation, he could dominate the whole legislative process.[41] The veto was sustained 27 to 15.

The *National Intelligencer*, speaking of the veto, said it was the introduction into federal government of a policy of repudiation, compounded by the fact that the government did have the resources to satisfy the claims.[42] The *Baltimore Sun*, departing from its usual policy of non-commitment, said that Polk's argument that the claims should be paid in money was the only sensible area of the veto. The paper did point out, though, that the claimants should have the right to accept payment in any form they chose.[43] One reason the *Sun* opposed the veto was because a million and a half dollars would have been allocated to residents of Baltimore, "some of whom are in quite indigent circumstances."[44] The only salvation for the country, in the paper's view, was the fact that Presidents were elected for relatively short periods. It felt that if the office of President were for life, the veto "would be attended by disastrous consequences."[45]

The *Jonesboro Whig* joined the chorus of indignation and said that Polk's conclusions were disgraceful in both logic and morals. Polk had been "insolent" in his language to Congress who, "with more honesty and more discernment, perceived both the legal and equitable character of the claim."[46] The paper said that the 1800 convention between the United States and France established the validity of the claims against the American government. The debt had been unjustly delayed by the government since its origin, and now Polk had used that very injustice as a reason for vetoing the bill. This was far worse, said the Whig, than pleading the statute of limitations.[47]

Announcing that the veto power was the mainstay of democratic government ,the *Richmond Enquirer* said that if Polk had approved the French Spoliation Bill, $25,000,000 would not have satisfied the claimants. It reported that most of the claims had fallen into the hands of a single individual, whom it identified as John H. Caustin, a resident of Washington. Caustin was described as a man of "great private worth, intelligence, and ability."[48] He had revived the claims in 1828 and had been fighting for their approval ever since. In the course of time, Caustin had supposedly influenced many people, among them William Preston of South Carolina, to change their minds on the validity of the French claims. This, said the *Enquirer,* indicated the dangerous influence that a single agent had in the claims question.[49] In the paper's opinion, the legislation would have been oppressive if it had passed, because it would have benefited the few against the many. Polk, therefore, took the proper course when he rejected it.

It is true that Polk's veto of the French Spoliation Bill was based solely upon financial and political expediency and had nothing to do with the respective roles of Congress and the President in foreign affairs, as did Jackson's veto of the Sicilian claims in 1835. It was based on an interpretation of the French-American conventions of 1799 and 1800. Polk adopted the thesis that the government had not assumed the claims in either of the conventions, and he further felt that this had been the accepted belief for over half a century. If he approved the bill, his action would repudiate the attitude of all the Presidents and Congresses since the days of Jefferson. He simply did not believe that, if the claims were just, the American government would have ignored them over such a long period.

Polk's veto demonstrated his adherence to Jacksonian principles. He was convinced that the issuance of land scrip to a few would have to be done at the expense of the many, an attitude which had ample precedents in Jackson's vetoes of the Maysville Bill, the Bank Recharter Bill, and the Land Bill. He also proved himself a student of Tylerism in the French Spoliation veto by contending that the holders of land scrip would have a power not easily controlled by the states in which the land was located. Thus, Polk was able to blend the nationalistic propensities of Jackson with the states rights beliefs of Tyler, a combination which tended to bring to fulfillment the postulates of Jacksonian democracy.

The last rejection that Polk effected was a pocket veto of a bill called an "act to continue certain works in Wisconsin and for other purposes." The bill, of House origin, appropriated $6,000 for Wisconsin, and more than half a million for "other purposes." Largely because of this discrepancy, Polk kept the bill at the end of the first session of the Twenty-ninth Congress. He gave his reasons in a message to Congress on December 15, 1847.

Polk presented a detailed history of internal improvements to that time with the objective of showing their ruinous nature. In the short time (about 20 years) that the internal improvements question had been discussed on the federal level, requests for about $200,000,000 had been made. Many of the requests had been motivated by speculative interests whose design was only to benefit a few to the detriment of the many. He called freely upon opinions that had been given on the subject by former Presidents, believing that Monroe (who had changed his thinking somewhat after his veto of the Cumberland bill in 1822) and J. Q. Adams had done the most to allow such a system to infiltrate the Congress. Jackson, however, had been instrumental in stopping the extravagance of internal improvements.[50]

Polk scolded Congress for the connotation it placed on the word "harbor." Congress used the word to denote places where commerce could be attracted by improvements. In the President's opinion, this definition *created* commerce rather than *regulated* it, and this was unconstitutional.[51] Congress could improve harbors only where commerce was already established. This, of course, put Polk in the position of arguing that nature must not be improved upon in the handling of internal improvements. This argument included even sites along the seaboard and it brought Polk much criticism.

In the veto, Polk offered some alternatives to internal improvements at federal expense. He said that states may lay tonnage duties for clearing harbors after permission from Congress was obtained. Raising internal improvement funds in this manner would be a cooperative effort by the state where the improvement was to be located and the federal government. He mentioned that tonnage acts had been passed by several states in the past: Massachusetts, Rhode Island, Pennsylvania, Maryland, Virginia, North Carolina, South Carolina, and Georgia had tonnage acts in their statute books. This plan would ensure that only important items were improved, and it would prevent the sectional abuses prevalent in a wide-spread system of internal improvements.[52] Lacking tonnage duties in the states, Polk asserted that the only other action that would make internal improvements legal was an amendment to the Constitution.[53] In making these suggestions, Polk was adhering relatively closely to Madison's and Jackson's repeated pleas for constitutional amendment. He was, however, the first President to emphasize tonnage duties as an alternative to federal internal improvements. His reflections in this respect, and his definition of what constituted a harbor, made this veto different from all the others that had been given.

While the veto was being read in the House, Thomas Clingman of North Carolina interrupted and moved that the reading be dispensed with, since it was not technically a veto message to the House. Because it was a pocket veto, the House could not act upon it. However, several members demanded to be allowed to speak on the measure. Samuel F. Vinton of Ohio disagreed with Polk's assertion that a high debt would have accrued through internal improvements. On the contrary, claimed the representative, such a program would have saved the country from several financial embarrassments. Here he was presumably referring to Tyler's administration.[54] Andrew Stewart of Pennsylvania suggested that a special committee be appointed to study the veto. In his opinion, the committee should be composed of one representative from every state in the Union. Nothing was subsequently done, however, on this proposal. Stewart went on to say that Polk's veto presented a new view of internal improvements because he denied help even to the seaboard, something that the former Presidents had not done. Polk was not convincing, either, said the Pennsylvanian, in contending that internal improvements built huge debts. Polk was certainly not afraid of high indebtedness as indicated by his prosecution of the Mexican war.[55]

Ohio Representative Robert C. Schenck made the strongest protest against the veto of the Wisconsin Bill. He facetiously reported that there were now several tests that had to be applied to the question of internal improvements. The first was a chemical test to determine whether the water where the improvement was to be was fresh or salt. Second, there was an ichthyological test to determine whether the fish where the improvement was to be made came from fresh or salt water. Third was the meteorological test, "to be found by watching the course of the tides and the distance to which they ascend." Finally, there was the geographical test, which determined the constitutionality of work upon "the question of whether it lies within a State, or is cut by the dividing line of two or more."[56] But Polk, said Schenck, applied a new test. The President "took the bold ground" that nature cannot be helped. If a harbor was deep enough only for schooners, Polk said it would be unconstitutional to deepen it for large ships. He caricatured Polk by saying that every vessel which henceforth traversed the shores of the United States should be given a copy of Polk's veto message. Instead of the usual sailor jargon of "by the deep six," "by the mark five," or "quarter less four," they would have to cry "con-sti-tu-tion-al," or "un-con-sti-tu-tion-al," as they measured the depth of the water over which they sailed into port.[57] Schenck's speech may have entertained the House members, but nothing could be done about Polk's veto.

The Wisconsin Bill, passed by a Democratic Congress, indicated again the growing trend toward internal improvements. While the bill was being discussed in the Senate, Arthur Bagby of Alabama moved that $150,000 in appropriations for the Ohio River below the falls be stricken. On this motion, only 6 Senators voted in the affirmative, while 38 voted negatively. Among those voting in the latter column was Senator Calhoun. These statistics disturbed such staid Democratic papers as the *Richmond Enquirer*.[58] A Democratic President had once again killed the internal improvements bill and as long as he and people of his party stayed in the presidential office, the system could not flourish, so the *Enquirer* thought.

Polk's recommendation of tonnage duties for financing internal improvements indicated that Presidents were being forced into the defensive on such questions. Until Polk's administration, the chief recommendation by Presidents on internal improvements bills was a constitutional amendment. Madison, Jackson, and Tyler never found it necessary to go beyond this suggestion because they were always reasonably sure that their rejections would be sustained. The mere fact, then, that Polk was obliged to emphasize methods other than amendment of the Constitution showed that Congress was beginning to accept internal improvements at federal expense without the authorization of a constitutional amendment.

In assessing Polk as a veto President, one must say that he drew more upon the philosophies of his predecessors than any other President in the ante-bellum period. It is true that he is remembered as a strong, independent executive, but he wanted to make sure that he had the force of precedent behind his veto conclusions. Therefore, his vetoes were quite similar in philosophy to those of Madison, Jackson, and Tyler, emphasizing the theories of the latter two. There were two areas, however, in which he brought out original thoughts. One was when he defined harbors in the Wisconsin Bill as only natural structures which could not be improved by man within the scope of the Constitution. The other was his discussion of tonnage duties as a legitimate method of providing for internal improvements. The latter suggestion assured the positive character of Polk's internal improvement vetoes, for it showed that Polk was not merely interested in destroying something but in helping to make it compatible with his interpretation of the Constitution. It also indicated that Polk was striving to maintain the initiative on a subject which had always been the cause of much friction between the President and Congress.

Polk used both expediency and the Constitution to rationalize his vetoes. The rejection of the French claims was based, by Polk's own admission, on reasons of expediency. There ran through the veto, however, an undertone of protecting at least the spirit of the Constitution as Polk interpreted it. To give land to a few people at the expense of the many was to violate the democratic concepts of equality. In the internal improvement vetoes, Polk used constitutional reasons (no specific power in the Constitution for internal improvements), and financial and political expediency (the Mexican war demanded most of the resources of the Treasury and internal improvements would lead to sectionalism). The internal improvement vetoes were Jacksonian in spirit, lacking, however, the personal animosity which prevailed in many of Jackson's rejections. They were Tyleristic also in that Polk was not willing to go as far in allowing internal improvements as Jackson. It will be remembered that this had been a notable difference between Jackson and Tyler. Finally, Polk's internal improvement vetoes marked the end of a period when a President could reject such bills and expect to be fully sustained by Congress.

Vetoes of Pierce and Buchanan
1853-1861

THE Whigs made the veto power a major issue in the presidential campaign of 1848. Their candidate, Zachary Taylor, pointed to the abuses of the veto by Jackson, Tyler, and Polk and promised never to use the power except to keep Congress in harmony with the Constitution or to protect the executive from legislative encroachments. The Democrats took the defensive on the veto power, arguing, as so often in the past, that the veto was indispensable to good government. For a President to pledge not to use it would be to abolish it temporarily.[1]

The veto was accordingly abandoned during the administrations of Taylor and Fillmore, although there were indications that Taylor would have vetoed the Texas bill in 1850[2] if he had lived to see it consummated. Fillmore, of course, favored the Compromise bills of 1850, so there was little possibility of the veto being used by him. For over four years, then, the veto power was in abeyance. This situation undoubtedly had an effect on Pierce when he came to office in 1853. For example, as internal improvements spread and as the Wilmot Proviso and the Compromise of 1850 became absorbing topics, the veto was relegated to the background. When it emerged, the old arguments either for or against it were no longer applicable. It could not be assumed in 1853 that the Democrats would, as a matter of course, defend the power, or that Whiggery would protest its use. One could not, in 1853, be labeled simply as a "Democrat" or a "Whig," for there were now too many shadings within both parties. Apparently, persons representing many shadings on the political spectrum combined to sanction progress in the form of internal improvements and commerce, for they were able to overturn most of Pierce's vetoes against these programs.

The veto was used for most conservative reasons in the administrations of Pierce and Buchanan. Their incumbencies may be described as the last great struggle in the nineteenth century against the inevitable progress of commerce and transportation. It was no coincidence that Congress began systemtaically overriding internal improvement vetoes during an era of rapid commercial expansion.

The trend observed during Tyler's administration was now, for the most part, completed.[3] Even the votes on the vetoes of Pierce and Buchanan that were sustained were always close enough to indicate that presidential objections could not long be tolerated. The two Presidents together vetoed 16 bills; Pierce 9 and Buchanan 7, although Pierce was the less successful of the two, for 5 of his vetoes were overturned.

The first dispute between Pierce and Congress occurred on May 3, 1854, when he returned to the Senate a bill providing land grants for the indigent insane. Known sometimes as the Dix Bill (because of the support given to it by humanitarian Dorothea Dix), it granted 10,000,000 acres of public land to the several states, apportioned according to congressional representation. The states could sell the land and use the proceeds to establish a perpetual fund for the indigent insane.[4]

Pierce was aware of the unpopularity that would result from his vetoing a bill supported by so many charitable organizations; therefore, he spent a week preparing the message. He used Madison's argument in the 1811 veto of the Episcopal Incorporation Bill that the federal government could not give legal sanction to something that was charitable in nature. If the federal government cared for the indigent insane, Pierce felt it would be only a matter of time until all the needy, not just those who were insane, would have to be assisted.[5] He also adopted Jackson's argument in the 1833 veto of Clay's bill[6] that lands ceded by states to the Union at its formation must be used for the common good.[7] Financial expediency, too, was a reason for vetoing the Indigent Insane Bill, because the public lands were security for the Mexican War debt; so no grant could be made before complying with this prior obligation.[8] Pierce attempted to avoid some of the criticism that he anticipated by intimating that he would approve land grants to railroads. Sometimes, he claimed, the profitable management of land required that portions of it be used to enhance the value of the whole, which was what any "prudent proprietor" would do. This did not, however, give sanction to wholesale appropriations of land by the federal government.[9]

The Senate reconsidered the bill on July 6. Pierce was attacked for his reference to the public land as security for the Mexican War debt, while instances of Pierce's approval of land grants to soldiers and to railroads were cited. There was little difference between granting lands for these purposes and granting land for the indigent insane. If Congress was a "prudent proprietor" as Pierce said, it could dispose of the lands in the manner it chose.

Pierce's defense came mostly from Southerners who believed that public lands were subject to the same restrictions as money. John Bell of Tennessee, a Whig, favored the bill, but admitted that it did open doors to unwarranted speculation and made it possible for the landless old states to be made subservient to the young states with large land resources.[10] The vote on reconsideration of the bill was close, 21 to 26.

The *New York Times* was a strong supporter of the Indigent Insane Bill. While Pierce was considering it, the paper stated that the President had earlier assured Miss Dix that he favored it. The *Times* blamed Representative David Disney of Ohio, Chairman of the House Committee on Public Lands, for propagandizing against the bill to obtain its veto.[11] Conversely, the *Richmond Enquirer* was ecstatic over the President's veto. It called Pierce a disciple of Jefferson and Jackson and said that he had no other choice but to oppose "every scheme for diverting the public lands from their legitimate uses." The public lands, said the *Enquirer*, could not be used for anything except payment of the national debt. Thus, the veto was a "memorable step" in the progress of the Democratic party because it halted the diminishing power of state rights. The paper dramatically claimed that it seemed to be the mission of the Democratic party to come into power at times of threats to the Constitution "and by the agency of the executive . . . veto to arrest unwarranted programs."[12]

Pierce was well known as a Northern Democrat with Southern inclinations; as such, his interpretation of the Constitution was a strict one. Unless Congress was specifically given power by the Constitution to act, it was forbidden. His state rights leanings, of long standing, caused him to believe that the states were the appropriate agencies for carrying out the program called for in the Indigent Insane Bill; he quoted the Tenth Amendment as the rightful authority in this respect. With these facts about Pierce in mind it should be concluded that his veto of the Indigent Insane Bill was a positive reaction, in which he relied mostly upon the Constitution, but to an extent also upon financial expediency. It took a considerable amount of political courage to reject a bill popular with so many people, especially members of his own party. Many Democrats voted for the bill in the first place, and, in the Senate, 4 Democrats voted to pass the bill despite Pierce's objections. If the vetoed bill had been returned to the House, the percent of Democrats for it would have been larger than in the Senate. So, while Pierce was able to hold his own in the Senate, it was the House from which he soon learned to expect trouble.

Pierce's emphasis on a strict interpretation of the Constitution continued as he considered another bill, of House origin, for the completion of certain internal improvements. He signed the veto on August 4, 1854, but did not give his reasons until December. As had many Presidents before him, Pierce gave a detailed history of internal improvements, making John Quincy Adams the villain for foisting such a ruinous system upon the American people. The only real difference between this internal improvement veto and all the others emanated from Pierce's argument that if the Founding Fathers had sanctioned programs of this sort, they would have made it quite clear in the Constitution.[13] He suggested that henceforth Congress pass individual bills for individual improvements,[14] a method which would eliminate some of the log-rolling so prevalent in bills for internal improvements. He also hinted again that Congress could appropriate for railroads and for the national security. He closed by suggesting that Polk's plan of allowing states to impose tonnage rates for internal improvements be employed.[15]

This internal improvements veto was a guide to Pierce's future reaction to similar bills. He was praised for his action by the *Richmond Enquirer* because early in his administration he had shown, as had Polk in the past, that he would not sanction programs "fraught with danger and difficulty." Pierce was morally and politically correct in preventing millions from being taxed to the advantage of the few.[16] After sporadic debate in the House, Pierce's veto was upheld on December 6, 1854, by a vote of 95 to 80. This was the first and only internal improvements veto of Pierce's to be so treated. His other five internal improvements vetoes were overruled by Congress, sometimes with an enthusiasm that hinted of vengeance.

The next two vetoes, however, were sustained by Congress. One was on the French Spoliation Bill which, it will be remembered, was vetoed by Polk in 1846. The subject was still the same; that is, the claims sought to satisfy those people (mostly insurance companies) who had not been included in the settlement with the French during Jackson's administration. As in the Indigent Insane veto, Pierce took his time in preparing this message, which he presented to the House on February 17, 1855. He admitted that no constitutional question was involved in the bill; however, like Polk, he argued that if the claims were just, they would have been paid long ago. In a short treatise on the veto power he argued that it was the President's personal feeling toward a bill that should decide whether he approved it or not.[17] Only an extraordinary case would cause a President to veto a bill for expediency alone. This was such a case, said Pierce, for if the bill passed, the French might originate claims against Americans for damages of the 1797-1798 war, thus leading to a raid on the Treasury Department. Because the bill might disrupt relations with France, and because it might allow abusive financial maneuvering, Pierce vetoed the second French Spoliation Bill. When the House reconsidered it on February 19, 1855, Pierce was narrowly sustained by a vote of 113 to 86. The vote was about 61 per cent in favor of overriding the veto.

Several Democrats were distressed over the President's veto of the French Spoliation Bill, and they assumed the Whiggish attitude of condemning "executive usurpation."[18] The Washington reporter for the New York Times overheard a Democrat, complaining of the veto, say that he would vote for the Texas Debt Bill if he thought the President would veto it, "so that the overshadowings of Mr. Pierce's disapprovals might result alike on all sections of the Union—the River and Harbor veto on the West, the French Spoliation veto on the East and Centre, and the Texas Debt veto on the South and Southwest."[19] The Richmond Enquirer called the Claims bill "shameless speculation" at the expense of the government. Pierce had once again interposed himself between the Constitution and a Congress willing to give up a substantial part of the national treasury. He had acted in the tradition—time-honored by now—of the Democratic party.[20]

The veto was discussed again shortly after it was sustained by the House. Representative Augustus Sollers of Maryland offered the rejected French Spoliation Bill as an amendment to a civil and diplomatic appropriation bill. The Chair, occupied by Harry Hibbard of New Hampshire, ruled Soller's amendment out of order, a decision which Sollers immediately appealed to the whole membership. John Kerr, Jr., of North Carolina said that if Soller's amendment were kept in the civil and diplomatic bill, Pierce would have no alternative but to use the veto again. Ohio Representative John L. Taylor supported Soller's amendment, and said he would be willing for all appropriation bills to die just to show the country how capricious Pierce was in using the veto. When the voting took place on the Chair's decision that Soller's amendment was out of order, the Chair was sustained by a large vote.[21]

Again showing that he would not be cowed by the business interests of the country, Pierce handed down another veto on March 3, 1855, on a bill calling for subsidies for ocean mails and dealing specifically with the E. K. Collins Line. The bill increased the governmental subsidy to Collins for carrying trans-Atlantic mails; freed the Line from the obligation of maintaining five ships in service; and took away Congress' power to terminate the contract by giving six months' notice.[22] The bill angered Pierce, who now concluded that the relationship between business and government should be made more distinct than in the past. He therefore vetoed the Collins Bill.

The House, which reconsidered the vetoed bill in the closing hours of the Thirty-third Congress, was a scene of great excitement. Theodore G. Hunt of Louisiana denounced the veto as "tyranny of the worst kind,"[23] and James H. Campbell of Pennsylvania called for a revolution.[24] The *New York Times*, lamenting the veto, said that the Collins Bill was to have been the means by which the United States attained a postal treaty with Great Britain.[25] The paper blamed the veto on Pierce's ignorance of good business practices and upon pressure from the interests of Cornelius Vanderbilt. Immediately after the veto, Vanderbilt applied to the Senate for the job of taking the mails to Liverpool. The *Times* was happy to report that the Senate indignantly turned Vanderbilt away by voting overwhelmingly against his proposition.[26] The *Richmond Enquirer*, as usual, supported Pierce's veto, saying that he had destroyed the Collins monopoly. It dramatized that the veto was not only a barrier against federal encroachments, "but a sort of . . . ratabane or strychnine, wherewith he [Pierce] cleanses the capitol of the beasts of prey and creeping things that plunder the treasury and feed upon the substance of the people."[27] When the House completed its deliberations on the returned bill on March 3, Pierce and the *Enquirer* were exonerated 79 to 99. That was the last time Pierce obtained a favorable vote on a veto.

Between May 19 and August 14, 1856, Pierce vetoed five internal improvements bills, for improvements on the Mississippi and Saint Clair Flats (both on May 19), Saint Mary's River (May 22), Des Moines Rapids (August 11), and the Patapsco River (August 14). The theme of the vetoes was the same as in his rejection of December, 1854:[28] no constitutional authority existed for federal internal improvements; the improvements called for were local rather than national; such a system would lead to logrolling and speculative tactics by Congress; and the result would be sectional animosities.[29]

The Mississippi and St. Clair vetoes met sharp opposition in the Senate, where they were considered on July 7. Louisiana's Judah P. Benjamin attacked Pierce by noting that the Mississippi River was the only outlet for 14 states and 5 territories, together comprising an area 22 times the size of New York.[30] The *New York Times* correspondent reported that it was amusing to watch the different Democratic reactions to the veto. Thomas G. Davidson of Louisiana was particularly bitter. One Congressman tried to comfort the Louisiana delegate by telling him that Pierce vetoed the bill "out of the kindness of his heart," demonstrated by the fact that if the Mississippi were improved and if war began, it would be easy for enemy ships to ascend to New Orleans and destroy it. Davidson and his Louisiana colleagues, however, did not find the argument convincing—or amusing.[31]

Other debate on the bill centered around attempts to postpone the vote until a full Senate could be convened. John Slidell of Louisiana strongly sensed that enough votes were present to override Pierce's objections, but it had to be decided whether it would take two-thirds of the whole membership or two-thirds of a quorum to repass a bill. The Chair ruled that the Constitution stipulated that a majority made a quorum to do business. Also, it was pointed out that when the first eleven amendments to the Constitution were approved by Congress, only a quorum had been present;[32] therefore, the whole membership need not be present when the voting occurred. The Chair's decision was upheld by a vote of 34 to 7.[33] Immediately following the ruling, the Senate voted on the Mississippi bill and passed it over the veto 31 to 12. It was sent then to the House where, with little debate, the veto was destroyed 143 to 55. The vote in the Senate on the St. Clair bill was 28 to 8 and in the House 130 to 55.[34]

In the midst of the discussions on the next veto, St. Mary's, the celebrated attack upon Charles Sumner by Preston Brooks occurred. The excitement of this event pushed the internal improvement veto into the background, and not until July 7, 1856, did the Senate override the veto 28 to 10. The next day the House concurred 136 to 54. The destruction of this veto led Elihu Washburne of Illinois to declare that at the first opportunity he would move to pass all other rivers and harbors bills upon which no action had been taken.[35] Apparently, then, once Congress succeeded in overturning one internal improvements veto, it was willing to enlarge the program considerably. The next internal improvements veto, Des Moines Rapids, was killed in the House on August 11 by a vote of 130 to 54. Five days later, the Senate confirmed the House's action 30 to 14. By the time of the last internal improvement veto, the Potapsco River, Congress was simply going through the formality of repassing the bills. It was reconsidered in the Senate on August 16 and passed over the veto 31 to 14; it was approved in the House on the same day 127 to 47.

Pierce's administration ended what may be called an era in American history: that period when Presidents could successfully stand in the way of commercial and transportation expansion. Pierce's conservatism was out of line with the times: his theories would have worked well in the first part of the century, but by the 1850's they were anachronisms. The relationship between business interests and the government, whether good or bad, was in reality much closer in the 1850's than at the opening of the century. Pierce attempted, therefore, to apply old interpretations to new situations.

He could not be called Jacksonian in his internal improvement vetoes, for Jackson constantly applied a broader interpretation to such programs than Pierce. Nor could Pierce be linked to Tyler in his rejections of this category, for Tyler approved bills for the Mississippi River similar to the ones that Pierce vetoed. Pierce was closer to Polk in vetoes of this type than any other President covered in this study: internal improvements, with few exceptions were unconstitutional. Pierce's inflexible stand helped cause the congressional reaction against him. A new generation of congressmen, asserting themselves in a most forceful manner, were now at the helm of government. This was demonstrated after Pierce's administration by the changes in both presidential and congressional attitudes toward interpreting the government's role in internal improvements. It is true that Pierce's successor, James Buchanan, vetoed two internal improvements bills, but it is noteworthy that both of them were pocket vetoes.

Buchanan's first veto, which was pocketed, dealt with a House-originated joint resolution to hasten delivery of federal mails from St. Joseph, Missouri, to Placerville, California. Introduced by James A. Craig of Missouri on June 10, 1858, the resolution provided a *pro rata* increase to the mail contractors for additional exertions in reducing delivery time from 38 to 30 days. Buchanan's opinion, on January 7, 1859, was that the resolution was unnecessary because the Postmaster General could order an increase in delivery time without authority from Congress. Moreover, the resolution sought to pay the contractors $49,000 more than they had asked for in the first place.[36] The delegates from Missouri and California were naturally disappointed over the veto, but most of the lawmakers agreed with R. M. T. Hunter of Virginia that the days of the overland mail were numbered. Steamers provided a safer and faster method of mail delivery than did the overland. Therefore, if the route between St. Joseph and Placerville were maintained, the pay to the contractors should be diminished rather than increased.[37]

The Overland Mail veto set the pattern Buchanan followed in his other rejections: that of strict thrift when dealing with government money. Like his predecessor, Pierce, Buchanan felt that Congress had no authority other than that specifically designated by the Constitution; therefore, he believed that Congress had no authority to subsidize business firms, to appropriate for internal improvements, or to grant public lands no matter how important or charitable the purpose.

Such was the case with the next veto, given to the House on February 24, 1859. It was on a controversial bill designed to cede 20,000 acres of public land to the several states, apportioned according to each state's representation in Congress. Another 20,000 acres would be given for each additional representative to which any state might be entitled when the 1860 census was taken.[38] The purpose of the land grants was to enable the states to establish colleges for studies in agriculture and mechanical arts.

Deeming the bill as both inexpedient and unconstitutional, Buchanan declared that it would deprive the Treasury of approximately $5,000,000 a year collected from the sale of public lands.[39] The distinction between the federal and state governments would be diminished to the detriment of the states. If the states ever depended upon the federal government for maintaining their systems of education and internal policy, "the character of both Governments will be greatly deteriorated."[40] The bill would injure the new states by causing the price of land to go so high that people would hesitate to settle.[41] Also, if the federal government gave the land, it would have no power to enforce the objects for which it was given.

The bill would interfere with existing colleges in the various states where agricultural and mechanical arts were already being taught. Even if appropriations of land could be made to the states for educational purposes, it would be logical to direct them toward the establishment of agricultural and mechanical professorships in already existing colleges.[42] Buchanan argued further that Section Three, Article Four of the Constitution did not give Congress the appropriate power for the College bill, as claimed by its proponents. Congress had the power to "dispose of . . . territory or other property belonging to the United States," but this did not mean that Congress could "give it away." It would be an anomaly indeed to argue convincingly that the Founding Fathers greatly limited Congress' power in all respects but that of the public land.[43] The President did intimate in the closing sentences of the veto that it would be constitutional to grant some portions of the public land to improve the value of the whole and to encourage settlement. Presumably he had in mind here, as had Pierce before him, granting lands for the construction of railroads.[44]

The College bill was reconsidered in the House on February 26, 1859. Justin Morrill of Vermont, the bill's sponsor, bitterly denounced Buchanan for committing, "if not a crime, at least a blunder."[45] The Vermont Representative said the bill was supported by both political parties, by petitions from at least 13 states, and by innumerable memorials, including one from the Trustees of the Pennsylvania Agricultural College.[46] The bill would have been approved, said Morrill, by all former Presidents, especially Washington. He cited Washington's opinion in his Farewell Address that the soil should become "an object of public patronage."[47]

Morrill then attacked each point of Buchanan's veto. The bill would not ruin the Treasury, because it would take two years to implement the colleges. The states would be in control of the colleges, so the bill would not, as Buchanan claimed, take away their power. Nor would the bill damage the development of the new states; on the contrary, it would benefit them by appropriations for the additional representatives they would have in the 1860 census. The bill did not "give away" the land as claimed by the President, because land values would be increased throughout the country. Finally, he cited past government endowments to asylums, claiming that if appropriations could be made in that field, they could be made in other fields as well. Morrill was the only outspoken House critic of the College veto. After his speech a vote was taken, with a result of 105 to 96. The defeat of the College bill was only a temporary success for the philosophy held by Buchanan; the bill passed during Lincoln's administration.

Buchanan's next two disapprovals would probably have been overridden if they had not been pocket vetoes. One was on a bill to deepen the channel over St. Clair Flats in Michigan, and the other was to remove obstructions from the Mississippi River. Pierce had had unhappy experiences in vetoes on similar projects, and Buchanan escaped them only through the expediency of pocket vetoes.

In messages on February 1 and February 6, 1860, the President explained his reasons for withholding the bills. First, they were financially unsound. The St. Clair Bill was for the removal of a sand bar between the mouth of the St. Clair River and the deep water of St. Clair Lake, a distance of about 6,000 feet. Appropriations had been made for this work during the Pierce administration and the project was almost completed. The real need, said the President, was periodic dredging to keep the depth of water at a constant level. The expense of this operation, trifling in Buchanan's opinion, should be borne by the interests using the lake and river.[48]

The bills were also unconstitutional, said Buchanan. He used Polk's argument that Congress could only regulate commerce, not create it, pointing out that when the Constitution gave Congress the power to create, it did so in unmistaken language. For example, Congress' power to coin money is creative, after which it has the authority to regulate it. The power to raise armies and navies is creative, while the power to control them is regulative. The Commerce Clause, though, gives no power of creation to Congress; only the power to regulate. The Commerce Clause thus presupposed the existence of commerce before Congress could exercise any power over it.[49] Buchanan also believed that unrestricted internal improvements would damage the relationship between the federal and state governments. He further relied on Polk by suggesting that a levy of tonnage duties would be a successful alternative to federally financed internal improvements.[50]

The St. Clair veto was discussed at length in the Senate, despite the fact that it was a pocket veto. The Senators paired off against each other. Zachariah Chandler of Michigan, for example, tried to shame Buchanan by noting that the Canadians had spent $20,000 on St. Clair, which was predominantly an American waterway. He saw nothing beneficial in Buchanan's argument for tonnage duties because ships did not stop at a site under construction.[51] Jefferson Davis of Mississippi, answering Chandler's arguments, said that railroads would soon surpass sea transportation, so Congress should be wary of expending great sums of money for water improvements.[52] Even so, tonnage duties still provided the most logical means of improving waterways. Davis was upheld in this opinion by Robert Toombs of Georgia, who said that tonnage duties were usually charged at ports of embarkation, so Michigan would have no difficulty in collecting from ships using St. Clair.[53]

Kentucky Senator Crittenden and Louis T. Wigfall from Texas became involved in an interesting argument in which they presented finely drawn interpretations of the Constitution. Crittenden, using Clay's old argument of 1842, said that ample precedent existed for federally financed internal improvements. The consensus of opinion in favor of such a program should now outweigh the dogmatism of a single President, and he called for a "judgment of the people" on the differences between Congress and the President on internal improvements.[54] Wigfall, following closely Calhoun's theory of concurrent majorities, opposed Crittenden's invocation of the "popular will." He said that the Constitution did not limit a President's action on a bill to mere popular favor, but to whether or not a President agreed with the legislation.[55] The fact that the Senators indulged in long debates even on pocket vetoes of internal improvement bills indicated further the President's loss of power in preventing internal improvement programs.

The *New York Times*, calling Buchanan nothing more than the great American mistake of the nineteenth century, was quite outspoken in its criticisms of the two vetoes. On St. Clair, Buchanan had "only a school boy's knowledge;" yet he pretended to know all. The great Northwestern trade, valued at $6,000,000 annually, relied heavily on St. Clair. Buchanan's veto, therefore, was politically motivated, since he was simply "venting his spite" on a section that had openly proclaimed its presidential preference to be Stephen A. Douglas instead of James Buchanan. The paper predicted that the vetoes would cost the Democrats dearly in the next presidential election.[56]

Oblivious to the congressional and press attacks against him, Buchanan continued his penchant for saving money in a veto sent to the Senate on April 17, 1860. It concerned a bill for "the relief of Arthur Edwards for transporting the mails from various places in Ohio to Detroit." The amount to be appropriated came to $80,405.23. Buchanan noted, however, that six years before, just after Edwards had concluded his services to the government, a bill for $25,180 had been presented and had been rejected by the Post-master-General. In June, 1855, Edwards took his case to the Court of Claims, where he stated that he was due $50,000 from the government. When the Court refused to rule in his favor, Edwards took his case to Congress. He claimed in 1860 an amount that was $55,000 more than he had in 1854 and $30,000 more than in 1855. The great discrepancies in the claims were the chief reasons for Buchanan's rejection of the bill.[57]

The *New York Times* supported the veto and explained that Edwards had been paid for what was called "way-bag" mail.[58] Included in the contract at no additional cost to the government was the "through" mail. It was the latter category that the Postmaster-General and the Court of Claims had rejected, and which Buchanan now vetoed.[59] In the Senate, John P. Hale of New Hampshire moved that the veto be given to the Committee on the Post Office and Post Roads for a revision of the figures. Florida's David L. Yulee, however, doubted if the Senate had power to refer the question to a committee. He was unsure if a precedent existed for such a procedure and if it did not, he did not favor starting one. Clingman, now in the Senate, mentioned the 1842 Tyler veto of the tariff bill which had been given to a special committee. That action, of course, had set a precedent for the House, but none existed for the Senate.[60] When the Senate took a vote on the returned bill, June 7, 1860, the President was sustained 22 to 30.

Buchanan climaxed his drive for thrift when he vetoed the Homestead Bill on June 22, 1860, his most controversial rejection. The bill stated that every married citizen who was the head of a household would be eligible to take 160 acres of government land, live on it for five years, and then buy it for 25 cents an acre. A resident alien could do the same thing if he were the head of a household, and if he announced intentions of becoming a citizen. The bill also ceded to the states all the public lands within their limits which had remained unsold during the last 30 years. The amount of such land came to 12,229,731 acres.[61]

The President found several things wrong with the bill, and he carefully enumerated them in his message. Congress' power to give away public lands to the states and to reduce drastically the price to individuals was questionable. Buchanan quoted extensively from his veto of the College bill of 1859 to prove his point.[62] The bill would operate unequally against the old settlers, who had paid $1.25 per acre for their land. If the bill passed, the old settlers could justly demand that Congress refund the difference between what they paid and what the homesteaders would pay. The bill would also reduce the price of the land which had been given as bounties to soldiers. The value of such land had already fallen to 67 cents per acre out of fear that the Homestead bill would pass. Furthermore, the bill would treat the various classes unequally, because only farmers would benefit from it, while the old states would suffer a population loss if the bill passed.

The bill would also lead to speculation, since it would be easy for capitalists to arrange settlement of the land in return for a share at the end of five years. The bill would discriminate unjustly between the citizen and the alien, because it would cause hordes of immigrants to declare their intentions to apply for citizenship just so they could become land owners. The Pacific slope might very well become inundated by Orientals if the bill became law. In addition, the bill would irreparably harm the Treasury Department because of the great loss of revenue which would ensue, and it would upset the present land system which had worked well up to the moment. Finally, the bill would go far toward ruining the independent character of the American farmer. It would introduce a "pernicious social system" of charitable governmental help to private individuals.[63]

The bill was reconsidered by the Senate on June 23. One speaker in opposition to the veto was Andrew Johnson of Tennessee, who read from Buchanan's inaugural address and said that in it the President intimated that he favored a Homestead bill. Johnson charged that Buchanan was inconsistent.[64] No doubt these charges caused echoes of remorse a few years later when Johnson himself became the victim. The vote in the Senate on repassing the bill was 28 to 18, falling just short of the required two-thirds.

Buchanan's rejection brought applause from one paper whose career to this time had been devoted to criticizing the use of the presidential veto. The old *Jonesborough Whig*, now known as *Brownlow's Knoxville Whig*, said:

The best act of old Buchanan's life, was his recent veto of the infamous Homestead Bill—a measure conceived in iniquity and brought forth in sin. Nay, it is the vilest Abolition measure ever introduced into Congress, intended to abolitionize the whole North-West, to defraud the old States out of their just and equal claims to the public lands, in order to divide it among the paupers of Europe, so as to manufacture free-soil votes for the political gamblers and sharpers who seek to aggrandize themselves at the expense of the peace and tranquility of the country.[65]

Editor Brownlow obviously did not stop to reflect that his advice of some years earlier to abolish the veto power would have made his statement impossible. This, apparently, was his only lapse in fighting the veto for, as we shall see, he continuously decried Johnson's use if it.

Buchanan's veto of the Homestead bill has ofen been credited with giving the Republicans the presidency in 1860.[66] It caused the Northern workingmen and the Northern farmers to turn sharply away from the Democratic party and look to the Republicans for sustenance. Buchanan believed that the bill would cause renewed agitation over slavery in the territories and might possibly lead to another "bleeding Kansas." The veto damaged almost beyond repair Democratic chances for the presidency in 1860. But if Buchanan had signed the bill, "he would have repudiated his whole presidential policy by endorsing a measure that he thought fiscally unsound, . . . condemned by his own party platform, and formally sponsored by the Republicans."[67] It is well known that the veto of the Homestead bill was only temporary, for it later received the approval of Lincoln.

Buchanan's final veto came on January 25, 1861. It was on a bill "for the relief of Hockaday and Leggitt," and it saved the government almost $60,000. In 1858 Hockaday and Leggitt had contracted to carry the mails from St. Joseph, Missouri, to Salt Lake City. They were to receive $190,000 a year for a weekly service. Under the contract, the Postmaster-General could curtail delivery to a semi-monthly basis whenever he felt it warranted. He did this in April, 1859, leaving the compensation to Hockaday and Leggitt at $125,000. Before the new delivery was to take effect on July 1, Hockaday and Leggitt assigned the mail contract to Jones, Russell and Company for a bonus of $50,000. In addition, their property sold for $94,000. This transaction left $144,000 for Hockaday and Leggitt for their mail delivery of 1858-1859. They therefore petitioned Congress for the difference between the amount of money they got and the amount they had originally contracted. Buchanan did not doubt that Hockaday and Leggitt had sustained considerable loss in the various transactions, but he believed that if the bill passed, it would annul all restrictions in the mail contracts, thereby enabling the Postmaster-General to curtail services when he felt it necessary.[68] The bill was reconsidered by the House on January 26, 1861, and the veto was sustained 81 to 67. Thus, as in his first veto, Buchanan left the presidential office still emphasizing governmental thrift.

Pierce and Buchanan were the last really conservative Presidents in the nineteenth century. Their veto policies admirably illustrated their drive for austerity programs, since all of their vetoes were on subjects dealing in various ways with Congress' power to appropriate and distribute the public domain. They had to compete with Congresses that were progressive in attitude, and although eleven of their vetoes were sustained, it became clear that the presidency was losing its ability to prevent programs of expansion. Their vetoes also reflected the last great influence of Southerners over the presidency in the nineteenth century. Both Pierce and Buchanan were closed constitutionalists, an attitude which endeared them to the South. They believed in a literal translation of the Constitution: do nothing unless specifically given the power. This interpretation, of course, was nothing more than what the other veto Presidents had believed. In this respect, therefore, Pierce and Buchanan acted positively in their rejections of legislation. Positive action can especially be seen in Pierce's veto of the Indigent Insane Bill in 1854 and in Buchanan's rejection of the Homestead Bill in 1860. Both Presidents literally challenged public opinion in disapproving bills they thought incompatible with the Constitution.

One may argue, however, that a veto should reflect the times in which it is given. If this is true, the two Presidents must be charged with a great deal of negativism in their approach to problems of government. Actually, for the first time in the century, Congress came closer to reflecting public opinion than did the presidency. This is seen in part by the fact that the sustaining majorities for the vetoes of Madison, Jackson, Tyler, and Polk were consistently larger than for those of Pierce and Buchanan. In reality, Pierce and Buchanan vetoes defeated their own purposes, for they helped to give victory to the Republicans in 1860. Once this occurred, most of the expansion programs rejected by Pierce and Buchanan were readily approved. Therefore, Pierce and Buchanan's outdated conservatism hastened the destruction of constitutional barriers to federally financed internal improvements, helped to destroy Southern influence at the national level, and figured materially in bringing about conditions that hurled the veto into disrepute.

Lincoln and Johnson: The War Vetoes
1862-1869

THE Civil War altered the procedures by which vetoes had usually been given by Presidents and considered by Congress. The vetoes of Lincoln and Johnson dealt directly with the war or with questions arising from that conflict. Only three rejections between 1862 and 1869, all by Lincoln, did not produce controversy, and these little known vetoes were on relatively unimportant subjects.

The first veto, June 23, 1862, was on a bill to lift prohibition on the circulation of bank notes below $5.00 in the District of Columbia. Lincoln believed that widespread circulation of irredeemable bank notes (banks having generally suspended specie payments) in the District would lead to a deterioration of the currency, which in turn would seriously hamper trade. He suggested as an alternative United States notes which would be as "safe as the government itself."[1] On July 2, nine days after this veto, Lincoln rejected a bill from the Senate to "provide for additional medical officers of the volunteer service." His reason for disapproval was that he had already signed a bill by the same title.[2] This veto was upheld 0 to 37. Lincoln's other uncontroversial veto, on a joint resolution from the first session of the Thirty-eighth Congress to "correct certain clerical errors in the Internal Revenue act," was pocketed. The resolution had not been signed by the President of the Senate and since its passage other errors in the law had been discovered. Lincoln suggested a new, more inclusive action on the subject.[3]

On two other matters Lincoln's relation to the veto seemed one of uncertainty, explained perhaps by exigencies of war. The first concerned a Confiscation bill passed in July, 1862. Lincoln's chief objections centered around clauses allowing forfeiture of Southern property beyond the life of the guilty party, and confiscation without a jury trial, which he believed inimical to the Constitution.[4] He therefore prepared a veto message while the bill was being debated in Congress. To escape the veto, the managers of the bill rushed through an "explanatory resolution" saying that forfeiture would not work beyond the offender's natural life.[5]

Lincoln accordingly accepted the Confiscation Bill and the joint resolution accompanying it. By this approval, he assumed that the joint resolution was an amendment to the Confiscation Bill—which it was not. He thought that by approving both, he could choose the parts that he would enforce.[6] In effect, Lincoln applied to the Confiscation Bill an item veto which, of course, did not exist under the Constitution. In doing so, he committed the same error of which Jackson had been accused in the 1832 Bank Recharter veto, that of choosing the laws or parts thereof to be enforced by Presidents. Although he signed the Confiscation Bill, Lincoln sent the veto message to Congress where it was read amid disrespectful merriment from the abolition members. Lincoln, of course, had to approve the whole bill or none of it, but he was attempting to effect a compromise to gain support for the war from certain parties. Afterwards the bill was never fully enforced by Lincoln, but his initial action on it displayed a lack of knowledge concerning the veto power of the Constitution.

Much the same can be said for Lincoln's disposition of the Wade-Davis Bill, which was passed on July 4, 1864. Most of the texts and Lincoln biographies say that this bill was pocket vetoed. This is not exactly true because he answered it in a proclamation of July 8. He said he did not want to be committed to an inflexible program of reconstruction and that the Wade-Davis Bill would destroy the work already begun in Arkansas and Louisiana. However, any state wishing to adopt its provisions could do so with presidential blessings.[7] As the word "veto" has been used in this study, Lincoln's action on the Wade-Davis Bill was not a veto. If a President acts under Article One, Section Seven of the Constitution, he either approves a bill or he rejects it. He cannot constitutionally do both. Presumably, Lincoln believed that he could sign the bill for individual states at any time during the remainder of his presidency and it would come into force for the states concerned. In this respect, he was much closer to *Le Roi S'avisera* than Jackson had been in 1832 on the Lighthouse and Portland Canal vetoes.[8]

To the extent that Lincoln approved the Wade-Davis Bill four days after Congress adjourned for states wishing to adopt it, he was at variance with his successor, Andrew Johnson. The latter pocket vetoed a joint resolution at the end of the first session of the Fortieth Congress and, in explaining it, he advanced the theory that approval after adjournment was unconstitutional. He said:

To concede that under the Constitution, the President, after the adjournment of Congress, may, without limitation in respect to time, exercise the power of approval, and thus determine at his discretion whether or not bills shall become laws, might subject the executive and legislative departments of the Government to influences most pernicious to correct legislation and sound public morals, and—with a single exception, occurring during the prevalence of civil war—[referring undoubtedly to Lincoln's action on the Wade-Davis Bill] would be contrary to the established practice of the Government from its inauguration to the present time.[9]

The course that Lincoln took on the Confiscation and Wade-Davis bills can probably be justified in the long run because of the Civil War. He was vitally interested in obtaining workable plans by which to correct unsettled conditions, although no ordinary rules could be applied because of the abnormal circumstances "wholly unforeseen by the Constitutional Founders."[10] In handling these problems, Lincoln did not hesitate to apply new interpretations to the Veto Clause of the Constitution. He was, by necessity, a compromiser, neither approving nor rejecting wholly the various plans of reconstruction submitted to him. This trait was not evident in Andrew Johnson, who defended his interpretations of the Constitution "as if they had been transmitted to him from Sinai."[11]

The struggle between Johnson and the Reconstruction Congress is well known. His vetoes indicated an unwillingness to allow Congress any participation in the reconstruction of the Southern states. In thus disallowing the element of compromise between himself and Congress, Johnson added a negative quality to his rejections. His sincerity of purpose and his determination were admirable, but often he simply made matters intolerable by his unyielding attitude. He expounded, often brilliantly, upon the Constitution in its entirety, from the undisputed enumerated powers to the philosophical foundations. But he overlooked or was not willing to concede the fact that the Constitution is a flexible document, that it can adapt itself to the times in which it operates, and that it is conducive to compromise.

This is not to argue that Johnson's lot would have necessarily been easier or that fewer wrongs would have been perpetrated by the Reconstruction Congress if he had compromised to a degree. It is only to claim that in his relations to Congress, Johnson abandoned several alternatives which the veto power could have given him. His lack of tact, for one thing, weakened any veto that he might give, while his assertion that reconstruction belonged exclusively to the executive department was another claim that caused him to lose the initiative to Congress.

The "black codes" were legislative definitions of the Freedmen's civil rights which, among other things, denied them the right to vote, to sit on juries, and to testify against white people.

That these black codes were allowed to operate in Johnson's restoration program was another factor that caused him to have trouble with Congress. In short, he put himself in a defensive position on the reconstruction question; the only weapon he could use in such a case was the veto and it fell far short of the mark. If he had approved some of the initial reconstruction measures, such as the Freedmen's Bureau, through subtle manipulations he might very well have built a vast patronage that would have weakened Congress' program. But in the name of constitutionalism, he vetoed 29 bills, and in rapid order Congress vindictively overrode 15 of them.

The first veto, on February 19, 1866, was on the Freedmen's Bureau Bill. The bill imposed military jurisdiction over all parts of the United States containing refugees and freedmen. In the eleven Southern states, whites were subjected to imprisonment if they denied Negroes "any civil rights or immunities belonging to white persons." The trials taking place under the bill would be without benefit of jury.[12] Johnson refused the bill as unnecessary because the Bureau established in March, 1865, was still in operation. The bill did not define the "civil rights and immunities" to be given to the freedmen, while the non-jury provision was in direct conflict with the constitutional stipulation that "no person shall be held to answer for a capital or otherwise infamous crime unless on a presentment or indictment of a grand jury." Finally, the bill was passed while the section to be most affected by it, the South, was unrepresented in Congress.[13]

The vetoed bill was reconsidered in the Senate on February 20. The message was received at 1:30 p.m., but it could not be read until 3:30 because Richard Yates of Illinois had the floor until that time. In the interim the galleries, lobbies, alleys, and corners of the Senate were filled with spectators, about half of them women, coming to hear debate on a veto that had engendered as much excitement as Jackson's Bank veto in 1832.[14]

The chief supporter of this veto, and of most of the others that Johnson subsequently issued, was Thomas A. Hendricks of Indiana, who said that several military reports indicated the inefficiency of the Bureau. General Grant had reported that the divergence of opinion among Bureau agents made the organization operate differently in various locales.[15] After an afternoon's debate, the Senate voted about 8 p.m. on the returned bill. The *New York Times* recorded the scene: "A sudden silence fell upon the murmuring galleries and the noisy floor. As this or that Senator gave his suffrage, the great crowd would turn in the direction of the votes, and indicate by smiles or dark looks their approval or disapproval of the act, but no vocal utterances disturbed the occasion."[16] When the vote was completed, the veto was upheld 30 to 18, just 2 short of the two-thirds necessary to override. The *Times* supported the veto of the Freedmen's Bureau because "it taught no theory, invoked no passions, and used the Constitution as the sole standard of appeal." The true task, said the *Times*, was to educate the Negro into fitness for freedom and self-reliance.[17] The veto, however, caused the radicals in Congress to launch plans to obtain enough votes to override subsequent reconstruction vetoes.

Johnson vetoed a Civil Rights Bill on March 27, 1866, "to protect all persons in the United States in their civil rights and furnish the means of their vindication." Johnson disapproved of the legislation because it made citizens of all persons born in the country except those subject to a foreign power and Indians not taxed. The bill also displaced state courts in favor of federal tribunals which could travel from one place to another in order readily to try offenders of the Civil Rights Bill. Believing that citizenship could not effectively be given *en masse* and that Congress did not have the power to stop discrimination in all aspects of human life, Johnson returned the Civil Rights Bill.[18]

In preparation for a reconsideration of the Civil Rights Bill, the Senate expelled Senator John P. Stockton of New Jersey on a technicality. This action assured more votes for the radical side. Senator Benjamin Wade spoke vehemently on the veto, accusing Johnson of usurping congressional authority by allowing Southern states to re-enter the Union. The Ohio Senator said it was imperative to override the veto,[19] which was accomplished on April 6 by a vote of 33 to 15, two more votes than were needed. The House concurred 122 to 41 three days later. Speaker Schuyler Colfax directed that his name be called so he "would have the pleasure of voting with the majority."[20]

Once again the *New York Times* supported Johnson's veto. The President's exposition, it said, was so sharp that it would make "learned men of law" blush to be told so many things by a layman. The message would be widely read outside of Congress, said the *Times*, and it would elevate the character of Andrew Johnson.[21] On the other hand, *Brownlow's Knoxville Whig*, now known as *Brownlow's Knoxville Whig and Rebel Ventilator*, attacked Johnson for pursuing a course of "double dealing." If Johnson's policy was allowed to prevail, in Editor Brownlow's opinion, "all union men will have to leave the South."[22] This was the first veto of Johnson's to be killed by Congress. It set a pattern that was followed freely during the remainder of the Tennesseean's incumbency.

The next two vetoes, however, were not overridden. It is proper to say "not overridden" instead of "sustained" in Johnson's vetoes, for "sustained" has a connotation of approval that did not exist. The cases where "not overriddin" was appropriate were explained by referrals to committees, by a momentary lapse in the application of the party whip, by larger, more vital interests of the Congress, or by absences of congressmen on the days the vetoed bills were reconsidered.

Such was the case with Johnson's May 15 veto on the admission of Colorado. The entry of that territory into the Union at the time would more than assure the radicals enough votes to destroy Johnson's vetoes. Johnson, however, did not mention this factor in his message to Congress. He gave as his reasons the unwarranted stipulation that Colorado must grant Negro suffrage, that the population there was small and transitory, that in recent elections the Coloradans themselves had shown doubts about statehood, and that the reconstruction question should be resolved before additional states were added to the Union.[23] Senator Wade furiously told the Senate that this was the first time a President had ever vetoed a bill for the entry of a new state. He wanted to postpone reconsideration of the bill until all its friends could be gathered in the Senate. The President was defended by Johnson of Arkansas, who said that as much right existed to veto the entry of a state as on anything else.[24] Reconsideration was postponed.

The next legislation which provoked Johnson was a bill allowing the New York and Montana Iron Mining Company to purchase Western mineral lands. The Company would preempt up to twenty sections of land at $1.25 an acre. In return the Company was required to produce at least 1,500 tons of iron annually. Johnson believed that the bill would halt the development of the West, that corporations should not have the same privileges of preemption as individuals, and that the land to be taken belonged to Indians. There was a difference, he said, between granting land for corporations and for railroads, the latter being valuable in connecting the remote parts of the country with population centers.[25] The *New York Times* called the bill an alliance between the radical Republicans and selfish business interests,[26] and said that it reflected a closeness of business and government that had been growing ever since the Pierce administration. The veto, not overridden, was referred to a committee.

A month after the Montana Mining veto, Congress passed a bill to continue the Freedmen's Bureau. It will be remembered that Johnson's first veto dealt with the Bureau and that Congress failed to override it by only two votes. By July, 1866, the radicals had just enough numerical power to defeat presidential objections to reconstruction legislation, but not enough yet to make them invincible. Johnson once again explained his political philosophy in great detail. He believed that the protection of the Negro should come from a sound basis through due process of law rather than by military tribunals.[27] In the Senate, Hendricks defended the veto, saying that the Bureau was oppressive and full of fraud. Senator Willard Saulsbury of Delaware believed that a "grateful people will remember Johnson" for his defense of the Constitution.[28] It required a "vigorous application of the party whip"[29] to get enough votes to override the veto. This was done first in the House on July 16 by a vote of 103 to 33 and the same day in the Senate 33 to 12. The defeat of this veto was a prelude to the wholesale interdiction of Johnson's reconstruction program which began early in 1867.

But for a little longer the President still retained a semblance of power. This was seen on July 28 when he again prevented preemption privileges to the New York and Montana Mining Company. He had first vetoed the bill on June 15 and Congress was now attempting to re-pass it under the guise of making "a survey district of Montana." Not enough votes were available in the Senate, to which it was returned, to destroy the veto.

In a deepening mood of hostility the Congress, now completely dominated by radicals, opened 1867 with a vigorous denial of a veto on suffrage in the District of Columbia. The bill was designed to give equal voting privileges to Negroes in Washington and Georgetown. Johnson said that referendums by the citizens of the District showed almost unanimously their dislike of the proposal. Congress' power over the District was not unlimited; the Constitution demanded that the referendum be honored. If the bill passed, the tremendous influx of freedmen into the District would cause a serious unemployment problem. The President called upon the writing of Chancellor Kent, Justice Story, and President Madison to support his thesis in this long and laborious veto.[30]

When the Senate reconsidered the bill, Justin Morrill said that while it was being discussed no objections of the people to Negro voting in the District was apparent. The President could not rightfully insist that the bill impaired local government, because none existed in the District. The District was the common property of all the country and as such, Congress' power to pass the bill was unquestionable.[31] Morrill's position was disputed by Edgar Cowan of Pennsylvania, who said that it was not the purpose of the Constitution "to make the people of the District slaves to the rest of the country." Thus, it was wrong for someone not knowing the local conditions to make laws of this nature. He said, moreover, that the Negroes in the District, some 30,000, paid no taxes and should therefore not receive voting privileges.[32]

The *New York Times*, which had supported Johnson in the past, differed with the President on the question of the Suffrage veto. Johnson's arguments were not convincing, said the *Times*, and his references to Kent, Story, and Madison had no direct bearing on the subject. Popular judgment would be with Congress in this instance, rather than with the President.[33] The veto was killed in the Senate on January 27 by a vote of 29 to 10; in the House the next day 112-38. The veto led to open talk of impeaching Johnson, that "officer now exercising the functions pertaining to the office of President."[34] James M. Ashley of Ohio offered a motion of impeachment of "Andrew Johnson, Vice-President and acting President of the United States." It would not be long before that motion received approval.

Johnson's next veto was the last during the years 1867 and 1868 not to be overridden. It came on January 28, 1867, on another bill to admit Colorado into the Union. The reasons Johnson gave in his previous veto of the Colorado bill were reasserted: the population in Colorado was still not sufficient for statehood and Congress had illegally placed restrictions on the Colorado Constitution.[35] This veto message was different from most of the others because no reference was made to the unrepresented Southern states.[36] The reception of the veto in the Senate, the house of origin, caused scarcely a comment. The Colorado bill was discussed sporadically until March 1, when the vote was 29 to 19 against overriding the veto.

Possibly Congress' reason for retaining the Colorado veto was that more than enough votes were now available to make innocuous any further moves by Johnson. This condition was assured on February 8 when the veto on a bill to admit Nebraska was overridden. Johnson had rejected the bill on January 29 because of congressional stipulations on the Nebraska Constitution.[37] In reconsidering the bill, the Senate quickly passed it 31 to 9, and the House concurred on February 9 with a vote of 103 to 55. Many radicals undoubtedly regretted later that the same vigor in overturning the Nebraska veto was not demonstrated on the Colorado rejection. The two Senators that Colorado would have had would probably have followed the example of the Nebraska senators and voted for conviction in Johnson's impeachment.[38]

In early March, 1867, the executive-legislative dispute reached a climax with the passage of several reconstruction measures.

The Tenure of Office Bill, requiring two-thirds permission of the Senate before the President released certain cabinet officers, was vetoed on March 2. The question of tenure of office had never been settled constitutionally, only by precedent.[39] Chancellor Kent, Justice Story, and President Madison had argued in the past that unless an official had a defnite tenure established by law, he served at the pleasure of the President. Henry Clay and Daniel Webster had fought the system of allowing a President unilaterally to dismiss a cabinet official.

It was clear that Congress passed the Tenure of Office Bill to protect Secretary of War Edwin Stanton. It is interesting to note that when Johnson and his cabinet considered the bill, even Stanton testified to its unconstitutionality [40] and helped to write part of the veto. In the veto message Johnson claimed that the bill was unconstitutional, politically motivated, and conducive to great difficulty because it was possible for a cabinet member to become unfit for service without committing an offense. In such a case the results might be disastrous if the President had to wait for Senate permission before dismissing a cabinet official.[41] The *New York Times* was not sure what Congress would do with the vetoed bill, since there seemed to be some opposition to it. However, this was not apparent when the Senate overrode the veto on the same day that it was returned by a vote of 35 to 11, and the House, also on March 2, overruled it 138 to 40. The votes showed that in the Senate 76 percent were in favor of overriding the veto; in the House, 77 percent. The radical majority had now achieved total domination over the government.

That this was true was illustrated by the "Great Reconstruction Act," which, along with three supplemental acts, established the congressional plan of reconstruction. All four acts were rejected by Johnson, but Congress quickly passed the bills over his vetoes. The initial reconstruction veto was on March 2, 1867. In the first paragraph Johnson expressed the wish that the veto might have "some influence on the minds . . . of patriotic and enlightened men . . . ."[42] Then he gave, at great length, his reasons for disapproving the Reconstruction Act: it was politically motivated; there was no law restricting the action of the generals which would be the equivalent of setting up a military dictatorship in the South; and it was a bill of attainder against 9,000,000 people.[43] Most of the message repeated the arguments of the Freedmen's Bureau and Civil Rights vetoes of 1866.

The *New York Times* correspondent reported that while the veto was read in the House there were none of the expected disturbances; there was only one sound besides that of the clerk's voice—a baby crying in the diplomatic box.[44] Editorially, the *Times* feared the bill because it would indeed establish a military despotism in the South. But coming from Johnson, arguments against the bill were not convincing. The state governments in the South which the bill destroyed were the ones established by Johnson. Therefore, Congress was simply undoing the work that Johnson had performed,[45] and forcibly claiming its jurisdiction over the reconstruction problem. The veto was destroyed in the House 138 to 51 and 38 to 10 in the Senate.

A supplemental reconstruction bill, giving the generals more extensive power over voter registration and elections, was vetoed by Johnson on March 23. Johnson spent many pages in explaining his opposition to the bill,[46] but the past actions of Congress and the lack of debate when the bill was passed indicated clearly what the fate of the veto would be. The bill extinguished the last chance of "passive resistance" toward reconstruction in the South,[47] as the veto was destroyed in the House 114 to 25 and in the Senate 40 to 7. Another supplemental act, exempting military commanders from civil rules, was vetoed on July 19.[48] With no debate at all, the House killed it 109 to 25 and the Senate 30 to 6. Also, on July 19 Johnson rejected a joint resolution on reconstruction which stipulated that majority votes in the Southern states would be enough to activate radical constitutions. This was to be the rule regardless of how small the minority taking part in the elections was.[49] On the day of the veto, it was overridden 99 to 22 in the House and 32 to 4 in the Senate. The reconstruction program of Congress was thus complete; the President was stripped of his power over the question.

Congress took another step in its course of vengeance by passing, in March, 1868, a Judiciary bill. Among other things, the bill weakened the appellate jurisdiction of the Supreme Court and interdicted appeals which had already been made. Johnson vetoed the bill because it gave unjustified power to lower tribunals and removed the last restraints against legislative despotism.[50] When the bill was reconsidered in the Senate, Thomas Hendricks and Charles R. Buckalew of Pennsylvania defended the veto. They said that the bill had been rushed through Congress without debate; therefore, a postponement of its reconsideration should be allowed to give members time to formulate arguments against it.[51] Other Senators, though, such as George H. Williams of Oregon, believed that the veto should be dispensed with quickly because any reconsideration would lead to time-consuming discussions at a time when the Senate should be heeding only the impeachment proceedings taking place against Johnson.[52] A vote was taken, therefore, on the returned bill, and it passed despite the veto 33 to 9 in the Senate and 115 to 34 in the House. The passage of the Judiciary bill meant that Congress now controlled not only the presidency, but the judicial branch as well.

By late spring, 1868, Congress was ready to readmit some Southern states in accordance with the radical plan. A bill passed to admit Arkansas was vetoed by President Johnson on June 20. To approve it, he said, would be tacitly to agree that the reconstruction acts were legal.[53] Moreover, the bill forbade Arkansas ever to change its Constitution on the subject of equality in voting, but Congress did not have the power to do this, said Johnson. The New York Times said that this initial veto of Johnson's since his impeachment was "uttered with as much determination and earnestness as on any previous occasion."[54] The President went over the same grounds of the past two years, showing that his opinions on reconstruction had not changed; on the contrary, they had been strengthened. It took but half an hour from the reception of the veto in the House to destroy it 111 to 31. The Senate voted 30 to 7 to override the veto.

Readmission of Southern states continued with an "omnibus reconstruction bill" to admit North Carolina, South Carolina, Louisiana, Georgia, Alabama, and Florida. Johnson vetoed it on June 25, 1868, using the same arguments as in the Arkansas veto.[55] The bill was reconsidered by both houses on the day of the veto, and the vote was 108 to 32 in the House and 35 to 8 in the Senate. The states thus restored to the Union, said the New York Times, would cause a "tidal wave" for Grant and Colfax in the upcoming presidential election.[56]

Congress passed a joint resolution in July, 1868, excluding from the Electoral College all the Southern states which were still unreconstructed, but the resolution was rejected by Johnson on July 20. His reasons were that the resolution assumed that the Southern states actually left the Union in 1861. If they did in fact leave the Union, then it must be argued that secession was legal. If secession was legal, then the war fought against the South was illegal, according to the President's reasoning.[57] He referred to the many people in the South who had remained loyal to the Union even during the war, and also to the many in the North who had championed the Confederacy. Yet the resolution was to work only on the South. If the resolution passed, Congress would take the power of electing a President from the people.[58] The resolution was reconsidered by both houses on the day the veto was given. With no discussion, the Senate defeated the veto 45 to 8; the House 134 to 36. Shortly after this action by

Congress, another veto was received on a bill discontinuing the Freedmen's Bureau. Dated July 25, the veto message said that the bill would interfere with the appointing power of the President, but the real reason was that if Johnson approved it, he would admit the legality of the Freedmen's Bureau. The harmless veto fell before the Senate 42 to 5 and the House 115 to 23. This was the last of the reconstruction vetoes.

A half year later Johnson vetoed more legislation that was related to the general problem of the freedmen, this time rejecting a bill transferring the duties of the Trustees of Colored Schools of Washington and Georgetown from the Department of Interior to the public school system. Johnson stated on February 13, 1869, that the Negroes themselves had voiced a desire to stay with the Interior Department. No good reason existed, therefore, for the change contemplated by Congress.[59] The veto was not overridden; instead, it was referred to a committee.

Johnson's final veto reflected the ever increasing beneficient relation between government and business. It was on a bill, passed in the interest of certain mines on Lake Superior, to increase the duties on copper and copper ores. The President believed the bill would adversely affect the revenues because it would curtail trade; it would favor a few at the expense of many; and it would impose a tax upon the American citizenry just to support the Lake Superior mining interests.[60] The day following the veto, the bill was reconsidered. The House, said the *Knoxville Weekly Whig* (Brownlow's paper), found the veto "so convincing . . . that the bill was promptly repassed."[61] The bill was passed in the House 115 to 56 and in the Senate 38 to 12. Thus ended the dreadful conflict between Johnson and the Congress.

The Civil War vetoes upset the normal pattern of the preceding years, a situation which is understandable in light of the unique circumstances facing the government. Lincoln's vetoes reflected his belief that the executive should take the largest part in the reconstruction program. He used the veto power, though, as a means of effecting a compromise of different opinions. His treatment of the Confiscation Bill and of the Wade-Davis Bill would have been unorthodox in ordinary times. Both Jackson and Lincoln were accused of choosing which laws they would enforce; also, both Presidents believed it was their prerogative to sign a pocket vetoed bill at any time during the remainder of their administration. Actually, when these accusations were directed at Jackson, they were largely overstated, since he did not often select legislation to be enforced[62] and he never implemented his belief vis-a-vis the pocket veto. Thus, as Polk had fulfilled much of Jackson's philosophy, Lincoln reactivated the issues of the Bank veto and the Lighthouse and Portland Canal vetoes. This did not necessarily mean that the general philosophy of the two Presidents was alike, for without the Civil War, there would have been neither Confiscation Bill nor Wade-Davis Bill. Hence, there would have been no vetoes productive of issues similar to those of 1832. Thus Lincoln's veto policy cannot be fully compared to that of Jackson or any other President because of the extraordinary times in which he acted.

Andrew Johnson may be compared most closely with Pierce and Buchanan because he did not have the ability to use the veto as a means of compromise. Compromise, of course, was impossible after the radicals won their majority, but Johnson might have conducted his affairs differently during the first part of his administration so that the veto could have been used as an offensive, rather than a defensive, tool in solving the problems of reconstruction. It might have enabled him to retain the initiative in his quarrel with Congress. Johnson's veto performance may also be compared with Jackson's rejection of the Bank in 1832. In that veto, it will be recalled, Jackson made any compromise with Congress impossible. But there was obviously one major difference between the performances of Jackson and Johnson: the anti-Jacksonians in 1832 had no hope of overriding the President's decision, while this condition was exactly reversed during Johnson's incumbency. Johnson may be further compared with Old Hickory in that his vetoes were addressed not so much to Congress as to the American people. He knew that his words would have no effect on radical congressmen, but he nevertheless wrote long and carefully detailed vetoes in hope that posterity would justify his position.

Johnson's action parallels that of Madison, Tyler, and Polk in that he consistently upheld a constitutional philosophy. In this respect, positive action can be attributed to him. But he also displayed a great deal of dogmatism. It should have been evident to Johnson, as to Pierce and Buchanan, that a veto should reflect the times in which it is given. By the time Johnson came to power, the veto had been used to approve parts of legislation and to suspend approval on others. This was not constitutional, but it was done. And since the Reconstruction Congress made its own rules, precedent and the Constitution notwithstanding, Johnson perhaps might have done likewise and thereby divided some of the opposition. Johnson, the "Boniface VIII of the presidency,"[63] was perhaps too straitlaced in his interpretation of the Constitution.

Congress was also guilty of upsetting the veto pattern of many years' standing. To this time, reconsideration of a vetoed bill had always implied a vote. But the only times that Congress voted on returned bills were in the instances of the Freedmen's Bureau and the second Colorado bill; the veto of the former being overridden, and that of the latter being sustained. The first Colorado bill, the two Montana bills, and the bill dealing with colored schools in the District of Columbia, were simply read in the house of origin, and then were either tabled or referred to a committee. If congressmen argued that reconsideration could come at any time, then tabling or referral was legitimate. But the Constitution stipulated that in reconsidering vetoed bills "the votes of both Houses shall be determined by Yeas and Nays, and the names of the persons voting for and against the Bill shall be entered on the Journal of each House respectively";[64] therefore, Congress acted unconstitutionally.

The overwhelming power of the Reconstruction Congress did not result solely from the political conditions which came in the aftermath of war. Strong economic forces also gave vitality to the legislators, as indicated by the Montana bills (Johnson's vetoes of these were not overridden) and by the Copper Tariff Bill which was passed despite his rejection. This alliance of the government with economic interests was the consummation of a drive first propounded by Clay's American System. In some ways it indicated that Whiggery was still alive in the 1860's, since many of the radical reconstructionists were old Whigs who, after the Civil War, had a better opportunity than before to pursue their economic programs. The extent to which this was true marked a reaction against the veto, which had done much to prevent economic expansion.

PART TWO

Introduction

THE uses of and reactions to the veto changed considerably after the Civil War. There were only eighty-five vetoes during the pre-war period, but between 1870 and 1944 there occurred well over a thousand. The phenomenal number of vetoes necessitated changes in the procedures used by the President in presenting them and by Congress in considering them. In addition, some of the alterations caused interesting and important controversies.

Private pension bills flooded the legislative hoppers after the war. These bills, along with private relief bills, were vetoed most often by the Presidents from U. S. Grant to F. D. Roosevelt. The volume of legislation was simply too great to allow any President to become involved in the long drawnout constitutional arguments favored by his ante-bellum predecessors. Postwar Presidents also tended more often to refer bills of questionable merit to their cabinets or other officials for a decision. This procedure led to the criticism that subordinates, rather than the President, were really vetoing bills. Furthermore, such a procedure violated the Constitution because the *President*, rather than a subordinate official, was required to state objections to legislation.

Postwar vetoes were more readily referred to congressional committees than were those discussed in Part I. It may be remembered that the question first arose during Madison's administration: was it legal for a committee of Congress to consider a returned bill when the Constitution stated that the "yeas" and "nays" of the whole house had to be taken? The precedent of referral was set by the House during Tyler's term and was well entrenched in both houses by the time of Andrew Johnson. Although referral was almost unanimously accepted during Grant's and his successors' administrations, some voices cried out against the procedure, saying that it was a waste of time because a committee could make no final judgment on a vetoed bill. Congress alone had this prerogative.

The practice of referral meant that quite often a vetoed bill, once it had gone to committee or had been tabled, was forgotten.

Thus, no vote was ever taken on the majority of the vetoes in the post Civil War period. Unless a bill evoked intense interest, Congress would raise no objections to its veto. This procedure, of course, saved a lot of time, but it was not strictly within the confines of the Constitution—if it does not exactly violate the letter of the Constitution, it does its spirit.

Pocket vetoes were used more often after the Civil War. Unlike the Presidents of the ante-bellum period, latter-day Presidents generally did not explain their reasons in their subsequent messages to Congress. Except in a few instances which will be noted, the pocket veto was not productive of controversy in the period to be considered.

Since changes occurred in the use of and the reaction to presidential vetoes, so it will be necessary for the style and organization of this survey to change. Presidents will be grouped as much as possible, while the main objective will be to discover major themes within their administrations which developed from the veto.

☆ X ☆

Grant, Hayes, and Arthur
1870-1884

An examination of the vetoes in the years 1870-1884 yields four distinct groups: private bills relating to the Civil War, bills in defense of the gold standard, bills to protect the executive authority from Congress, and bills to prevent passage of strict immigration laws. There were well over a hundred vetoes, both regular and pocket, during the period. Most of them were given by Grant.

President Grant was the first Executive faced with large numbers of private pension and relief bills. He found that many of them were fraudulent or that serious mistakes had been made in their drafting. Three essential groups of private bill vetoes were given by Grant: those on fraudulent grants for relief of corporate and individual contractors, those pardoning deserters, and those relieving army officers from various disabilities.[1] Only the vetoes of private bills that led to important constitutional controversies or that set precedents will be discussed.

Grant's first private bill veto occurred on January 11, 1870, on an act to relieve Rollin White. The bill, agreeing with White that he had been deprived of royalties for improvements he had made in repeating pistols, authorized a hearing before the Commissioner of Patents. Grant consulted his Chief of Ordinance, Major General A. B. Dyer, and was informed that White had been given ample royalties from the Company of Smith and Wesson. The President based his veto of four lines on the letter from General Dyer.[2]

The *Hartford* (Conn.) *Daily Courant* reported that the veto caused amusement in some quarters because it was composed entirely of attached documents.[3] However, Senator Matthew Carpenter of Wisconsin found nothing humorous in the situation. He charged that Grant's message was not constitutionally acceptable since he gave no objections to the bill. Furthermore, even if General Dyer's competency in the case were admitted, he had misinterpreted the bill by claiming that Congress was trying to grant a patent when in reality all it desired was a new hearing for White before the Patent Commission.[4] The Senate debated the veto periodically until May 31, 1870, and then killed it 41-13.[5] The House, however, did not agree with the Senate's judgment, and on June 22 it upheld Grant's action by a 12-168 vote.[6] With the White veto Grant established a pattern in dealing with future bills of this type. He called freely for the advice of his subordinates, using their testimony, if appropriate, as reasons for disapprovals. After the veto of the White bill, Congress did not question this procedure as being constitutionally doubtful.

A most interesting event occurred on August 15, 1876, when Grant vetoed two bills, then later changed his mind. The first was a private relief bill for Major Junius T. Turner. This veto was referred by the Senate to the Committee on Military Affairs. Weeks later, while the veto was still in committee, Grant sent a message stating that the Turner veto was based on a misapprehension of the facts and that the veto should be returned.[7] There was no debate on this request, and no action was ever taken on it, or on the Turner veto itself.

On August 15 Grant had also made an identical request on a veto involving the sale of a portion of the Otoe and Missouria Indian reservation. As the Senate was considering the veto, a presidential message arrived stating that, since rejection had been premature, the return of the bill for signature was requested.[8] Senator Aaron Sargent of California said that the President "has no more right to recall a bill after having vetoed it than he has . . . to tear a leaf out of the statute book. . . ."[9] The Senate refused to consider Grant's second message, stating that it was only for information and had no legal importance. The Senators did, however, re-pass the bill unanimously.[10] The House concurred with a 120-18 vote against the veto the same day.[11]

That Grant was obliged to reverse himself on these two vetoes indicates that the advice given to him was poor. This could have become as interesting a constitutional question as Jackson's *Le Roi s'avisera* if the lawmakers or the President had chosen to pursue it; the question, however, did not arise again. It is yet another aspect of the Veto Clause that remains unsettled—does a President have a legal right to withdraw a veto once it is given? The opinion of Grant's Congress was that he does not. But Congress often changes its mind.

The most important of Grant's private relief vetoes affected those bills which asked the government to pay for private property damaged or destroyed during the Civil War. Grant firmly maintained that the government was not responsible.

The initial veto came on June 1, 1872, on a bill for the relief of J. Milton Best.[12] The bill appropriated $25,000 to repay Best

for the destruction of his residence in Paducah, Kentucky, which
had been accomplished on orders from the federal commander.
Grant claimed that it was recognized internationally that property
destroyed during times of national peril is not subject to restitutions
by the government. It would set a dangerous precedent, said Grant,
if Best's claim were honored. The President ended his veto by
asserting that unified legislation was obviously needed.

Grant was commended for the Best veto by the *New York
Times*, which claimed that the bill opened a door to "an immense
number and amount of claims." These should be granted, if at
all, only by a competent tribunal.[13] The veto was returned to the
Senate where Timothy O. Howe of Wisconsin moved that the
matter be sent to the Committee on Claims. The motion passed,
and the veto was not acted upon again.

Grant rejected a bill similar to Best's on June 7, 1872, which
authorized a claim by Thomas B. Wallace of Lexington, Missouri.
Grant said that the bill had the same character as the one for
Best, and for the same reasons he could not approve it.[14] Still
another veto was given on January 29, 1873, on a bill for the
relief of East Tennessee University.[15] Admitting that the loyalty
of the East Tennesseans was unquestionable, this did not entitle
them to relief in Grant's opinion. He said: "If the precedent is
once established that the Government is liable for the ravages of
war, the end of demands upon the public Treasury cannot be
forecast."[16]

On February 11, 1873, Grant rejected a bill for the relief of
those "suffering from the destruction of salt works near Manchester,
Kentucky, pursuant to the order of Major General Carlos Buell."
The salt works were destroyed by the Union Army, said Grant,
"while engaged in regular military operations." The "sole object
of their destruction was to weaken, cripple, or defeat the armies of
the so-called Southern Confederacy." Therefore, this was a necessary act of war and, as such, the government was not obliged to
provide compensation for the loss of property.[17]

Relief vetoes of this type always made a distinction between
property seized by the government for peaceful purposes and
property destroyed because of war, since nothing in the Constitution
enjoined the government to pay for necessary war damages. For
example, Best's residence had been destroyed so that the federal
artillery could get a better firing range on the Southerners. All of
the other destructions were of a similar nature; that is, they enabled
the Union to terminate the war. Because of the necessity for the
destruction, an unseemly precedent would be set if the government
now paid for it. Grant could see endless claims against the treasury

if the practice once started. Therefore, his vetoes in this area settled a question that could have become serious later.

Grant established the precedent by which private bills would be handled. As stated previously, most of the vetoes from 1870 to 1945 were on private bills of one sort or another. The greatest numbers came, of course, under Grover Cleveland and Franklin D. Roosevelt. On the whole, these vetoes reflected the desire of Presidents to guard the Treasury against unwarranted intrusions, since it was estimated by the *Courant* that twenty-five percent of the claims were fraudulent. The vetoes, too, sometimes reflected the political battles between Republicans and Democrats, or among factions within one party. Possibly one reason for so many private bill vetoes is that the lawmakers rarely refused to sponsor a bill for one of their constituents, although they fully expected a presidential veto. Thus, the President would suffer the onus of having prevented a pension, while the congressman would gain support for at least having tried to secure passage of the bill. This may also explain Congress' failure even to reconsider the vast majority of such vetoed legislation.

The second broad area of vetoes during the Grant-Arthur period dealt with retention of the gold standard. Grant opened the fight with a veto on April 22, 1874, against an act to "fix the amount of United States notes in circulation." Passage of the bill reflected, first, Congress' efforts to relieve adverse economic conditions, and second, the power of Western congressmen who tended to favor "soft money."

The "inflation bill", which was discussed in Congress for several weeks, increased the maximum value of greenbacks in circulation from \$383,000,000 to \$400,000,000[18] and also provided for an additional issue of \$46,000,000 in bank notes.[19] Proponents of the bill argued that the notes "were merely replacements of outstanding issues."[20] Thus, the actual increase was \$18,000,000, a figure which in their opinion was not excessive. Opponents, however, claimed that a new issue of paper money during a time of peace[21] was an economically unfeasible procedure. Moreover, they charged that the \$18,000,000 would be only an "entering wedge" for runaway inflation. "If it became a law, they [the opponents] contended, there would be other issues of paper currency, and Congress would have to manufacture money on a large scale every time there were a few business failures."[22] Former Secretary of the Navy Gideon Welles expressed Eastern condemnation of the measure: "Congress is stupid and weak, without sense, honesty or character on questions for currency and finance."[23] Regardless of party affiliations, Westerners generally favored the bill. The Ohio River was the dividing line between the two factions.[24]

The inflation bill confronted the President with a dilemma. To approve it would mean supporting those who sought artificially to sustain the economy, while a veto would run counter to prevailing public opinion, would lose the West for the Republicans, and would expose, to the country's close scrutiny, the factional infighting within the Republican party.[25] Grant's first impulse was to sign the bill, and he wrote a message giving his reasons. He believed initially that the bill would not cause an undue expansion of the currency and thus would not have an adverse effect upon the government's credit.[26] A concerted campaign was begun by Eastern conservatives to convince Grant that the bill would ruin the economic soundness of the country. New York and Boston delegations to the White House, however, received no satisfactory promises from Grant, and they left believing that he would approve the measure.[27] At the last moment, though, Grant reread his message of approval and decided that his own arguments sounded unconvincing. He therefore set the first message aside and penned the most important veto of his career.[28]

The bill, he said, was a departure from sound principles of finance. Grant referred to his annual message of December, 1869, in which he had pledged a gradual return to specie payments, and to an act of March 1869 which promised to pay the public debt in coin or its equivalent. Since this act was still in force, it must be honored.[29] In the final part of the rejection, Grant wrote: "I am not a believer in any artificial method of making paper money equal to coin when the coin is not owned or held ready to redeem the promises to pay, for paper money is nothing more than promises to pay, and is valuable exactly in proportion to the amount of coin that it can be converted into."[30] Grant thus used the same arguments as Hayes did later; i.e., that the bill would repudiate debts already in existence that should be re-paid in the same medium as that in which they were borrowed.

The veto came as a surprise to all parties. The Eastern conservatives were jubilant while enraged advocates of soft money claimed that the veto was a victory for Wall Street. They lost no time in informing Grant "that he had opened a Pandora's box that would be as deadly as the repeal of the Missouri Compromise."[31] When news of the veto arrived, stocks on Wall Street rose about one-half of one percent while gold declined approximately one-eighth.[32] Businessmen cheered the presidential rejection, saying that it would stop speculation, would cause stock to increase and gold to decline in value, and would increase the value of government securities in foreign markets.[33] That the latter argument was true was indicated by the applause of foreign bankers, brokers, and bullion dealers. French bankers believed that the veto was the best thing Grant had done since he captured Richmond,[34] and the *London Post* thought Grant deserved as much praise for the veto as for his campaign at Vicksburg. The English paper was confident that the South and the West would ultimately be grateful for the presidential disapproval.[35]

Events immediately after the veto, however, indicated that the *London Post* had misjudged the domestic reaction in the United States. Westerners threatened to rise up and destroy those responsible for the veto;[36] promises of a "soft-money" caucus were rampant;[37] a document was prepared by Senator Oliver Morton from Indiana and others to show Grant's inconsistency in matters of finance;[38] and it was rumored that the Westerners and Southerners would try to pass some radical inflation measures under a suspension of the rules.[39] None of these excesses came to pass, however, and the veto was upheld in the Senate on April 28 by a vote of 34-40.[40]

The inflationists were somewhat mollified by congressional peacemakers, led by Speaker of the House James G. Blaine, who promised them further opportunities to consider financial legislation, coupled with a reminder of "Charles Sumner's fate three years before when he had crossed Grant."[41] Thus, for the time being, the inflationists were checked. The veto was regarded as "the turning of the corner by the American people, and setting the face of the Government toward specie payment and honest money."[42] Grant, as a result of his veto, must be given credit as the President most responsible for putting this country on a gold standard.[43] And finally, "by vetoing the major legislation of the western Senatorial leaders, Grant had created strains and resentments that were to shape the resumption battle for the next half-decade."[44] The truth of this statement was amply demonstrated during Hayes' term, when he was compelled to veto the Bland-Allison act.

Under President Hayes, the cheap money question took the form of an argument over free silver instead of unrestricted greenbacks as it had under Grant. Silver mines, so vividly described in Mark Twain's *Roughing It*, were producing unheard of quantities of the metal. Naturally, as the production of silver increased, the market for it fell. By 1876 the "soft money" advocates began decrying the demonitization of silver which had occurred three years before as the "Crime of '73," and demanded the reinstatement of the silver dollar. Richard P. Bland, a Missouri Democrat, led the silver fight in the House of Representatives. His counterpart in the Senate was William B. Allison, a Republican from Iowa.

On November 5, 1877, a Bland sponsored bill which provided

"for the free coinage of silver brought to the mints in the same way as gold was coined",[45] was passed by the House. The vote, 165-34, showed the tremendous support for free silver in the Lower House. In the Senate, however, the bill was amended by the Allison directed Finance Committee. The amendment effected a compromise in the free-coinage clause so that silver would not be taken to the mints to be turned into money. Instead, an amount which would vary from a minimum of $2,000,000 to a maximum of $4,000,000 would be bought each month by the Secretary of the Treasury. The silver would then be coined into dollars.[46] The amendment was accepted by the House, although a few of the extreme silverites, led by Bland, were disappointed. They nevertheless voted for the measure which granted partial, instead of free, coinage at a ratio of 16.1.

President Hayes had watched the bill carefully as it made its way through the legislative halls. A hard money man by reputation, it was expected that he would disapprove of the Bland-Allison measure. He wrote in his diary on February 3: "It is now almost a certainty that the Silver bill will pass in such a shape that I must withhold my signature. I am not so opposed to silver coinage that I would veto a bill which guarded the rights of creditors, and operated only in futuro. But I cannot consent to a measure which stains our credit. We must keep that untainted."[47] His concern, of course, was that the public debt would not be re-paid in the same manner as it had been borrowed. Hayes believed the public debt was a contract between the government and the creditor, and contracts cannot legally be broken without the consent of both parties. Since the Eastern and foreign holders demanded gold redemption, Hayes felt it would be a repudiation of the public debt to do otherwise. Because of their insistence on gold, the bondholders were regarded by the silverites as "shylocks,"[48] and this only intensified the struggle.

The February 28 entry in the President's diary described the differing opinions of his cabinet. His Secretary of the Navy, R. W. Thompson, opposed the veto because he was an "old time" Whig and did not believe in vetoes based on expediency or policy. When Hayes explained that the bill impaired contractual obligations, Thompson replied that Congress had the authority to impair contracts because of its right to alter the legal tender.[49] Secretary of State W. M. Evarts contested Thompson's reasoning, claiming that the President is a part of the law-making power and thus has the right to reject legislation and thereby force a two-thirds approval by Congress.[50] The division of the Hayes cabinet was: "For a veto decidedly Evarts, Key, Schurz, Devens—4.

For a veto with some doubts Sherman[51] and McCrary—2. Opposed
to a veto, Thompson."[52]

Hayes's message on February 28, 1878, was short and pointed.
He could not approve a measure that sought to repay debts with
a money cheaper than that which was borrowed. The country's
indebtedness was based on gold; therefore, the country should
repay in gold. If there must be a silver dollar, it should be worth
just as much as the gold dollar. To enact a law providing otherwise would be repudiation.[53]

The veto was hastily disposed of in the House. After some
parliamentary maneuvering designed to gather the friends of the
bill, the House overturned the rejection 196-73.[54] Shortly afterward the Senate concurred with a 46-19 vote.[55] The President
fully expected Congress to override his veto, since the division in
both Houses was on a sectional, rather than a partisan, basis.
Only a few of the lawmakers, predominantly from the East,
had opposed the measure.[56]

The significance of the Bland-Allison controversy has been
summarized by Professor Eckenrode:

> The measure was a weak substitute [for the economic ills of the
> day] and thus destined to failure from the beginning. . . . The Govern-
> ment purchases of silver had some effect in keeping metal prices up
> but not very much. The government was, month by month, a buyer
> of silver in a falling market, which meant that at the end of some years
> it was greatly a loser by its enforced purchases. The price of silver,
> artificially buoyed up by this measure, continued to trend downward
> as less of it was used in Europe. Silver producers had to look to
> backward countries such as Mexico, China and India [who were on
> the silver standard] for their principal market.[57]

By 1896 the silver question had become a major political issue,
the Democrats of the South and West usually favoring and the
Eastern dominated Republicans opposing free coinage. Ultimately,
the gold standard was adopted and both Grant and Hayes deserve
accolades for this accomplishment. Professor Eckenrode argues
that if Hayes had not resolutely opposed the Free Silver
bill, the Bland measure would probably have passed without
amendments, thus aligning this country with the "single-silver
standard group, with all of its backwardness."[58] Hayes must be
credited with positive action in his veto of the Bland-Allison bill.
Reacting from personal principles long established, he used the
veto in a way which, through precedent, had become perfectly
legitimate.

The third group of vetoes during the Grant-Arthur period
protected the Executive department from what the Presidents con-

sidered to be congressional encroachments. All three Presidents—
Grant, Hayes, and Arthur—expressed themselves on this subject.

Grant's first veto of this type occurred on April 18, 1876,
when Congress lowered the presidential salary from $50,000 to
$25,000 a year. He felt himself "constrained to [veto the bill]
from a sense of duty to my successors. . . ."[59] A salary of $25,000
did not defray the expenses of the Executive for one year, since
the sum was not now "one-fifth in value of what it was at the
time of the adoption of the Constitution in supplying demands
and wants."[60] The *New York Times* and the *Hartford Courant*
supported the veto. The *Times* said that in relation to the salary
of a Congressman, the President's pay was not out of proportion.[61]
The *Courant* believed that Grant could not consistently have done
other than veto the measure. The bill would have applied only to
Grant's successors, and his rejection of it was an example of his
statesmanship. The bill was passed, thought the *Courant*, "for
political claptrap," in the hopes of forcing the President into an
embarrassing veto.[62] The President was not intimidated by so-
called "liberals," though, and invoked the veto to protect the
presidential salary from congressional restrictions. The veto was
returned to the Senate and was referred to the Committee on
Civil Service and Retrenchment. No action was ever taken on it.

Grant's second veto on January 26, 1877, shows how closely,
even jealously, he guarded the prerogatives of the Executive. This
veto was on Joint Resolutions directing the Secretary of State to
respond to letters of congratulations from the Argentine and
"Pretorian Republic" on the United States' first centennial of
independence. Grant sympathized with the motives behind the
resolutions, but he could not avoid concluding "that their adoption
has inadvertently involved the exercise of a power which infringes
upon the constitutional rights of the Executive."[63] Furthermore,
no copies of the resolutions had been forwarded to the President,
so he had been unable to study their tone, language, or purport.
He closed his veto message by stating that "as regards the resolution
relating to the Republic of Pretoria, I cannot learn that any state
or government of that name exists."[64]

The veto of such resolutions might appear to be extreme or
even petty. Its tone indicated that Grant might possibly have
thought that Congressmen were joking with him, especially on the
resolution about Pretoria.[65] Grant's veto can be defended on the
basis that it was necessary to keep foreign policy a function of
the Executive branch, since the Secretary of State, an executive
officer, must be directed by the President. In some ways this
veto compares with the one on Sicilian Claims given earlier in

the century by Andrew Jackson. It may be recalled that Jackson argued that Congress may not alter, either by increasing or abridging, the foreign policy powers of the President.

President Rutherford B. Hayes also defended his office against what he considered to be infringement by Congress. The fight became particularly bitter and affected legislative-executive relations for years to come. The controversy centered around Democratic and Liberal Republican efforts to change the Federal election laws. When changes failed of enactment through the regular legislative process, the Democratic-Liberal Republican Coalition adopted the expedient of adding riders to appropriation bills. Thus it was necessary for Hayes to veto the entire bill in question, causing great turmoil among the political factions.

The struggle began on April 29, 1879, when Hayes returned a House originated bill on Army appropriations. The sixth section of the measure repealed an act of February, 1865, which authorized the use of Federal troops to keep peace at the polls during national elections.[66] Hayes pointed out that but for this rider, he would have quickly approved the Appropriations bill.

The President had anticipated such an event for some time, as the entries in his diary indicate. He viewed the riders as "the first attempt in our history to break down the functions of the Executive by coercion."[67] He believed that it was just as logical for the Federal government to protect Federal elections as for a State to protect State elections. Though many felt that Federal supervision of elections was a form of suppression retained from the Civil War, Hayes believed it essential to prevent fraud, and he further believed that the present House of Representatives was composed largely of people elected through fraudulent means.[68]

The President's diary of April 28 recorded the Cabinet's approval of the Army appropriation rejection. Hayes said there was a great deal of betting on whether he would sign or veto. Hostile Republicans, he wrote, "profess to be in doubt" about the outcome of the bill "and hope I will sign. Their number is now small—only the implacables—the patronage brokers."[69]

His veto stated that the rider made a vital change in the election laws which was not necessary for the successful operation of the army.[70] Thus, there were actually two bills before him instead of one. Hayes felt that Congress should return to the earlier practice of letting each law stand or fall on its own merits and should not make the approval of one dependent on the other. Such procedures, said Hayes, will "establish a precedent which will tend to destroy the equal independence of the several branches of the

Government,"[71] and will seriously damage the spirit of the Constitution.

On the 30th, Hayes was happy to note that the veto was fairly well received, and the House refused to override, 121-110,[72] on the following day. The *Hartford Courant* viewed the attachment of the election rider to the Army appropriation bill as an improper attempt to coerce the President. The Democrats had promised to repeal all federal election laws, especially the supervision of elections and the juror's test oath, during the present session. The President's stand was firm, however. Thus, "the Democratic statesmen are now obliged to consider the most available and graceful method of backing out of their dilemma."[73]

The House Democrats immediately framed another measure— this time a separate one—making it unlawful to employ any part of the army or navy at general or special elections.[74] The bill was met by another veto on May 12, 1879. Hayes said that it repeated the provisions of the previous act and that it favored the states and discriminated against the Federal government.[75] Thus he could not approve it. The President had been anticipating this veto for some time as he testily related in his diary of May 11, the day before the veto was formally given:

The Democrats have not been conservative or, as I think, politically wise. They have passed an affirmative new measure which repeals for the day of election many valuable laws. They call them war measures, and seem to think that as the War is ended these laws should now be mustered out. We are ready to muster out the soldiers, but we don't muster out the flag nor the powers of the law and of the Constitution which enabled us to gain the victory. We don't muster in again the evils that caused the War. Besides it is for the victors to say what shall remain— not for the vanquished.[76]

As with the first veto of this nature, Hayes was happy to report that the second was fairly well received. He summarized his vetoes, and anticipated others, in his diary entry of May 15:

My first veto maintained the prerogatives of the Executive, and the separate and independent authority of each branch of it [the Government] against the grasping ambition of the House of Representatives. The second maintained the right of the Executive branch to exercise power enough to enforce the laws, and now I am likely on the Civil— the Legislative, Judicial and Executive appropriation bill with its rider repealing the election laws, to have an opportunity to do something for purity and fairness in elections.[77]

The veto was sustained on May 13 by a vote of 128-97.[78]

The third election law veto was submitted by Hayes on May

29, 1879, against a civil appropriations bill to which the offending rider was attached. The rider, however, was not as stringent as the former one in that it did not demand the complete abrogation of the federal election law. Federal supervision of elections was to remain, "but its function was reduced to mere observation and report."[79] Since Hayes felt that the election laws should be strengthened instead of weakened, he refused the bill, using the same reasoning as in the two previous vetoes.

The bill was reconsidered in the House on the day it was returned. The amount of acrimony surrounding the subject is evident in Hayes's quotation of a congressional committee on the New York elections of 1876:

This election of 1876 will stand as a monument of what good faith, honest endeavor, legal forms, and just authority may do for the protection of the electoral franchise.[80]

This statement was greeted by derisive laughter on the Democratic side and by applause from the Republicans, accompanied by cries of "Read that Again!" At the end of the reading the regular Republicans indicated their approval with noisy demonstrations. With no debate at all, the veto was sustained by the House, 114-93.[81] Then the entire question was sent to the Judiciary Committee for further study and recommendation.

The fourth act dealing with the election laws was vetoed by Hayes on June 23, 1879. This was an appropriation act for "certain judicial expenses." The offending section forbade the payment of any official who enforced federal election laws in the states. The rider did not repeal the election laws but, as Hayes pointed out, it defeated their enforcement.[82]

The President again asserted that riders were dangerous additions to normal legislation. The veto, according to Hayes, threw his adversaries "into the greatest confusion." He was happy to report that seventeen Democrats and all of the Greenbackers in the House had supported the veto and had gone on record against legislative riders.[83] The veto was upheld 102-78.[84]

A bill similar to the one just discussed was rejected on June 30, 1879. The act appropriated the fees of United States marshals and their general deputies, granting $600,000 for this purpose. Appropriations for general judicial expenses had already been made by Congress and approved by Hayes since his June 23 veto. The June 30 bill prohibited the marshals and deputies from making contracts with anyone for the enforcement of the election laws until Congress had specifically made the necessary appropriations.[85] Hayes regarded this as still another effort to destroy the federal election laws. Of course, in vetoing the bill, he prevented any appropriation for the marshals, although a special message, asking the Representatives to make necessary provisions for them, accompanied the veto. The Congressmen refused, however, and it was not until the next session of Congress that the marshals were provided for. The veto was quickly dispensed with in the House, being sustained by an 85-63 vote.[86]

With this, his fifth veto in respect to the election laws, Hayes was generally conceded to be the victor in the fight over rider legislation. In the next session, however, it was again necessary for the President to apply the veto to appropriation bills because of congressional efforts to destroy or weaken the federal election laws. The first veto on May 4, 1880, was against a deficiency bill.[87] The President explained his motives in his diary: "I vetoed the Deficiency Bill on account of the permanent legislation attached to it in regard to the election laws. It was a measure of coercion thinly disguised."[88]

The final veto concerning the election laws occurred on June 15, 1880, on a bill to regulate the pay and appointment of deputy marshals. The objectionable part of the measure, said Hayes, was that the bill replaced the special marshals, called to duty during an election, with deputy marshals, to be appointed by the citizenry instead of by the marshal.[89] Nor would the marshal have the power to remove the deputy. This appointive and removal authority would be wrested from him, and thus his position would be considerably weakened. Hayes felt this constituted still another unwarranted attack on the federal election laws.

Even if Hayes had supported the repeal of the federal election laws, he probably would have vetoed it because of the manner in which it was presented. The Democrats and Liberal, or "implacable," Republicans in the House were offering him an "either-or" proposition. Either approve appropriation bills with the repeal provisions, or bring to a halt the financial operations of the government. Hayes, however, reversed the tables and put the blame for such tactics on the Congressmen. He maintained that Congress, or even a part of it, does not have the power to coerce the President, even though it might control the purse strings of the country. Hayes was therefore safeguarding the independence of the executive department, something for which there was ample precedent extending back to the administrations of Andrew Jackson.

Hayes proved himself a positive user of the veto in respect to the rider question since he believed that riders were unconstitutional because they attempted to coerce the President. The departments of government must maintain their separation and independence from each other, and Hayes used the veto to assure that this separation was maintained. The cost was high, of course, since he lost much personal popularity, and he became, as it were, a "President without a party," but this only confirms the positive nature of his executive refusals of congressional dictates.

A final example of a President safeguarding his prerogatives occurred under Chester A. Arthur in the Fitz-John Porter case. Porter, accused of being responsible for the Union disaster at the Second Battle of Bull Run, had been court-martialed and cashiered from the service in 1863. In 1878 a Hayes-appointed commission exonerated Porter from any wrong-doings at the battle. Congress passed a bill in 1884 restoring to Porter the same grade and rank which he held at the time of his discharge, and allowing the President to place the General on the retired list.[90] President Arthur, writing objections himself, said that the bill interfered with the nominating powers of the President and would serve "no useful purpose upon the statute books."[91]

The reading of the veto was listened to with intense interest. Upon its conclusion, there was great applause on the Republican side of the House.[92] Then General Henry Slocum, representative at large from New York, moved that the bill pass in spite of the veto, and the House complied 168-78.[93] The result of the vote caused wild demonstrations on the Democratic side as they waved their handkerchiefs and tossed papers into the air to show their jubilation.[94] The Porter bill, however, was lost in the Senate by a 27-27 tie[95] and did not become law under Arthur. It was only during Cleveland's term that the bill received presidential sanction. Other examples could be cited to show how Presidents guarded the integrity of their offices against what they feared were congressional encroachments. Those discussed will, however, suffice to show that the question was a vital one in the immediate post war period, and that vetoes, once again, helped to build the power of the Chief Executive.

The final group of vetoes in the Grant-Arthur era concerned the immigration problem. Presidents Hayes and Arthur were the Chief Executives most involved with immigration during the post war period. In the 1870's Chinese population on the West Coast reached high proportions, as it had risen from only a few in 1868 to 116,000 by the early seventies.[96] Chinese immigration was protected by the Burlingame Treaty of 1868, the fifth section of which paid homage to "the inherent and inalienable right of man to change his home and allegiance . . .," while the sixth section granted to China the "most favored nation" treatment.[97] The Chinese immigrants, however, competed in a real way with the

West Coast common laborers, while eastern industrialists of Pennsylvania and Massachusetts in particular brought in oriental labor to break strikes.[98] Fanned by West Coast radicals like Dennis Kearney, and encouraged by hypocritical politicians, the Chinese question had become acute by 1879. Thus a bill dealing with Chinese immigration was passed near the end of the forty-fifth Congress. It prohibited ships from bringing more than fifteen Chinese on each trip, and instructed the President to renounce sections five and six of the Burlingame Treaty.[99] President Hayes had been watching the bill closely as indicated by his diary entries. On February 23, 1879, he recorded, "As I see it, our treaty with China forbids me to give it [the bill] my approval. . . . We have accepted the advantages which the treaty gives us. Our traders, missionaries and travellers are domiciled in C[hina]. Important interests have grown up under the treaty, and rest upon faith in its observance."[100] He sympathized with the residents of the West Coast, but honor required that the treaty be upheld.

Hayes's veto of March 1, 1879, was written by W. M. Evarts, Secretary of State,[101] and repeated essentially the position Hayes had expressed in his diary. In the veto he emphasized his belief that a nation cannot honorably annul a treaty or any part of it unless some great insult has been given to the national honor as in the 1789 case with France. Moreover, Congress under the Constitution may not dispense with, or modify, a treaty since this is a function of the Executive department.[102]

The bill was reconsidered in the House on the same day it was returned. The vote was 110-96,[103] far short of the necessary two-thirds to override the presidential rejection. The effect of the veto, in part, was to pacify the Chinese question for a time and to cause the interested parties to seek more peaceful readjustments.[104] But the entire question had become so political in nature that it could not remain dormant. James A. Garfield, the Republican presidential candidate in 1880, became the victim of a forged letter which represented him as being opposed to the treatment given the Chinese by the West Coast residents. The result was that of a total of nine electors in California and Nevada, only one Republican was chosen.[105] Thus the question, ever growing in political intensity, constituted a serious problem for President Arthur.

On April 4, 1882, he vetoed a bill suspending for twenty years Chinese immigration to America. In addition, passports and personal registration were to be required of each Chinese immigrant.[106] Arthur accompanied his veto with scores of documents which showed that the legislation was in violation of the Burlingame Treaty.[107] A nation can repudiate a treaty only when the treaty conflicts with great and paramount interests,[108] said Arthur. Furthermore, the twenty-year suspension was unreasonable, while it was unfair to require passports and registration for Chinese when immigrants from other nations were exempted from these procedures.[109] Arthur also spoke of the advantages accruing to the United States over the past several years from the labor of Chinese workmen, and closed the veto by asserting that our West Coast trade depended in large part on friendly relations with Asian countries.[110]

The Senate, to which the vetoed bill was returned, became the scene of controversy as the Senators tried to decide how to dispose of the bill and its disapproval. Senator John T. Morgan of Alabama argued that it would be unconstitutional to refer the bill to a committee, as was suggested by several members,[111] since a committee cannot give the required "yeas" and "nays" on the question. The motion to refer was finally defeated 18-32.[112] Commenting on the veto, John Sherman of Ohio said that the Chinese were not desirable immigrants, and that the vetoed bill did nothing more than change our policy of open invitation to the Chinese policy of excluding foreigners.[113] Morgan said that the Burlingame Treaty hampered American progress, and he accused Arthur of encouraging Chinese officials to use their influence in Congress to help defeat the measure.[114] It was therefore obvious, claimed Morgan, that the President gave more credence to Chinese testimony than to the opinion of Congress. With the exception of Thomas Bayard of Delaware, supporters of the veto did not participate in the discussions. The vote was finally taken, and the veto was sustained 29-21.[115]

Shortly after these events, Arthur signed a bill suspending Chinese immigration for ten years. The Chinese Minister protested, and in 1883 a test case was brought before an American court, which decided that although exclusion was in violation of the Burlingame Treaty, Congress had the right to alter a treaty any way it saw fit.[116]

A second exclusion veto was given by Arthur on July 1, 1882. The bill required the same compartment space in steamships as existed in sailing vessels for the transportation of passengers.[117] Arthur claimed that the bill would prevent nearly all of the large steamships from carrying passengers anywhere but on the main and steerage decks because these were the only ones with the requisite space.[118] Though somewhat surprised at the veto, the House made no effort to override. Instead, it composed a new bill which met the President's objections.

Arthur lost much popularity and support from large sections of voters during these proceedings. The *San Francisco Daily Examiner* said that Arthur was "handy with his vetoes" in the exclusion question. It related that a Wisconsin delegation, calling upon the President, had informed him that if he vetoed the Passenger bill "which was for the protection of immigrants, he would be repudiated by one-half of the German voters in the Northwest."[119]

The immigration struggle was by no means ended by the vetoes of Hayes and Arthur; on the contrary, it was just beginning. Presidents Cleveland, Taft, and Wilson would have to deal with the problem along with all the prejudices, provincialism, and politics that it entailed. Like Hayes and Arthur, they would use the veto, feeling that restrictions either violated prior treaty arrangements or ran counter to basic American ideals.

The three Presidents discussed in this chapter were forceful and positive in their use of the veto power. Because of his conflict with Congress over the rider issue, Hayes may be considered the strongest of the three. This struggle did not merely reflect a difference of opinion between the President and Congress over the contents of a bill, but it was also concerned with principles central to the American system of government. Arthur probably came closest to giving a negative veto when he rejected the Fitz-John Porter bill. This question had become so politically involved that Arthur may have been thinking about something besides principle when he vetoed it. Grant employed the veto power most often during the period and, although the majority were on private bills, his rejections demonstrate that, at least in some respects, he may be considered to have been a powerful Executive. Any Chief Executive who gave forty-four regular vetoes and about the same amount of pocket vetoes, while Congress overrode only three of them, was not a weak President. It should be recalled, too, that one of his vetoes was overturned at his request.

There were fifty-nine regular vetoes during the period from Grant to Arthur. The ones discussed in this chapter adequately reflect the opinions of the time, since they were on questions of great national interest, and made headlines in many of the nation's newspapers. Other important matters, such as internal improvements, have not been treated here. Both Grant and Arthur vetoed internal improvement bills, and in the case of the latter, Congress overrode one. But the question was not as vital as it had been earlier and therefore it did not attract as much attention as the subjects which have been discussed.

During the next five administrations, the Presidents were largely concerned with vetoes of private pension and relief bills. It is now necessary to turn to those Presidents who presided over the fortunes of the country during the last quarter of the nineteenth and the first years of the twentieth centuries.

Grover Cleveland through Theodore Roosevelt
1885-1909

PRESIDENTIAL vetoes of legislation during the period from 1885 to 1909 covered a myriad of subjects and only two clear patterns emerged: protection of the Treasury against unwarranted intrusions, and the maintenance of personal principles. With the exception of Cleveland's rejections of pensions, silver coinage, and the internal improvement bill, none of the vetoes was concerned with the major events of the day. The rise to world power and the onslaught of reforms during the period definitely relegated the veto to a place of secondary importance.

Grover Cleveland's vetoes are perhaps better known than those of any other American President. During his first term 1885 to 1889, he rejected 413 bills and joint resolutions, 109 of which were pocketed, and only two were overridden. He was the first President to scrutinize closely the private bills for pension and relief, and his veto of 343 such bills amounted to 83 percent of the total.

Many applicants for pension benefits had already been refused by the Pension Bureau. They then appealed to Congress, usually through a lawyer or an insurance company. Congress thus established itself as a "rival pension court," hampering the work of the Pension Bureau.[1] Even before Cleveland was inaugurated it was generally agreed that one-fourth of the pension list was fradulent. The pension roll had grown to 325,000 by 1885,[2] and Cleveland was determined to arrest its growth. In his pension vetoes, he was guided by three specific objections: much of the evidence was *ex parte*, the examining physicians were local people anxious to help a friend, and the measure of a pension was the *physical* fitness of the applicant, which meant that such factors as his mental capacity or private income were ignored.[3]

On the other hand, many Congressmen and Senators, usually Republicans aligned with the Grand Army of the Republic, accused Cleveland of playing politics with the pension question. For example, it was charged that the Pension Bureau was often unfair or was unduly influenced by applicants, while it did not always place the facts before the President. These Congressmen felt that

Cleveland discriminated unfairly, since it appeared that he favored high ranking officers rather than enlisted soldiers. Furthermore, the President frequently expressed his ill-concealed bad temper in his private pension vetoes. A widow of a veteran who applied for a pension claimed that medical tests showed her husband died of rheumatism, a condition resulting from his army service. One physician, however, said that the veteran's death could be attributed in large part to alcohol. Thus, "the President [saw] fit to advertise this officer, who served honorably, to the country as a drunkard."[4] Cleveland's sarcasm was usually justified, however, because of the numerous attempts to take money from the public treasury, and to waste the time of Congress.[5]

The President attacked his antagonists by asserting that the universal theory seemed to be that "no man who served in the army can be the subject of death, or impaired health, except they are chargeable to his service." He mentioned some of the startling claims that had come before him. Apoplexy was attributed to insignificant wounds received in service, heart disease was caused by chronic diarrhoea, consumption resulted from hernia, and suicide was caused by army life in general.[6] Cleveland deeply resented Congress' overruling of the Pension Bureau, holding that the private bills reflected an undue influence of attorneys and insurance companies over the lawmakers.[7] He also objected to the large numbers of bills sent to him at the same time. In one day Congress sent him 240 special bills, 198 of which had already been rejected by the Pension Bureau.[8] The House set aside each Friday to consider pension bills, and the Senate enacted 400 such bills in a single day.[9] The President, however, demanded "reasonable time for the inspection of all legislation;" this prevented many "vicious private bills from being hurried through."[10] While it may have done this, it also kept many worthy petitioners from getting pensions. Cleveland shifted the blame for this to Congress, since it sent him so many bills that each could not be considered with care.

No effort was made to override a pension veto until July, 1886, and by this time Cleveland had given 33 such disapprovals. All of them had been either tabled or referred to committees, and only a few would be taken up for further consideration. The veto that was considered by Congress in July was against an act to pension Joseph Romiser.

The veto, on July 5, 1886, claimed that Romiser did not have the proper records on file with the Pension Bureau, and that the wounds for which he hoped to receive a pension were not service connected.[11] Romiser's case was argued in the House by

Louis E. McComas of Maryland, who accused the President of making a "grievous blunder" in refusing Romiser's pension. Romiser had been accidentally wounded by one of his own comrades, but the President and his followers had the temerity to claim that this was not "in the line of duty." McComas gave a vivid description of Romiser's wounds:

The heavy minie-ball broke the jaw at its ramus, making its exit through the molar bone below the eye. There was exfoliation of the bone, terrible deformity of the face, followed by months of lingering suffering and twenty-five years of neuralgia, and a legacy of pain for life.[12]

Edmund Morrill from Kansas stated that the Romiser pension had been approved unanimously by the Committee on Invalid Pensions. The President's veto was undoubtedly based on a "misapprehension of facts; therefore, it should be overridden."[13] Favoring the veto was John H. Reagan of Texas, former Confederate Postmaster General, who presented the ludicrous argument that before a wound should entitle a veteran to a pension, he would have to receive it in an actual battle. Otherwise, "his case is the same as that of any other citizen at home in any vocation who may be similarly wounded."[14] The majority of the House was convinced that the President had committed an error, not of principle but of fact, in the Romiser case. Accordingly, the veto was overridden 175 to 38.[15] The Senate took up the question on August 3, and in a short time overrode the veto 50-0.[16]

Congress rarely overrode a pension veto, and it was almost as rare for Congress, or even one House, to take a vote on the rejection of a private pension bill. Out of the hundreds vetoed by Cleveland, the reconsideration of only eleven was ever voted on. This lack of effort by Congress again seems to indicate, as it did in Grant's time, that Congressmen were willing to sponsor any number of private pension bills, but fight only half-heartedly for their passage. Thus they could protect their vote at home while the President, rather than the individual Congressman, would be given the blame for the lack of pensions.

Attempts to place pension laws on the books came to a climax in February, 1887, when a bill sponsored by Senator Henry W. Blair of New Hampshire was sent to the President. This measure, general in application, provided that any disabled veteran who had served 90 days in the army during any past war would be eligible for a pension of $12.00 a month. "Disabilities from old age and other nonmilitary causes were to suffice as qualifications for the stipend. Included in the 'Pauper's Bill' were dependent parents of soldiers who had died in service."[17] The bill was strongly supported by the G.A.R. and Claim Agents, and by Republican leaders catering to the "soldier vote."[18] Enough "weak-kneed Democrats, influenced by the "bloody shirt," were persuaded to vote for the measure to assure its passage.[19]

Cleveland returned the bill to the House on February 11, in one of the most important rejections of his presidential career. He noted that this was the first pension measure that had been passed for present disabilities alone, without considering their origin. Since the Civil War, 561,576 veterans had been granted pensions. In addition to these, more than 2,600 pensioners had been added to the rolls through private legislation, "many of them of questionable merit." If the bill passed, it would equalize the 90 day soldiers who had easy jobs and the gallant heroes of the major battles. But Cleveland believed that the pension roll should be kept a "roll of honor."[20]

Moreover, the bill treated the beneficiaries as objects of charity, and Cleveland believed the true veteran would object to this classification. The bill further complicated the pension question in which there was already a "widespread disregard of truth and good faith."[21] Finally, Cleveland believed that Congress had no way of knowing how many people would become eligible for a pension under the bill, which meant that it was impossible to ascertain the costs that would be involved. The country was living in peace time under war-imposed taxes, and the effect of the bill would probably be to increase them further.[22]

The House considered the vetoed measure on February 24. Representative Andrew Curtin of Pennsylvania defended the rejection because the bill would make eligible approximately 20,000 to 25,000 former Confederates. These men were rebel deserters and prisoners who joined the Union armies near the end of the war.[23] The bill would not benefit the true living veteran, although it would slur the memory of the heroic dead. Curtin thus hoped the veto would be sustained.

Future President William McKinley of Ohio said there was ample precedent for the measure. He drew applause from Republicans as he cited laws of 1818, 1820, and 1832 which provided general pensions. He also quoted Andrew Jackson's plea of 1829 that Congress extend the pension laws for the benefit of the Revolutionary soldiers.[24]

Competing with McKinley for applause from the Republican side of the House was William P. Hepburn of Iowa. He called the veto "cruel," and accused the Southerners in Congress, who were generally against the bill, of using their influence with the

President to cause his veto. He said that the great daily newspapers were biased in their reporting of the bill and its veto, since the papers, in Hepburn's opinion, were the spokesmen for the wealthy.[25] The House vote was 175-125.[26] Far from the necessary two-thirds, the vote was not enough to override the presidential objections.

Some authors say that Cleveland was not successful in his pension vetoes because, despite his care, hundreds of unworthy pensions were granted. Also, he failed to get much needed reform in the general pension system.[27] Because of his vetoes, many who should have received pensions did not. Cleveland was certainly aware of this, but he shifted the blame for it to Congress. Other authors maintain that Cleveland did stop the most flagrant abuses of the pension system. His vetoes of minor pension bills gave him the needed prestige to destroy the potentially dangerous Blair bill of 1887.[28]

Whatever his successes or failures, Cleveland outdid all other Presidents in the nineteenth century in using the veto. He holds the percentage record for having vetoed more bills than any other Chief Executive. He was non-partisan in his pension vetoes, and in most instances, despite claims to the contrary, he made no distinction between high and low ranked veterans. Therefore, his vetoes were positive reactions. It took political courage to withstand the powerful pressures of Congressmen and of the Grand Army of the Republic. Under his successor, Benjamin Harrison, pension legislation found a much better friend in the White House.

A few days after the pension veto, Cleveland returned a House sponsored measure with provisions not unlike the Blair bill. It sought to relieve some Texas farmers from drought conditions, appropriating $10,000 worth of seeds to the farmers. In his message of February 16, 1887, Cleveland said that public funds could not be used for charitable purposes. Such aid would increase the paternalism of the federal government and would weaken the sturdy character of the recipients. The state was capable of furnishing support for those most seriously affected by weather conditions. Included in the veto was a statement that several of Cleveland's successors, especially Herbert Hoover, would use many times: ". . . [T]hough the people support the Government, the Government should not support the people."[29]

Little discussion of the veto occurred in the House. Representative Samuel W. T. Lanham of Texas spoke briefly against it. He claimed that precedents had been set by laws of 1875 and 1883 for assistance of this type. If the Department of Agriculture was a constitutional body and if its services were nation-wide, the distribution of seed to needy farmers was a legitimate procedure. Moreover, the proposed assistance was not charitable but was an aid to good conservation practices.[30] Cleveland, however, viewed the Texas Seed bill as embodying the same principles as the pension legislation. The government simply could not be utilized to rescue everybody who found themselves in financial straits. This would injure the foundation of the government.[31] In his opinion, Cleveland upheld almost a century of presidential belief. With but few exceptions, every Chief Executive before him had believed exactly the same thing. The House quickly agreed with Cleveland and sustained his veto overwhelmingly 83-159.[32]

One of Cleveland's disapprovals seemed to belie his actions of preventing privilege. This was in a veto of March 11, 1886, when Congress tried to reclaim some land granted to Iowa in 1846. The bill directed the Attorney General to begin suits to assure the title of the government to such lands. The President reasoned that if the lands in question were public, "the declaration that they are so by enactment" was unnecessary.[33] The motivation of Congress in passing the bill was to allow a number of squatters to seek a redress of grievances in federal court against the Des Moines Navigation Company, which controlled the lands. To do this, the lands would have to be declared public.[34] In this first attempt to legislate on the Des Moines River bill the Senate, with its Republican majority, overrode the veto, 34-15. In the House, however, Representative Louis E. Payson of Illinois refused to allow the vetoed bill to be returned to the Judiciary Committee for study. This forced many Democrats to sustain the President without investigating the bill's true merits.[35] Thus, the veto was upheld in the House 161-93.

The question was resumed early in 1889, and this time it was thoroughly debated by the President and Congress. The President repeated essentially what he had said in 1886, emphasizing that several courts had ruled that the United States had no jurisdiction over the lands, and he felt it would be improper to overrule a judicial decision.[36]

Speaking against the veto in the House was Adoniram Holmes of Iowa. He accused the Des Moines Company of spoilsmanship, of tearing down property, and in general of doing more harm than good. The bill would only permit the actual settlers to take their case to a federal court.[37] Stephen White of New York, however, argued that if the bill passed, it would be a legislative decree defying twenty years of Supreme Court decisions.[38]

White's statement was refuted by John H. Gear of Iowa, who maintained that the Supreme Court decisions had amounted, in effect, to legislation. Gear made a lengthy and somewhat unstable speech in which he called the Des Moines veto an "alarming use of executive power." He quoted Hamilton, Kent, Story, Clay and Webster, in their contentions that the veto should be used only for extraordinary reasons. Cleveland's rejections, said Gear, were based upon expediency, with the Constitution being omitted altogether.[39] Gear's speech was reminiscent of some that Clay and Webster gave during the first part of the century. Of course, Gear should have known that to attempt restriction of the President's veto power was futile indeed. Very few people in 1889 were willing to challenge the right of a President (they might challenge his judgment but not his right) to return for any reason legislation of which he disapproved. The House agreed with the President and sustained his veto 147-104.[40] Thus, the Des Moines Company retained the lands in question.

Somewhat akin to the "pension grab" and the public land question was the attempt to appropriate for public buildings. Cleveland vetoed twelve such efforts in his first term. Appropriations in this area showed, as did the pension legislation, the amount of strife between Republicans and Democrats, and the effort by Congressmen to gain favor with the local electorates by sponsoring a public building bill. Few attempts were made to override Cleveland's vetoes on this question. The Senate did vote to pass a bill, despite a presidential veto, for a public building at Sioux City, Iowa, but the House refused to agree.[41] In vetoing legislation of this type, Cleveland reasoned that most of the buildings were not essential to the smooth functioning of the government. As stated in his veto of the Zanesville, Ohio, public building bill, Cleveland believed that such expenditures should be solely for necessity instead of ornamentation. An Ohio delegation visited Washington in an effort to change Cleveland's mind on the Zanesville building, but their visit was to no avail, and they finally agreed to introduce another bill calling for smaller appropriations.[42] Immediately after the Zanesville veto several Senators talked of attaching public building riders onto civil appropriations. There was little chance that such efforts would succeed, however, for it was clear that the President "would unquestionably veto the whole bill. . . ."[43] Thus such a movement never materialized.

Only one of the public building vetoes was overridden. Cleveland vetoed a bill on July 9, 1886, during his first term, which provided for a public building at Dayton, Ohio. Cleveland said that the only governmental offices at Dayton were the Post Office and the Internal Revenue Service and therefore he could not believe that $150,000 was needed for the work of the government in Dayton.[44]

The vetoed bill was debated in the Senate on March 3. Senator William Mahone of Virginia argued that to date twenty-one bills had been passed for enlarging and twenty-nine bills for beginning public buildings. These projected improvements were scattered throughout eleven states and territories. Mahone accused the President of inconsistency in approving these several bills that were at variance with his much vaunted "economy in public affairs." He also quoted statistics and population figures which purported to show that many buildings approved by Cleveland were located in cities much smaller than Dayton.[45] This argument convinced most of the Senators present and the veto was overridden 39-18.[46]

In the House, Representative Charles M. Anderson of Ohio argued that Dayton's population of between 55,000 and 60,000 entitled it to a public building, since there were 116 government buildings located in towns smaller than Dayton. It was apparent, said Representative Anderson, that the Ohio city was being slighted. The House then voted on the veto, overriding it 133-64.[47]

Cleveland is also remembered for his vetoes of internal improvements legislation. However, unless his public building and land vetoes of his first term can be called internal improvement vetoes, he was not prominent in this respect until his second term, when he vetoed a major bill for rivers and harbors. He used a pocket veto at the end of the Second Session of the 49th Congress to destroy appropriations for rivers and harbors. To be sure, there were many efforts to pass internal improvements bills, particularly in the Senate, where attempts were made to "load" the river and harbor bills with high appropriations. Some observers also feared the logrolling tendencies of the House, believing that only the President could stop this aspect of the treasury raids. But the House, which was controlled by Democrats, began killing Republican-sponsored additions to internal improvements bills. Thus Cleveland was not exposed to large numbers of unfavorable river and harbor bills.[48]

Cleveland was replaced by the Republican Benjamin Harrison in 1889. Under Harrison, pension legislation that would surely have been vetoed by Cleveland was approved. This was also true of many public buildings bills. Harrison's vetoes were, on the whole, neither controversial nor exciting. He vetoed forty-four bills and joint resolutions, most of which concerned pensions and public buildings, while only one was overridden.

The only controversial veto was against a bill enabling William McGarrahan to submit his claim to Rancho Panoche Grande in

California to the Court of Claims. The controversy was between McGarrahan and the New Idria Silver Mining Company. McGarrahan claimed that he was the legitimate owner of the mine and that the New Idria Company had taken it through fraud. Harrison vetoed the bill on July 29, 1892, but it was not considered in Congress until January 17, 1893. At that time the veto was upheld 29-18 after a moderate amount of debate.[49]

Harrison was harshly attacked for his veto of the McGarrahan bill. The *Cleveland Plain Dealer* called McGarrahan an Irishman "without friends, position, or money." The silver mine had been wrongly taken from him, and the only thing the bill would do in his behalf would permit him to take his case to court. However, the President of the New Idria Mining Company was D. O. Mills, who happened to be the brother-in-law of Whitelaw Reid, Harrison's running mate in the upcoming presidential election. Though Harrison had voted for the McGarrahan bill while in the Senate, his present political fortunes required a turnabout.[50]

The *Washington Post* half-heartedly defended Harrison's actions by saying that he did not have enough time to fully consider the McGarrahan bill before the close of Congress.[51] The *Omaha World-Herald*, however, decried the veto, saying that McGarrahan had suffered the injustice for over 30 years, while the bill in support of him had been before the Congress for 10 years.[52] The *Plain Dealer* was not to be outdone in invective, as it blasted the President in its editorials. The McGarrahan veto was "an outrage on honesty and fair justice," it said. Harrison was now running for a second time with all the odds against him; thus, he had to ingratiate himself with influential men. President Mills of New Idrian had promised lavish contributions to Harrison and Reid's campaign. Harrison was therefore swapping truth and justice for political influence.[53] The editorial was closed with the fond hope that Congress would destroy the veto. But this did not occur when the Senate considered the veto early the following year.

Harrison's last veto was overridden. The bill provided for an increase in U. S. attorneys and marshals serving Alabama, and was part of a general appropriations bill made by Congress at the last minute.[54] This probably accounts for both its veto and its subsequent re-passage. The President stated that in effect four districts were already being served by U. S. attorneys and marshals. He believed two sufficient for the job, yet the bill called for two more.[55]

Speaking against the veto in the House was future governor William C. Oates of Alabama. He said the bill did not require any additional appropriations from the Treasury Department, since the federal officers would be paid from the fees they would collect. William W. Dickerson of Kentucky, claiming that his state had only one judicial district, doubted Alabama's need for three. Oates replied that the additional personnel were needed to control internal revenue violations. "If the gentleman will give us greater facilities for the prosecution of illicit distillers it may enlarge the market for the sale of lawful whiskey made in his State."[56] The size of the vote, 184-55, indicated that Oates had carried his points well.[57] The Senate complied with the House action on the next day, destroying the veto by an overwhelming vote of 58-1.[58] Harrison thus left office on a note of discord with his Congress.

As previously stated, Harrison's vetoes were nondescript. His rejection of the McGarrahan bill cast him in a negative role. Whether the charges were true or not, at least they appeared to be and, ofcourse, impression is often the greater part of reality. His vetoes of pension and public buildings were not as numerous as Cleveland's, but they were positive, although extremely limited, attempts at economy in government. The importance of these vetoes was diminished by the furor of the McGarrahan case, in which it was easily argued that Harrison had used his power for political expediency. His defeat in 1892 brought Cleveland to power for a second time. Cleveland's vetoes were not as numerous during his second administration as in his first, but nonetheless they were a powerful factor governing the relations between the President and Congress.

Cleveland's second term was not as successful as his first. He vetoed 170 bills and resolutions, five of which were overridden. His vetoes on the crucial issues reflected his general unpopularity during the period. The first major veto was against a bill for the coinage of silver bullion, or seigniorage, of which about $55,150,000 had accumulated by 1894.[59] The Westerners favored the measure, believing the amount trivial in relation to the number of Bland-Allison dollars already circulating.[60]

Cleveland was under pressure to sign the Seigniorage bill because it would aid party unity, and heal the breach with the Westerners which had occurred since the repeal of the 1890 Sherman Silver Purchase Act.[61] The President, however, viewed the question as a matter of principle and did not approve the bill, returning it to the House on March 29, 1894. The main points of his veto message were that the bill would undo the work of the Repeal Act. A further infusion of silver into the economy would re-open the silver question and would result in many disadvantages. Thus the Seigniorage bill was "ill advised and dangerous." Instead of dumping more silver on the market, said the President, the government should be strengthening its gold reserves.[62]

Tempers were high in the House as the vetoed bill was reconsidered. Speaker Charles F. Crisp of Georgia insisted that a contested-election case be disposed of before the Seigniorage bill was considered. He ruled that the Constitution required only that the bill and its veto be read immediately; consideration could then take place at a stated date. Efforts by Charles Boutelle from Maine to appeal this decision were sharply denied by Crisp.[63] On April 4 the question again came up, and once more there was much disorder in the House. The Silverites, led by Bland, perhaps realizing the hopelessness of their case, were eager for an immediate vote. Several disruptive incidents occurred as the roll was called. Thomas Reed of Maine said that Nelson Dingly, also of Maine, had been prepared to debate the vetoed bill, but that Crisp had peremptorily demanded a roll call. There was so much noise on the floor and in the galleries that some members did not know the question being voted upon. A sharp exchange occurred between Crisp and Reed, the latter continually interrupting the roll call to protest the action of the Speaker.[64] Crisp was not to be moved, though, and John L. Wilson of Washington shouted out: "Tyranny! Tyranny!"[65] When the roll was completed, the vote was 141-114; thus, the veto was sustained and the Silverites had lost yet another battle. The country had moved a step closer to the gold standard, and Cleveland must be credited with assisting this objective. He abandoned what would have been a convenient and conciliatory move in favor of his stated principles and, as such, his veto of the Seigniorage bill must be viewed as a positive action.

Cleveland's next significant veto, on February 28, 1896, was against a bill allowing the territorial government of Arizona to lease lands reserved for educational purposes. The leasing would be limited to five years and it would be under the strict control of the territorial governor and the superintendent of public instruction.[66] Fearing the bill would probably lead to timber depredations by the lessees, Cleveland stressed this point in his veto message.

Representative John Lacy of Iowa charged that Cleveland was interfering with the constitutional power of Congress by vetoing the bill. The Constitution gave power to Congress to legislate for territories; thus, the President's veto was an intrusion of a congressional right.[67] He pointed out that Oklahoma had been given similar privileges in 1894, and that the system had worked well there. In one year's time (1895) Oklahoma collected $88,276.97 from her leases. This money could be put into a trust fund to provide quality education for future generations. Oscar W. Underwood of Alabama supported Lacy's contention, saying that the Arizona land was good pastureland and the territory could derive much income from using it properly. These two arguments sufficed for the other members, and the veto was overridden 199-38.[68] The vetoed bill was considered in the Senate on March 2, where it was referred to the Committee on Public Lands. That committee never reported on the bill.

Three bills on pension legislation were overridden during Cleveland's second administration. Several others were voted down in one House but not in the other. As in his first administration over half, 96 to be exact, of Cleveland's vetoes dealt with pension and relief. Much the same conditions prevailed as had previously. Petitioners, having been turned down by the Pension Bureau, appealed to their Congressmen for special legislation. In most instances Congress simply referred the vetoed bills to committee and they were subsequently forgotten. Two of the overridden vetoes dealt with widows of Civil War veterans. Congress apparently had softened its view toward such cases, but the President had not.

The bill granting a pension to Francis E. Hoover caused considerable acrimony between the President and Congress. The legislation increased Hoover's pension from the $12.00 a month which had been granted to him in 1890 to $50.00. The President retorted that Hoover's maladies could not be attributed to his service, and that if the bill were approved, it would be an "unjust discrimination" against thousands of similarly situated former soldiers.[69] Hoover suffered from varicose veins which had been caused, said his supporters, by physical exertions in the 1864 pursuit of John Bell Hood through Tennessee. The disease had become permanent around 1892 and now the applicant's spinal column was perfectly rigid, making mobility and means of support completely impossible.[70]

Representative Snyder S. Kirkpatrick of Kansas spoke when the House reconsidered the Hoover veto. Kirkpatrick did not so much defend Hoover's right to a pension as he deplored Cleveland's vetoes in general. He claimed that Cleveland discriminated in the disbursement of pensions. Generals and their widows were rarely required to trace their disabilities to service injuries; only enlisted men and officers of the line had to prove a connection. More importantly, the President had no right to limit Congress' power to grant pensions, whether of a private or public nature. Passing pension bills was the prerogative of Congress, and if this particular bill did not stand, a serious limitation on congressional authority would have occurred. This was clearly outside the Constitution.[71]

Franklin Bartlett of New York defended the veto. He drew attention to the amount of money spent each year through the General Pension Act of 1890, or the Pickler Act, as it was commonly called. The cost was between 61 and 62 million dollars for this one bill alone, while the other provisions for veterans cost additional millions. He also claimed that all the evidence in favor of pensions was *ex parte*, and thus was not truly reliable.[72] Bartlett's appeal was insufficient, however, and the House overturned the veto 196-47.[73] Without debating the question, the Senate complied 36-9 on June 10.[74]

The two other overridden pension vetoes were considered early in 1897. One involved Mrs. Rachel Patton, who had collected $20.00 a month since her husband fell in the line of duty in 1863. She had married after 13 years of widowhood, and naturally the pension was stopped. Her second husband deserted her in 1889 and she re-applied for her pension. Since her second marriage had ended in divorce, Cleveland did not feel she was entitled to a resumption of a pension.[75] Considerable debate occurred in the House when the vetoed bill was returned. Representative Benson Wood of Illinois, giving the report of the Committee on Invalid Pensions, said the tax-payers should be grateful to Mrs. Patton since her remarriage had saved the government $4,800 in pension money. He cited precedents justifying the resumption of the Patton pension—bills similar to this that had been signed by Presidents Jackson and Tyler.[76] The only defense of the President's veto came from George C. Crowther of Missouri, who made the inane suggestion that the pension should not be granted because Mrs. Patton, by her re-marriage, had deserted the memory of a dead soldier.[77] Constantine J. Erdman of Pennsylvania, in a more reasoned appeal against the pension, said that if the Patton pension were restored, all such widows should be treated likewise.[78] When the vote was taken, the result was 137-60. On March 3 the Senate confirmed the House action by a vote of 37-10, thus making the bill law.

A second pension veto was also overridden by the House on February 9. This veto concerned Mrs. Caroline D. Mowatt, the widow of Alfred B. Soule who had died in 1866. At that time she received a pension of $25.00 a month. She married Henry T. Mowatt in 1869, and the pension was accordingly discontinued. Mowatt died in 1878, but the widow did not re-apply at that time for the pension. Cleveland showed his displeasure when he claimed in the veto message that it was unreasonable to replace her name on the pension rolls eighteen years after the death of her second husband. "If she is to be again pensioned because her second husband does not survive her, the transaction has more the complexion of an adjustment of a governmental insurance on the life of the second husband than the allowance of a pension on just and reasonable grounds."[79] The House, unconvinced by Cleveland's reasoning, chose instead to be influenced by the statement of Cyrus Sulloway from New Hampshire, who claimed that Cleveland had signed thirteen bills exactly like this one in his presidential career. The veto was killed 143-55.[80] The Senate overrode the veto 39-7 at the mid-point of the fifty-fourth Congress.

Cleveland's experiences with pensions bills by no means ended the problem. Every President following him has been obliged to use his power to stop pensions which he believed unworthy. Indeed, the bulk of the vetoes given since the Civil War has been on pension and relief bills. The reason most often given for these vetoes was that they were financially inexpedient, although Harding and Coolidge would later make out a case that such legislation was unconstitutional. The entire situation was one in which it was easy to play politics. Congressmen quickly took advantage of any situation that might ingratiate them with the home-town constituency, rarely giving much thought to the consequences in the Treasury Department. Surpluses in that Department, brought about in part by protective tariffs, encouraged many Congressmen to sponsor pension and relief bills.

The most significant of Cleveland's vetoes in his second term, and perhaps of his entire presidential career, involved internal improvements. He returned the bill to the House on May 29, 1896. He pointed out that 417 items had been provided for, and that if the bill passed, the government would be committed to a total expenditure of around $80,000,000. The expenses were too high, the improvements "improvidently planned," and the entire proposal made the government appear to be the "giver of gifts."[81]

It is interesting to note that neither the President's veto nor Congress' reaction to it was based on constitutional grounds, but rather on the fact that the internal improvement bill was too expensive. The constitutional arguments of Jackson's and Tyler's time were by now definitely things of the past. There was little debate in the House on the returned bill. The House Committee on Rivers and Harbors approved passage despite the veto and Representative John Shafroth of Colorado, in connection with the veto, stated his plans to introduce a constitutional amendment allowing the use of an item veto. In his opinion, this would save government from $30,000 to $50,000 a year.[82] The veto was overturned in the House on June 2 by a vote of 219-61,[83] a majority of more than three to one against the veto. Even many avowed opponents of internal improvements voted against the veto because they "had supposed that Cleveland could suggest a bill of particular and specific objects which would confound the proponents of the bill." When Cleveland did not, his supporters lost heart.[84]

Debate in the Senate lasted about three hours, with several Senators showing anger at Cleveland's veto. Senator G. G. Vest of Missouri disputed the President's claim that the bill would cost $80,000,000. He cited statistics to show the growth of the country, claiming this as justification for increases in internal improvements. The Senator complained about the failure of Chief Engineer Brigadier General W. P. Craighill to answer his letter of inquiry and his telling the President that many items in the bill were local and should not be approved on this basis.[85] Sherman said that internal improvement bills like this should never be vetoed because they contained so many mandatory provisions for the good of the country.[86] William M. Stewart of Nevada said that Congress' right to pass internal improvements bills should never be questioned, and that all vetoes, especially those on appropriations, should be overridden on principle.[87]

The discussion took an even angrier turn when Richard Pettigrew of South Dakota gained the floor. Pettigrew wanted an amendment to limit the President's power to veto certain types of legislation or, failing that, to allow a simple majority to destroy a presidential disapproval.[88] Then, at the end of a speech that sharply differed with Pettigrew's position, David B. Hill of New York introduced a resolution for the enactment of an item veto. Following this resolution came another from Marion Butler of North Carolina, who formally presented Pettigrew's suggestion of allowing a majority to override presidential vetoes. Butler claimed that the veto power as it now stood "is a dangerous evil."[89] Of course nothing ever came of these various proposals, and the veto power remained intact.

Cleveland's supporters on the issue were few, only five voting to sustain the veto. William Bate of Tennessee said that lurking behind the internal improvements bill was another high tariff which, when passed, would probably be more excessive than the McKinley Act of 1890. Thus the laboring classes would again be taxed to pay for internal improvements which were wanted primarily by the monied interests.[90] The final speech in favor of the veto came from Hill, who chided Stewart for his belief that vetoes should be overridden on principle. The veto power was a constitutional one and could not legally be limited as the Constitution now stood.[91] Defenders of Cleveland were engaged in a futile cause and the veto was overridden 56-5.[92] The defeat of the veto showed the influence over Congress of powerful business interests. This influence had grown steadily since the administration of Franklin Pierce, when it may be recalled that several improvement vetoes were overridden. The transition was completed well before Cleveland took office.

Cleveland's last important veto dealt with the immigration question. Hayes and Arthur had first considered this touchy problem in their vetoes of 1879 and 1882, all of which were sustained. The Immigration (or Lodge) Bill was presented to Cleveland during the last week of his administration. It was the first effort by Congress to impose a literacy test on would-be immigrants to the United States and marked the beginning of a drive that would be completed only over the vigorous protests of President Woodrow Wilson in 1917. The bill barred immigrants over sixteen who could not read and write either English or some other language.[93]

Cleveland's veto, given the day before he left office, claimed that the Lodge bill marked a radical departure from past practices. The bill was unnecessarily harsh and oppressive, and the ability to read and write was one of the poorest tests of good citizenship.[94] The same pressures, primarily from the South and West, that were at work for restriction of immigration during Hayes' and Arthur's presidencies were present on this occasion. Congressmen, anxious for further ingratiation with their constituencies, reflected in their votes the provincialism and bias of the electorate. It thus took much political courage for Cleveland to reject a bill that was so popular. His veto message used language that would be adopted freely by Taft and Wilson when they found themselves obliged to deal with the same type of legislation. The House overrode the immigration veto 195-37, but the Senate upheld it by referring the matter to the Committee on immigration.

The end of Cleveland's terms as President marked the beginning of a period in which the veto's role in American politics was virtually non-existent. McKinley's and Theodore Roosevelt's administrations were highly significant from the viewpoint of America's development as a world-power and as a progressive nation. It was these very factors, however, that caused the veto to be relegated to a place of obscurity. McKinley exercised the power 42 times, 36 of which were pocket vetoes. Most of his rejections dealt with private bills for pension and relief, and in only a few instances did Congress attempt to override them. The vast majority of his vetoes were either referred to committees or were tabled.

The only significant veto given by McKinley was against a bill which he believed would exploit the rights of the Navajo Indians in Arizona.[95] The rejection, dated May 3, 1900, said that the opening of the land to miners and prospectors would disturb the peaceful relations of the past few years, and would also destroy the economic and social progress made by the Indians.[96] On May 4 the House referred the vetoed bill to the Committee on Indian Affairs, and no subsequent effort was made to override the President's action.

As was true in McKinley's term, during the administration of Theodore Roosevelt the country was too involved in momentous struggles for world power and domestic reforms to be interested in presidential vetoes. Roosevelt rejected 82 bills and resolutions. Forty of these were pocket vetoes, and only one of his rejections was voided by Congress. Again, the overwhelming majority of Roosevelt's vetoes concerned private legislation which sought relief or a pension from the government.

The only veto of Roosevelt's to be overridden was in May, 1908. The bill extended the time for construction of a dam across the Rainy River, which was located on the border between Canada and Minnesota and extended for some 80 miles into the Lake of the Woods. In this veto of April 13, 1908, and in a subsequent one of January 15, 1909, dealing with the construction of a dam across the James River in Missouri, Roosevelt noted the danger of granting monopolies in the development of electrical power. Waterways belonged to the people, and care should be taken to preserve that ownership against unscrupulous men. The government thus had the right and the duty to scrutinize carefully all efforts at building dams, including the imposition of a cost and time limit.[97]

When the House reconsidered the bill, J. Adam Bede of Minnesota reported that the conditions of the War Department had been complied with by the Rainy River Construction Company. Roosevelt had become convinced of this since the veto, and he would sanction its destruction. However, Bede noted, the President had shown a "complacent" attitude in getting the bill passed over the veto. Consequently, Bede "promised to stand by the President in all his policies, including the 'conservation of natural resources,' by swapping the Philippines for Ireland and raising our own policemen."[98] The Representative said the Rainy River project had not been completed because of the "recent panic." In the rear a Democrat, Albert Burleson of Texas, shouted: "A Republican panic." Retorted Bede: "Well, we adopted one or two of your planks and ran the country into a panic."[99] So in a somewhat jovial mood, brought on by the ready wit of Adam Bede, the House destroyed the veto 240-5. The same day the Senate unanimously complied 49-0 with the House action.

The best known of Roosevelt's vetoes was against a bill of February, 1909, providing for the thirteenth and subsequent decennial censuses. The measure permitted Representatives and Senators to designate persons for census positions after they underwent a simple, non-competitive examination.[100] Roosevelt, ever the reformer, could not permit such a measure because it would give the lawmakers vast patronage powers, would prevent the gathering of a competent census force, and would be more expensive than operating through the Civil Service.[101] The President was shown statistics which revealed that the thousands of appointments contemplated in the bill would virtually re-instate the old spoils system. Of course, such an eventuality was repugnant to Roosevelt.[102] Although the veto was anticipated for several days, "few expected that the message would be such an arraignment of professional politicians and the spoils system."[103] The returned bill was referred to the House Committee on the Census, and no effort was ever made to override the rejection. Roosevelt thus departed from the White House still the reformer that he had been when he first came to office. Though he did not need to employ it very often, he indicated that he would never hesitate to use the veto power to foster his program of social and economic reform.

Of the Presidents discussed during the period considered in this chapter, only Cleveland and Roosevelt can be compared. Each fought against special privileges. Most of the efforts to obtain pensions were just as much attempts at privilege as were schemes to monopolize public building projects. The difference, then, was not of kind, but degree. The only exception to this would appear to be Cleveland's veto of the Des Moines River Lands Bill, in which he helped a big corporation retain its control over landed property. This can be explained by Cleveland's decision not to upset many previous years of legal adjudication on the subject, and by the legal claim that the company had to the lands. He returned to his usual pattern in his veto of the Arizona School Land Bill, stating his great fear that the lands would be depleted and shorn of their economic value.

Cleveland and Roosevelt may also be compared to a considerable extent with pre-Civil War Presidents. Like Jackson, Cleveland frequently lectured Congress on the financial impropriety of certain legislation. Like Pierce and Buchanan, he showed a fierce determination to protect the public treasury from unworthy individuals and corporations, although his general philosophy was not as tightly constructed as that of his two predecessors. Roosevelt, like Madison, kept a close watch on the men the government commissioned for its business, and he took care to see that the privilege was not abused. Also like Jackson, Roosevelt believed that the President served the people first and Congress second. This position meant that the President was burdened with the enormous responsibility of thwarting the desires of special interest groups. And also like Jackson, though not to the same degree, Roosevelt never hesitated to use his veto to accomplish this end.

Under Harrison, Congressmen were bent on spending money and the President was not inclined to stop them. The items that Cleveland usually vetoed received the ready approval of Tippecanoe's grandson. While McKinley was in the White House, Americans were preoccupied with international events, and even if they had not been, McKinley's vetoes would not have stirred them either to wrath or jubilation. It was only with the advent of William Howard Taft that great interest in the veto was reawakened.

William H. Taft and Woodrow Wilson
1910-1921

BECAUSE their vetoes are similar in at least three significant respects, Presidents Taft and Wilson will be discussed in the same chapter. First, their major vetoes evoked an extraordinary bitter reaction from certain members of Congress: Taft's from the insurgent faction of his own party, and Wilson's from the opposition. Second, neither President compromised on subjects that really mattered to him, and their veto policies clearly showed that they would never yield on matters of principle. Third, although from different parties, Taft and Wilson's disapprovals of major congressional action were based on similar premises. Taft vetoed one immigration bill and Wilson vetoed two, basically giving the same reasons, and both vetoed appropriation bills primarily because riders were attached.

Taft and Wilson were essentially conservative in spirit. Taft opposed the swiftness of Progressive changes, believing that true and lasting reform came slowly; as a result, he thoroughly despised most of the Republican insurgents. Since he could not accept their tariff views, the tariff question became the first major issue in which his veto was used. Theodore Roosevelt had not committed himself on the problem, but Taft bared "his chest to the arrows of the tariff controversy."[1] The 1908 Republican platform promised tariff revisions by "the imposition of such duties as will equal the difference between the cost of production at home and abroad, together with a reasonable profit."[2]

In 1909, after much political wrangling during which Taft threatened more than once to use his veto, a tariff bill became law. Although he was not completely satisfied with the Payne-Aldrich legislation, Taft convinced himself, and spent much time trying to convince others, that the basic tenet of the 1908 platform had been applied. The platform had not specifically stated that tariff revisions be "downward," but the Payne-Aldrich schedules were lower than those of the 1897 Dingly Tariff which they replaced.[3] Nonetheless, Taft realized that revision of the tariff merited further consideration, and he therefore planned to use to its fullest extent the three man Tariff Board (increased to five at the half-way point of the Sixty-first Congress) created by the Payne-Aldrich Act. Before the Board could reach any definite conclusions, however, the insurgents and Democrats struck.

In April, 1911, Taft called a Special Session to deal with Canadian tariff reciprocity. In August, near the end of the session, an Insurgent-Democratic coaltion passed several bills calling for specific reductions in the Payne-Aldrich Tariff. Taft applied a veto to each of these attempts, thereby eliciting a storm of invective from the disgruntled members of the Congress.

The first of these vetoes was given on August 17. The bill revised the unbelievably complicated Schedule K of the Payne-Aldrich Tariff, the subject of which was wool. A House bill, sponsored by Oscar W. Underwood of Alabama, lowered the rate on wool from an average of 47.24 percent[4] to the revenue level of 20 percent. A similar Senate bill raised this to approximately 35 percent. A Senate-House conference compromised at 29 percent and sent the bill to President Taft.[5] The President's veto message said that the revisions were antagonistic to the platform pledges of 1908 because they did not reflect the principle of imposing duties equalling the difference between home and foreign production.[6]

Taft emphasized the importance of the Tariff Board, which he had charged with the duty of compiling a glossary of terms to be used in connection with tariff revision. He spoke highly of the Board and said that its report was due in December. He thus argued that Congress should await the Board's findings before altering the tariff. "There is no public exigency," he proclaimed, "requiring the revision of Schedule K in August without adequate information, rather than in December next with such information."[7]

The veto was read in the House to the great applause of the regular Republicans. Cheers rose from the Democratic side when Majority Leader Underwood announced his intention of calling up the bill immediately for re-passage over the veto.[8] The first major speech was by Ollie James of Kentucky. He vigorously attacked the Tariff Board in which Taft put so much faith. He identified the members thusly: Professor Henry C. Emery of Yale "who has never given any special attention to the tariff;" Alvin H. Saunders, "editor of the *Breeder's Gazette* . . . [who] has changed his vocation now and has become a breeder of procrastination;" (great applause on the Democratic side), George M. Reynolds, a banker, "who knows nothing of the tariff;" Professor Thomas W. Page of the University of California, "who has had no training or experience along the tariff line;" and finally William

M. Howard, a former Congressman from Georgia, who was a "great lawyer and a great orator," but no expert on the tariff.[9] The Kentuckian ended his tirade amid the accolades of his colleagues by asserting that "Taft will go down in history as the lone and spectacular figure who ever occupied the presidential chair in all the tide of this Republic's life who planted his ponderous corporosity in the way of remedial legislation for the American people."[10]

The Republicans' opportunity to cheer came as fellow Kentuckian John W. Langley sharply took exception to James' words. "We do not produce as much wool in the tenth Kentucky district as they do in various other sections of the country," he asserted, "but we want to be just to the millions of people employed in this industry." The Republicans of Kentucky, he said, were devoted to the principle of protection simply for its own sake. Langley expounded upon the Republican argument that drastic reductions in the tariff would seriously hamper basic American industries and would lead to an unemployment problem. The retention of a protective tariff was just as much in the interest of the American working man as it was of the American producer.[11]

The other speeches encompassed the broad spectrum of tariff beliefs. They extended from the vigorous defense of the veto power by Henry Cooper of Wisconsin and the staunch support of Taft's message by Frank Mondell of Wyoming to the dreadful picture painted by Georgia's Thomas W. Hardwick of children shivering in the cold because their parents could not pay the high prices of the Wool Trusts, and the eloquent scriptural quotations against high tariffs by Thomas (Cotton Tom) Heflin of Alabama. The House rang with the excitement of the great debate.[12] In the end, though, with both sides promising that the tariff would be the major issue of the next presidential campaign, Taft's action was sustained 227-129.[13]

The Democrats and their insurgent allies had not yet completed their attack on the tariff. On the same day the wool veto was debated and upheld, the House reconsidered a bill which would place several agricultural implements on the free list. Believing that reductions should await the findings of the Tariff Board, Taft disapproved the bill. It retained duties for raw materials and machinery but put finished products on the free list, an action which would be harmful to home manufacturers. Finally, the bill allowed home production to be undersold by Canadian imports without providing for United States reciprocity.[14]

The only lengthy speech on the Free-List veto was by Representative Sereno Payne of New York, a co-author of the 1909 legislation. He said of the Free-List bill, "No more bungling piece of tariff legislation was ever brought into the House by any party or by any act of men since the foundation of the Government." The bill placed on the free list articles of high-grade manufacture, but "everything from which they are made now bears a duty."[15] Defenders of the bill spent a short time criticizing the President and reading into the *Congressional Record* newspaper editorials against high tariffs. Then the vote was taken and the repassage attempt failed, 227-126. The bill was only three negative votes short of being handled the same way the wool reduction bill had been.[16]

The final attempt at tariff revision took the form of reducing duties on cotton goods and certain other materials. These embodied Schedules A and C of the Payne-Aldrich measure. While the bill was being discussed in the Senate, the "unholy alliance" between the Democrats and the insurgents was temporarily broken and a hasty *entente cordiale* was formed between the Democrats and the "standpatters" of the Republican party. The Midwestern agriculture-oriented Senate insurgents were not willing to vote for the very low cotton rates of the House bill. The "standpatters," to prevent any compromise which might increase rates to an amount that Taft could approve, voted for the original House measure. Thus, the bill was sent to the President "for the usual veto."[17]

Taft only repeated the arguments contained in the two previous tariff vetoes. Taft was immovable in his demand that Congress await the report of the Tariff Board. He said, "The important thing is to get our tariff legislation out of the slough of guesswork and logrolling. . . ."[18] When the veto arrived in the House, Underwood stated frankly that the Democrats lacked the two-thirds majority necessary to override it. He congratulated the "patriotic and progressive" Republicans who had voted with the Democrats for tariff revision, but even with their support the necessary two-thirds was lacking. The vetoed bill was then sent to the Committee on Ways and Means.

With the defeat of the cotton bill, further attempts at tariff revision in the Special Session of the Sixty-second Congress ended. The battle was renewed in the second session beginning in August, 1912, when the House re-passed the downward revision (29 percent) of the woolen schedule and the iron and steel schedule (22.40 percent). Taft vetoed both measures on advice from his Tariff Board. Arguments in the House were nearly the same as they had been in 1911 except that now the Democrats charged

Taft with seeking large campaign contributions from big corporations for his "favors." The Republicans accused the Democrats of purposely enacting tariff legislation that the President could not approve so they could use his vetoes as an issue in the upcoming presidential campaign.[19] The woolen veto was overridden 174-80 by the Democratic majority, still allied with the insurgent Republicans.[20] By the same distribution of votes, the iron and steel veto was destroyed 174-83.[21] The Senate, however, refused to accept the House action on either of the bills, so tariff reform was still impossible. No meaningful reform was enacted until the Underwood Tariff of 1913 was passed during Wilson's administration.

Taft's action on the tariff gave even further credence to the belief that he was no friend of Progressivism. His loathing of the insurgents became more and more obvious as each succeeding vetoed bill was returned to Congress. Not since Tyler's time had there been such an uproar and such a spewing out of vindictiveness on the tariff problem. The two Presidents suffered through situations that were much alike. Tyler tried to hold down the tariff against those who were supposed to be of his own party; Taft endeavored to retain a high tariff in opposition to a large segment of his own party.

Summarizing the Special Session, Speaker Champ Clark of Missouri said that the "standpatter" Republicans were completely demoralized, as was shown by their great rejoicing when the Democrats and insurgents failed "by a scratch" to re-pass the tariff bills, though the Democratic majority was only sixty-three. Thus it was that Taft, who came to office behind a huge majority vote, was "glad to escape the humiliation of having his vetoes overridden in a House containing a majority of only sixty-three. We honestly and persistently endeavored to relieve the people of some of their burdens of taxation, but the President would have none of it. To use a sporting phrase, 'he blocked the game'."[22]

The Special Session was characterized by another battle besides that of the tariff. This controversy started with the effort to admit Arizona and New Mexico into the Union "on equal footing with the original States." The offending clause in the enacting legislation bestowed upon the Arizona electorate the power of judicial recall. Taft viewed the provision as an unseemly attempt by the reforming elements in Arizona to control the courts, which had given friendly decisions to big corporations.

Taft's theorizing in this veto was reminiscent of Madison's Minority Checks and Calhoun's principle of Concurrent Majorities. He said:

A popular government . . . is [one] of the whole people, by a majority of the whole people under such rules and checks as will secure a wise, just and beneficient government for all the people. It is said you can always trust the people to do justice. If that means all the people and they all agree, you can. But ordinarily they do not agree, and the maxim is interpreted to mean that you can always trust a majority of the people. This is not invariably true; and every limitation imposed by the people upon the power of the majority in their constitutions is an admission that it is not always true.[23]

Thus, the judiciary must be separate from the more popular branches of government; it must not be subjected to the "gusts of popular passion."

The recall provision of the Arizona constitution said that 25 percent of the electorate could force a recall election after a Judge had been in office for six months. The petitioners would have to summarize in 200 words their charges against the Judge, and the latter, in the same number, would have to answer them.[24] The supporters of recall argued that it would be used only to strike down a judge who discriminated against the "humble and oppressed" in favor of the rich corporations. Taft replied, however, that impeachment could be instituted more easily than recall. The recall provision would create a "legalized terrorism" against the Arizona Judiciary; it would give vent to the muckraking press; and it would prevent good men from seeking judicial posts.[25]

Supporters of the measure quietly canvassed the Congress to see if they had enough votes to override the veto,[26] and when they found they did not, the bill was sent to the Committee on Territories. Senate tempers rose as a House-revised measure was considered on August 17, 1911. The judicial recall provisions were omitted in the altered bill. Senators Moses E. Clapp of Minnesota and Joseph Bristow of Kansas savagely attacked Taft for his veto of Arizona statehood. The veto "was against the solemn verdict of an overwhelming majority of the people of Arizona," said Clapp, calling the presidential action "wholesale debauchery of the electorate of a sovereign state."[27] Bristow said that the veto was an arrogant assumption by Taft, and John Sharp Williams of Mississippi reminded the Senators that his state had had harsh conditions imposed upon her re-entry into the Union which were not voided until "state sovereignty was restored."[28] Senator James A. Reed of Missouri joined in the assault on the veto by attacking Postmaster General F. H. Hitchcock, who was present at the session along with Attorney-General G. W. Wickersham, Secretary of War H. L. Stimson, and Commerce Secretary Charles Nagel. Hitchcock listened in silence

as Reed accused him of asserting undue political influence against
the Arizona Progressives, saying that Taft and Hitchcock had
"juggled" postoffices and judicial appointments in Arizona to
stop the spread of recall sentiment.[29] But the Senators were arguing
after the fact because the new bill without the recall provisions,
rather than the veto, was being considered at this meeting. The
bill, already having passed the House, represented a compromise
between Taft and the Congress, since it provided for recall of
all state officers except those serving a judicial function.[30] Though
Taft's reputation as a Progressive was further hurt by his rejection
of Arizona statehood, he again demonstrated his conservatism and
his sincere belief that Progressives were trying to do too much
too quickly. The only true and lasting reforms, he could have
reminded his Congress, come slowly and only after careful deliberation.

There were few differences between Congress and the President
resulting in important vetoes after the Special Session of 1911 until
just before Taft left office, although his intervention against
several appropriation bills onto which riders had been attached
did attract widespread attention. The first was in August, 1912, on
an appropriation for the executive, legislative, and judicial departments. The rider would have changed the procedures of the
District of Columbia Civil Service by giving department heads
discretion to retain or dismiss workers at seven year intervals. In
Taft's opinion, this would undermine the Service's tenure system.
Another rider to the bill abolished the Commerce Court, giving
jurisdiction over matters affecting interstate commerce to a three
man court to be established in each of the judicial circuits.[31] In
dealing with the veto, several Representatives defended the right
of Congress to attach riders to appropriation bills. Their argument
was that since Congress controlled the purse strings, it could
place conditions upon how the money was to be expended.[32]
These points were not sufficient, however, and Taft was upheld
147-107.[33] Shortly after this, another bill was sent to the President
with the Civil Service tenure section omitted, but with the abolition of the Commerce Court still present. Of course, Taft could
not approve this measure. Accordingly, Congress returned the
appropriation bill to the President for the third time, now without
either of the objectionable riders, and Taft finally gave his approval on August 23, 1912. Again a President had used his veto
power to force the passage of what he considered was proper
legislation. Taft's final veto of an appropriation bill because of a
rider came on the last day of his presidency. The bill was for
"sundry civil expenses," and it contained a large appropriation

for enforcement of the antitrust laws. The proviso forbade the prosecution of any business combinations "having in view the increasing of wages, shortening of hours, or bettering the conditions of labor. . . ."[34] Taft saw in this "subtle" proviso the danger that although a combination might be *formed* with these benevolent purposes in mind, there was nothing to control such a combination after the period of formation.[35] The veto was accordingly returned to the House where, on March 4, 1913, it was overturned 264-48. In the Senate, however, no vote was ever taken on it, presumably because of the expiration of the Sixty-second Congress.

Taft also rejected some bills that in many respects were similar to the internal improvement legislation of an earlier day. The major difference was that before much of the struggle had been based on the Constitution, but now the question was primarily concerned with arguments between state and federal authorities regarding jurisdiction over the improvements. In the Dixie Power Company veto of August 6, 1912, Taft prevented the construction of a dam across the White River near Cotter, Arkansas. He believed there was not yet enough commerce on the river to justify federal improvements, and the ownership of the dam was scheduled to be transferred to the State government, although no provision was made for remuneration of federal expenses.[36] No effort was made to override the veto. The Coosa River veto of August 24, 1912, was against efforts to allow the Alabama Power Company to build a dam for commercial purposes. Taft feared that too much authority would be extracted from the federal government if the bill passed.[37] Again, no attempt was made to override the veto. Of course internal improvements were not as controversial in 1912 as they had been in the previous century, and Taft's vetoes dealt, not with the constitutionality of such measures, but with the preservation of federal jurisdiction.

Two of the most significant of Taft's vetoes occurred in February, 1913. One concerned a renewal of legislation designed to restrict immigration, similar to that vetoed by Cleveland in 1897. The legislation grew from a 1907 law which established a commission on immigration to conduct an investigation into immigration procedures. The results of the investigation were contained in the Dillingham Report, named for William P. Dillingham of Vermont, chairman of the Commission and co-author of the 1913 measure.[38] The law still received the support of organized labor, but now certain sociological groups interested in the welfare of the recently arrived immigrants joined in its advocacy. Like its predecessor, the bill required that heads of families and those over 16 years of age pass a literacy test. The test required them to read at least 30 words in English or another language. An exception to this allowed any alien already in the country or admitted under the Act, or any citizen, to bring his parents to this country if they were over 55 years old, regardless of their ability to read and write.[39]

Taft's veto of February 14 expressed regret that he differed with Congress and much of the country on this vexing problem. In his opinion, the bill contained several excellent amendments to the Immigration law, such as extending the list of communicable diseases, the holders of which would be excluded. The imposition of a literacy test, however, invalidated the whole legislation. The test was unfair because under it one qualified immigrant could bring in unqualified members of his family. On the other hand, an unqualified head of a family might make ineligible all of his qualified children. Delays would result at all ports of entry and this would bring protests from foreign countries, most especially from Canada and Mexico. And finally, to exclude someone because he was unable to read and write would deprive him of the opportunities he sought in America in the first place.[40]

Senator Dillingham defended his bill when its veto was returned to the Senate. He said that the tendency of the new immigration, unlike that of the old, was to go, not to the farms, but the cities where they became factory laborers at low wages. The old immigrants usually sought naturalization, but the new ones stayed only so long as it took to make a certain amount of money, then returned to their country of origin. Therefore, the new immigrants were not as interested in contributing to the welfare of the United States as had been the old ones.[41] The veto was defended by William J. Stone of Missouri, who claimed that many members of the Camorra and the Mafia could pass the literacy test,[42] and by James P. Clarke of Arkansas, who said he would not exclude anybody capable of worthwhile contributions merely because of the misfortune of illiteracy.[43] The veto's defense, however, was not good enough, and the Senators passed the bill 72-18.[44] It then went to the House for necessary action.

House supporters of the bill believed that enough votes could be obtained to emulate the Senate's action.[45] They objected to Commerce Secretary Nagel's letter upon which Taft had justified his veto. Nagel said the literacy requirement was "based upon a fallacy in undertaking to apply a test which is not calculated to reach the truth, and to find relief from a danger which really does not exist."[46] He disliked the "group" system whereby qualified dependent children of an unqualified head of a family would be excluded.[47] Those favoring the bill were displeased with Nagel's apparent belittling of the legislation.

Representative John L. Burnett of Alabama, co-author of the legislation, led the House fight for its adoption. The literacy test was not the perfect answer to the dilemma, he said, but it would be most effective against those immigrants who should be denied access to the United States. The literacy test, it was argued, was a humane practice, because many aliens in America lived in conditions which were just as bad, or perhaps even worse, than in the old country. Opponents of the bill continually quoted a poem by Louis S. Amonson, "A Message to Congress from the Men at the Gate." Its first stanza was:

> We've dug your million ditches,
>   We've built your endless roads,
> We've fetched your wood and water,
>   And bent beneath the loads.
> We've done the lowly labor
>   Despised by your own breed;
>   And now you won't admit us
>   Because we cannot read.[48]

The pro-restriction forces in the House did not have enough support, so the work of the Senate was undone by a 213-114 vote.[49] Thus the immigration question remained to create problems for yet another President. President Wilson was obliged to veto two Burnett-Dillingham bills, the second of which was voted down with an attitude that approached vindictiveness.

The last of Taft's important vetoes was overridden. This was against the Webb-Kenyon bill, the passage of which was an important victory for the Anti-Saloon League. The bill prohibited the shipment of liquor into states where its sale or use was legally forbidden—approximately 71 percent of the country.[50] Taft did not like the measure because it gave the states too much control over interstate commerce. The bill amounted to a delegation of one of Congress' powers, i.e., the Commerce Clause, which was beyond the scope of the Constitution. A letter from Attorney-General Wickersham, accompanying the veto, outlined the major points of opposition to the bill and cited several court decisions in support of the President.[51]

The veto was discussed in the Senate on the same day as it was given, February 28. Speaking against it, Senator Porter J. McCumber of North Dakota stated that Congress had previously outlawed other articles in interstate commerce, and he used the White Slave Act as an example. Even without precedents, McCumber argued, Congress' power over interstate commerce was all embracing, and it was competent to delegate powers as it saw fit.[52] Other supporters of the measure contended that the Webb-Kenyon bill conferred no more authority upon states in the regulation of liquor than it did in bad meats, poisons, and explosives.[53] There were no major speeches in support of the veto, and within two hours, the Senate overrode Taft's rejection 63-21.[54]

In the House, Henry Clayton of Alabama led the supporters of the bill. He said the legislation only reflected the police powers of the states, which had preceded the Commerce Clause. Clayton cited court decisions upholding state power over traffic in intoxicating liquor "according to their sovereign will."[55] The major refutation of Clayton's thesis came from Augustus Stanley, representing Kentucky and its liquor concerns. The Kentuckian also cited past judicial decisions which showed that Clayton was wrong in assuming that all of them upheld the power of the states, and called upon such giants as Webster, Marshall, and Taney to prove his contention.[56] Stanley closed his address by calling the bill a "hybrid" measure—half federal and half state. Toward the end of the debate it became more than clear that Protestant, Anti-Saloon sentiment in the House was too strong to overcome. Accordingly, the Senate's action of the previous day was confirmed 246-95.[57] The Webb-Kenyon bill thus became law and it foreshadowed the day, not too distant, when federal prohibition would exist throughout the nation.

It is clear that Taft's vetoes reflected his conservative, legalistic attitude toward government. In considering the tariff question, for example, he admitted that many schedules were in need of reform, but he feared the type of revision championed by the Democratic Insurgent coalition. It was entirely possible that changes in the tariff could make matters even worse than they were already, so he insisted on a thorough study of possible alternatives before committing himself to a definite course. This propensity toward "philosophical" Progressivism did not win Taft very many friends, but the reforms that did receive his sanction were solidly based.

His legalistic approach was evident in the veto of the Arizona Statehood bill. He could not allow the Judiciary to be placed at the mercy of an anti-corporation voter minority. The appropriation veto of March 3, 1913, revealed another aspect of his philosophy. He would not allow business combinations even if organized for such benevolent purposes as improving labor conditions by raising wages or shortening hours. Thus, just as he protected corporations from their detractors in Arizona, he defended the public against what in his judgment was actually a selfish attempt at business combinations.

Another side of Taft is seen in his vetoes of the various dam bills. Here, as in the case of Cleveland, Taft did not base his arguments upon the Constitution. He believed that if these bills were passed the states would receive more authority than the federal government should concede. Taft, therefore, practiced a healthy federalism, almost as had Theodore Roosevelt, though the latter's reputation was much greater. Concern over delineating jurisdiction between state and federal government was also evident in Taft's veto of the Webb-Kenyon bill.

Finally, Taft's veto of the Immigration bill was squarely in line with the precedent set by Cleveland. Political consideration did not motivate the veto, since the presidential campaign was already over, and Taft had carried only two states. The immigration question transcended party lines; almost as many Republicans as Democrats wanted it, so Taft's veto could not have been along partisan lines. Therefore, one must ascribe positive reasons for this, as well as for all of Taft's other rejections. He never acted on impulse, but rather only after a close and careful study of the issue at hand. This was not as exciting as Theodore Roosevelt's way of doing things, but in the long run it was equally as effective. Taft's successor, Woodrow Wilson, though a Democrat, also belonged essentially to the "philosophic" school of Progressivism. Accordingly, his vetoes, like Taft's, had the definite ring of political conservatism.

Wilson's first major quarrel with the Congress was over the reintroduction in 1915 of the Burnett-Dillingham Immigration bill. Its provisions were identical to those in a bill that Taft had vetoed two years before. Like Taft, Wilson believed there were many admirable things contained in the legislation, but the presence of the literacy test dictated his disapproval,[58] since it would deny worthy immigrants the education for which many of them came. Several people reminded Wilson of his statements on immigration in his *History of the American People*. In that book he had talked about "undesirable foreigners," and had indentified them mostly as Southern Europeans.[59] He had, however, changed his mind "in the right direction" by 1915 and he now upheld the historical bases upon which this country was founded.[60] Despite the outward evidence of his "conversion," Wilson wrote a letter to Mississipian John Sharp Williams saying that he was embarrassed to differ with so many people on the immigration problem. During the presidential campaign, though, Wilson had promised certain ethnic groups that he would disapprove any restrictive legislation.[61] This letter tends to show that there was a considerable political motivation in Wilson's veto.

The vetoed measure was debated in the House on February 4. It took the Representatives five hours and twenty minutes to dispense with it. The major points for passing the bill despite the veto were: immigrants depressed wages because they flooded the labor market; they led strikes; the veto favored the steamship trusts, which earned huge sums of money each year by bringing immigrants to the United States; with the end of war, the United States, particularly the West Coast, would be inundated by immigrants; the literacy test was not unreasonable; and the United States could not now afford to be as liberal on immigration as at times in the past.[62] Supporters of the veto brought out these objections to the bill: much of it was inspired by the so-called "patriotic" organizations who continually talked about the "Rome Lobby" in this country; thus, the bill was a tribute to hatred and provincialism; the bill would damage our relations with foreign countries; and the literacy test was far from being a qualification for good citizenship.[63]

In spite of the determined effort by Burnett and the bipartisan coalition supporting him,[64] the bill failed in the House 261-136.[65] The Republicans voted almost three to one against the veto. Burnett gave notice that the bill would be re-introduced into the next Congress, and he hoped to make it a campaign issue in 1916. He claimed that the European war had given a new impetus to restriction, and efforts would be continued to prohibit the "undesirables" from coming to the United States.[66]

Though these efforts continued, it was not until 1917 that the bill was passed again. There was little that was new in the bill or its veto, which Wilson sent to the House on January 29. By now the bill did have a "religious persecution" clause, which stated that any foreigner could waive the literacy test if he came here seeking religious freedom. Augustus P. Gardner of Massachusetts said this provision was inserted primarily for Jewish people.[67] Another addition to the bill was the establishment of "zones" from which immigration would not be permitted. According to Senator Reed these involved areas containing 300,000,000 people, affecting mostly Sourthern Europeans and Asians.[68] The African was not included, said Hardwick, because so little immigration had come from that continent in the past.[69]

On February 1, the House overrode the veto 287-106;[70] party lines were almost completely ignored and Republicans and Democrats were equally divided in favor of the immigration bill. Both Republican leader James Mann of Illinois and Democratic leader

Claude Kitchin of North Carolina voted to override. Of the 287 votes for repassage, 149 were Democratic, 131 Republican, four Progressive, one Prohibitionist, and one Independent.[71] This bipartisan unity was an indication that the Senate, which had originally passed the bill 64-7, would comply with the House action. There was only a slight possibility that the Senate might sustain the veto because of the grave international situation. Some observers believed that the Senators would fear the creation of international complications if the bill became a law.[72] These speculations did not materialize, however, and on February 5, by a 63-19 decision, Wilson's veto was overridden.[73] Thus, the drive that had begun during Cleveland's presidency had now reached fulfillment.

The bill's passage was the prelude to severe restrictions on immigration during the post-war period. Efforts to establish the quota system first became obvious in 1921 when a bill to that effect went to President Wilson. He received it at the end of the Sixty-sixth Congress, so he prevented its passage by a pocket veto.[74] Immigration restriction, of course, reflected the conservative, isolationist attitude that Americans possessed during the immediate post-war period. The passage of the 1917 bill gave the necessary impetus toward establishing the quota system during the 1920's.

Wilson's other important vetoes dealt almost exclusively with World War I and its attendant problems. For example, one veto involved efforts to repeal daylight saving time, which had been instituted during the war. Farmers complained that their labor forces operated under the same rules as industrial workers, with the result that sufficient crews could not be kept long enough during the day.[75] The farmers, unable to set the working hours of their employees, suffered unwarranted hardships. The first attempt to change this system came in an agricultural appropriation bill in July, 1919. Wilson stopped it by asserting that serious economic losses would be entailed by repeal at that time.[76] During the following month, Congress passed a specific bill to repeal daylight saving time. Again, Wilson vetoed it. He pointed out that the farmers might very well be under disadvantages in relation to an adequate labor force because of daylight saving time. However, industry needed it, and the disadvantages of its repeal would be greater to industry than would be the disadvantages to the farmer because of its retention. After all, the farmer used the products of industry, so in many respects agricultural interests would benefit from the continuation of the time system. Wilson referred to studies which showed that industry was more efficient during natural daylight than in artificial light;

thus more helpful to the economy.[77] Congress, however, was not
to be denied victory this time. It was heavily representative of
the rural districts, and on August 19 the House overrode the
veto 223-101. The next day the Senate confirmed this action
57-19.[78] Repeal of daylight saving time, a war expedient, was
thus effected.

As it turned out, daylight saving was only one of several differences between the Congress and the President dealing, one
way or another, with World War I. Wilson's controversy with a
majority of his Congress over ending the war with Germany is
well known. Doubtless he would have approved many bills that
either repealed or continued certain wartime practices if there
had not been the semantic argument about whether the war was
over, or when it ended. A good example of this was the passage
of the Volstead Act in October, 1919, which continued wartime
prohibition until national prohibition became effective in January,
1920.

Wilson argued that demobilization of the armed forces ended,
for all practical effects, wartime prohibition. It was not proper to
make permanent a law that had been designed for temporary
purposes. To uphold the Volstead Act would cause many liquor
concerns to lose money on the stock they were holding in anticipation of repeal.[79] Indeed, a Kentucky judge had recently ruled
that wartime prohibition in itself, to say nothing of its extension,
was unconstitutional, since it amounted to a "confiscation of private
property without just compensation."[80]

There was only one slight possibility that Wilson's veto would
come through the House and Senate intact. If the German Peace
Treaty were to be ratified, Wilson could declare peace and formally demobilize the army and navy. Such an event would automatically annul the wartime prohibition law.[81] As it was, without
ratification, many thought the President was not authorized unilaterally to end the prohibition measure. The House, in an uproar
during the reading of the presidential message,[82] overrode the
veto 175-55 in a short time.[83]

Senator Thomas Sterling, Republican of South Dakota, directed
the bill's reconsideration in the Senate. Supporters said that the
war with Germany was not technically over and that all wartime
measures should be enforced until it was. Opponents believed that
Congress had acted in bad faith by shortening the time allowed
for national prohibition to go into effect.[84] Wartime prohibition
should have ended automatically with the Armistice, but it was
now being argued because Congress believed the war was still
in progress, and Wilson, at least on this occasion, believed it

was not. The Senate destroyed the presidential disapproval 65-20.[85]
This action assured that there would be no great "wet spell"
throughout the country before the 18th amendment became law.
During most of the overriding procedure, the galleries were almost deserted in both the House and the Senate. "The crowds
that used to sit through weary hours of prohibition debate had
not heard, of course, that the final fight was at hand, and John
Barleycorn's wake, if it was that, was unattended."[86]

The Volstead struggle was not carried out along party lines.
Both Republicans and Democrats (Southern Democrats almost
en masse) voted heavily for its passage over the veto. It was a
different matter, however, with the next crucial test between
Wilson and the Republican dominated Congress. This occurred
in May, 1920, when a Joint Resolution was passed ending the
war with Germany. Known formally as the Porter-Knox Resolution, Congress' action attempted to show that a war could be
ended by something other than a treaty, and it repealed all wartime legislation.[87] Republican interpretation of the Resolution
was that Germany had conceded United States' demands by the
Treaty of Versailles. "The only controversy remaining is the
one between Chief Executive and the Senate over the terms of
the treaty." Thus, the war was over and the country demanded
a removal of wartime restrictions and prohibitions. If the President would not exercise his responsibility, then Congress must.[88]
The veto of the Peace Resolution showed an apparent contradic-
tion in Wilson's actions. He had rejected the Volstead Act because it continued a wartime prohibition.

Everyone knew that Wilson would reject the Resolution, because not to do so would be to accept the Republican position
of refusing to ratify the Treaty of Versailles. The President said
the Resolution would "place an ineffacable stain upon the gallantry
and honor of the United States," and it did not exact from
Germany any action setting right the "infinite wrongs" upon the
peoples it attacked.[89] An important political observer, the *Washington Evening Star*, was disappointed in Wilson's veto. It had
hoped that the President would restate his case concerning the
Versailles Treaty "in a way to serve the San Francisco Platform,"
soon to be written. Since he did not, however, the phrasemakers
at the upcoming Democratic Convention faced a problem. Apparently, the "tweedledummers," and the tweedledeers" would
have to stay close to each other during the proceedings.[90]

In the House on May 28, Stephen Porter, Republican of Pennsylvania, spoke for his Resolution by asserting that its effects
would be only to repeal wartime legislation and to "hold all of

the rights of the belligerents in abeyance" until a peace treaty was signed and ratified.[91] Then Tom T. Connally of Texas claimed that the Resolution was unconstitutional because only the Senate confirmed actions to end wars. Moreover, Connally believed that the Republicans did not actually want to repeal the wartime laws, but merely desired to give that impression to the public.[92] Other speeches on the subject were short and not much different from those by Porter and Connally. When the vote was taken, the veto was sustained 220-152.[93] This vote was definitely partisan because the sectional motivations of the Volstead action were missing.

The tiresome fight between Wilson and Congress resumed in full fury at the beginning of 1921. Republican Senator Asle J. Gronna from North Dakota, Chairman of the Senate Committee on Agriculture, initiated a resolution to revive the War Finance Corporation which, during the war, had helped to finance agricultural goods intended for export. The Gronna Resolution authorized the issuance of $1,000,000,000 of debentures to stimulate agricultural exports. The Westerners and Southerners were solidly in favor of the Resolution because it gave them an opportunity to dispose of products which they were having a difficult time marketing.[94]

Wilson's veto, however, disagreed with the advantages claimed by the Resolution. The Resolution was designed, said the President, to reverse the trend of falling agricultural prices by making it easier to trade with the European countries, as had been the case before the war. This was an admirable goal, but the condition of Europe, though steadily improving, was not such that prewar practices could be automatically resumed. The burdens of war, he asserted, are not lifted when the fighting stops; war leaves behind it a legacy of economic ills and suffering from "which there is no escape." Patience is required in rebuilding war-torn institutions; therefore, rehabilitation must be genuine instead of artificial. Thus, the resumption of the War Finance Corporation, two years after the Armistice, would impede the *natural* restoration of the American and European economies.[95]

Alabama's Underwood, now in the Senate, argued on January 3 that the American economy was in better condition during the war than it was now, and he could see nothing harmful in the Gronna Resolution. After a very short discussion, the Senate, divided along sectional lines, destroyed the veto 53-5.[96] The next day the House considered the measure and, with no debate, followed the Senate 250-66.[97] It was then announced that the Corporation would be revived immediately, although it would be about two months before the first loans could be made to farmers. At the time, the W.F.C. had an account with the Treasury Department of $375,000,000. To reach the sum required by the Resolution, the Treasury intended to issue corporation bonds.[98] The enactment of the Gronna Resolution was one of the first direct governmental aids to farmers throughout the land. The question would be discussed periodically during the 1920's and would reach a sensational climax under Calvin Coolidge in 1928.

Wilson's final veto of importance occurred during the closing weeks of his presidency. This was against a Joint Resolution which called for the cessation of enlistments until the army was reduced to 175,000 men. Wilson believed that the 280,000 figure previously established was necessary, stating that the War Department recommended a minimum of 500,000 soldiers for the country's defense.[99] The veto was discussed in the House on February 5, 1921. Otis Wingo of Arkansas attempted to postpone a vote, but to no avail. No Republicans supported Wilson's veto, while 92 Democrats voted against it.[100] Thus, by the overwhelming vote of 271-6,[101] the veto was destroyed in the House. The 67-1 vote in the Senate toward overriding was even greater than in the House.[102] The vote showed clearly how powerful the Congress had become in dealing with the Executive branch, and also how isolationist-minded the country was in 1921.

Many other Wilson vetoes could be cited to show his conservative, unyielding, and often dogmatic, views of government. His rejection of the Railroad Control measure in July, 1919; his refusals to allow cities or companies to pre-empt federal property, as seen in his rejections of the Cemetery and Park bill of August, 1916; the Milk River Valley Gun Club bill of February, 1921, and his vetoes of various appropriation and budget bills because of riders, all indicate his efforts to protect the public against monopoly, his strong desire to effect governmental thrift, and his determination to preserve executive independence. These vetoes, however, were not as well known or as exciting as those dealing directly with the war.

In summary, the major issues of Wilson's time fluctuated between partisan and sectional interests. After 1918 the Republican Congress could pass any law it wanted, but it was never assured of a two-thirds majority to defeat vetoes unless the question affected the interests of more than one section. This, of course, explains the success over the veto of the Daylight Saving Time repeal, the Volstead Act, and the Gronna Resolution, which affected the occupations and the prejudices of people, and which the lawmakers were obligated to reflect. The passage of the Peace Resolution, however, which would have completely undermined not merely Wilson but the office of President itself, reflected only the quarrel of words between Democrats and Republicans on ending the war. Thus, the Republican majority could pass such a Resolution, but without the help of the Democrats, they could not overturn its veto. By 1921 the country's mood, regardless of any personal feelings for the President, was definitely isolationist, and it was opposed to the more obvious symbols of the Great War. Accordingly, both Democrats and Republicans joined forces in reducing the size of the army.

In some ways, President Wilson was like Andrew Johnson, though the rank bitterness surrounding the latter was never quite as pronounced with the former. Wilson was perhaps too unbending in his belief that he was right on the German war question and that Congress was wrong. If he had been more inclined to compromise, conditions which led to the vetoes might never have occurred, and the subsequent hostilities with Congress, might have been avoided. Wilson's idealism and his belief in parliamentary government are well known. With such attitudes it was probably inevitable that he would have trouble with the Legislature, even if it had remained solidly Democratic.

From the tariffs of Taft to the war of Wilson, the vetoes narrated in this chapter clearly reflect the major issues of the country. The impulse toward reform in all areas was extremely strong during the period. The growing feeling that government should intervene on behalf of needy citizens, especially the farming elements, was manifested in the halls of Congress. Against such demands, the presidential veto was becoming powerless by Wilson's time, and it would become even more impotent during succeeding years. The Presidents of the 1920's, Harding, Coolidge, and Hoover, set themselves squarely against these reformist and subsidy tendencies. But whatever successes they enjoyed were only partial and, of course, only temporary.

☆ **XIII** ☆

Harding, Coolidge, and Hoover
1921-1933

THE vetoes included in this chapter were among the most spectacular which occurred during the entire course of United States
history. The trend toward economic relief for certain classes,
noted in the closing months of Wilson's presidency, came dramatically to the front in the 1920's. Crusading lawmakers launched
one determined attack after another to win the government's
favors for their constituency. With equal resolution, the Presidents stood in their way, first blocking one bill and then suffering
defeat on another. As the battle raged, it became evident that it
embraced issues which penetrated far more deeply into American
life than mere partisan factors ever could.

The three Presidents of the period, their political philosophy
epitomized by Calvin Coolidge, firmly held that there should be
"more business in government and less government in business."[1]
They were Hamiltonian in their outlook, believing that the country's well-being depended on the soundness of business and industrial enterprises. Thus, they were highly protective toward
industry, but almost completely dedicated to free trade in the
agricultural sphere. Therein lies much of the veto story of the
1920's. The vetoes divide almost naturally into five areas: pensions,
farm relief, government competition with private industry, general
relief, and Philippine independence. Because the philosophy of
the Presidents was essentially the same on all these matters, the
vetoes will be treated more topically than chronologically in this
chapter.

It is generally agreed that the most forceful presidential act of
Warren G. Harding was his 1922 veto of the Soldier Bonus Bill.
He had appeared before the Senate in 1921 to urge against the
passage of any bonus or "adjusted compensation" measures. His
personal appeal had been successful, but 1922 was a congressional
election year, and the "soldier vote" exerted much influence.
Therefore, two major bonus proposals emerged from Congress.
One would give veterans an extra dollar (a dollar and a quarter
for overseas duty) for each day of service. The other which

received Congressional approval would, in effect, issue to each veteran a paid-up twenty-year insurance policy that would equal the amount of the first proposal.[2] Instead of receiving cash under this plan, veterans were given certificates which would mature in 1945. In addition, they could borrow up to one-fourth of the certificates' face value.[3] Supporters of the legislation claimed that it would compensate the veteran for the low wages he received during the war.

The measure, known as the Fordney-McCumber Adjusted Compensation Act, was vetoed by Harding on September 19, 1922, a few days before the adjournment of Congress. He reasoned that the bill did not provide any revenue "from which the bestowal is to be paid . . ."[4], that it would be impractical to distribute funds to a class numbering only 5,000,000 out of a population of 110,000,000,[5] and that increased taxes or borrowing would be necessary to finance the project. The only way in which such veteran demands could have been met, according to Harding, was for the United States to have imposed indemnities against the Central Powers.[6]

There was little doubt about the veto's fate in the House where it was considered on September 20. After only a few minutes of debate, it was overridden by the large majority of 258-15.[7] It was evident that most of the Congressmen coupled the passage of the Bonus bill with their political futures. The elections were not far off, so "Democrats [vied] with Republicans in the rush on the Treasury."[8]

There was speculation about the Senate's ability to override. The original Senate vote for the Bonus bill was 47-22, but there had been so many absentees or failures to vote that it was now impossible to say what would happen in the bill's reconsideration.[9] When the veto arrived in the Senate, sixteen Senators who had initially voted for the bill were absent. North Dakota's McCumber, Chairman of the Senate Finance Committee and a co-author of the measure, spoke bitterly of roving Senators in Hong Kong and on the Pacific.[10] Heflin of Alabama, speaking on the same subject, remarked that when some Senators came into the Chamber he had not seen them for so long he "felt like having them sworn in again."[11]

The debate was continued by Henry F. Ashurst of Arizona, who said that the bonus would enable the veterans to escape the merciless grasp of the rent profiteers. Through the bill the veterans could borrow enough money to build small homes or to buy small farms.[12] McCumber criticized the presidential veto because it allowed the judgment of one man to hamstring the majority will of the people's representatives.[13] Heflin threatened to talk all night if the vote were not postponed until the next day to enable friends of the measure to be present. After a time, however, Heflin turned to his favorite habit of attacking W. P. G. Harding, former Chairman of the Federal Reserve Board, for his alleged favors to Wall Street. Then suddenly he stopped and yielded the floor and did not carry out his threat.[14] When the speeches ended and the vote was taken, the result was 44-28,[15] only four short of defeating the veto.

With this, the first of the bonus vetoes of the 1920's, the battle that ultimately led to such events as the Bonus Expeditionary Force in 1932 was begun. The business community applauded Harding's veto because it was proof of his economizing. Businesses, of course, regarded economies in government as promises of reduced taxes. No one should have been surprised at the veto, for Harding had publicized his views on the subject. The *New York Times* stated its editorial support of Harding's rejection, finding it admirable. The President had earned a "breathing spell" for the country in the frenzied questions of bonuses.[16] The paper asserted, ironically enough, that Harding wanted to avoid the scandals that had been connected with Civil War pensions.[17]

The bonus forces by no means conceded a victory to the President on this occasion. They continued to build up their strength, and in 1924 they again submitted their proposals, this time to an even sterner President, Calvin Coolidge. The initial attempt at pension legislation under Coolidge dealt with war veterans going back to the War of 1812. The measure was sponsored by Holn O. Bursum of New Mexico. Coolidge returned the bill on May 3, 1924, claiming it would cost $58,000,000 during the first year and up to a total of 415 million dollars for the first ten years.[18] This would increase the burdens on the taxpayers at a time when such pressures should be relieved. Congress made no effort to override the presidential rejection.

World War I, however, was closer to the minds and politics of Senators and Congressmen, and largely for that reason they destroyed the presidential disapproval of a second effort at passing an adjusted compensation bill. The bill, similar in content to the Fordney-McCumber proposal of 1922, issued "bonus certificates" which amounted to a paid-up twenty-year life insurance policy for each veteran, the value to be determined by the number of days spent in service. In his veto of May 15, 1924, Coolidge said the bill would require the government to reserve $114,000,000 annually in anticipation of the insurance's maturity in 1945.[19] Moreover, the Act allowed veterans to borrow a maximum of around 25 percent of their certificate's face value, and there was no way of anticipating what this would cost the government. The President spoke against efforts to "capitalize patriotism." Gratitude for what the veterans did in the War, he said, could not be computed in terms of dollars.[20]

The veto came under heavy attack in the House, where it was discussed on May 17. Royal C. Johnson of South Dakota said the Act was a money-saving device since it gave the government 20 years to pay its veteran debt instead of having to grant pensions immediately.[21] Fiorello LaGuardia of New York, saying that he was "hurt, offended, and saddened" by the veto, claimed that Coolidge had placed a question mark upon every honorable discharge earned by World War I veterans.[22] Nicholas Longworth of Ohio stated that government civilian workers during the war had received bonuses of $240.00 a year; therefore, adjusted compensation should be passed for the veteran "because it is just."[23] The House vote, 313-78, was nearly 80 percent in favor of destroying Coolidge's rejection.[24]

Though the House vote against the veto was overwhelming, it was questionable whether the Senate would override or sustain. The firmness of the veto might impress upon Senators, even those who had voted for the original measure, the importance of economy in government.[25] One paper believed that Coolidge's veto was really a call for a national referendum on the bonus question, and that Senators would agree that the problem should be freed of "political jugglery."[26] These speculations came to nought, however, as the Senate, on May 19, agreed with the action of the House. The vote in the Upper House was 59-26, slightly over the 66⅔ percent needed for overriding.[27] Thus the Bonus Act, or Adjusted Compensation Act, became law.

Bonus agitation continued throughout the 1920's. Proposals were made to increase the loan value of the certificates to 50 percent, while some members of Congress pressed for immediate full cash payment. However, none of these proposals was enacted into legislation during the remainder of Coolidge's presidency. A bill did pass to grant pension increases to widows of the Civil War, but Coolidge pocketed it at the end of the second session of the Sixty-ninth Congress. He also pocketed a bill half way through the Seventieth Congress which would grant preference to veterans in civil-service examinations. It was not until Herbert Hoover's presidency that the veteran question was again involved in a series of Executive-Legislative quarrels that attracted world-wide attention.

The first dispute of this nature came in May, 1930, when Hoover returned a Senate-originated bill granting pensions to Spanish-American war veterans, to soldiers who participated in the Philippine insurrection, and in the China Relief Expedition. Dated May 28, 1930, Hoover's message said that the minimum service for qualification under the Act had been cut from 90 to 70 days, and that in the interest of justice to the taxpayer, the veteran should be required to prove his need.[28] The measure added $11,500,000 annually to the Spanish-American pension rolls, at a time when governmental economy was most necessary.[29]

The Senate debated the vetoed measure on June 2. Royal S. Copeland of New York called the veto "cruel," and William E. Borah of Idaho said the Spanish-American soldier had been more inconsiderately treated than all other veterans. Ashurst, speaking of Hoover's opinion that many veterans were in need because of "vicious habits," replied that "suffering is suffering" regardless of what produced it. Arthur H. Vandenberg of Michigan reminded the Senators that the Spanish-American war veterans were volunteers and this was an additional reason to grant them pensions.[30] Voting for the bill had been unanimous when it was first passed, but during its reconsideration, 18 members—all Republicans—voted to sustain the President. Those voting against the veto, however, numbered 61, so the bill was easily re-passed.[31] In the House, on the same day, with debate more parliamentary than germane, the Senate's position was affirmed. The vote was 299-14.[32] Thus, Hoover had suffered his first major setback since becoming President.

In February, 1931, Congress renewed its efforts to change the loan basis of adjusted compensation. It will be recalled that the 1924 measure allowed loans of up to 25 percent of the certificate's face value. The proposal now was to increase the amount to 50 percent. To this date, about $330 million had been loaned. The face value of existing certificates was $3,426 million, representing 3,478,956 holders. The average contemplated loan was $500.00, so it was possible for the government to commit itself to a billion dollar expenditure under the Act.[33] It was a foregone conclusion that Hoover would use his veto.

To ascertain the actual needs of veterans, Hoover ordered the Veteran's Bureau to conduct an investigation. Among the findings it was claimed that in one unnamed city 159 out of 20,000 veterans were in actual need. In another city with a population of over 140,000, there were 1,700 needy veterans. These cities were located far from Washington and they were regarded as typical.[34] The bill before the President, however, allowed all veterans, whether affluent or poverty stricken, to borrow considerable sums from the government. When the suggestion was made to require proof of need, proponents of the legislation always inveighed against "pauper oaths." Thus, a major motivation in the bonus legislation was to "curry favor with the entire veteran population."[35]

In the House, on February 26, only about ten minutes elapsed between the reading of the veto and the time the vote began. Within an hour, the veto was destroyed 328-79,[36] all the negative votes being cast by Republicans. While the country watched with interest, about 500 veterans, attracted by the prospects of additional loans from the government, marched on the District of Columbia. They naturally rejoiced at the House action, and waited eagerly for the Senate to comply.[37] That hope was fulfilled on February 27, when the Senate, after considerable discussion, re-passed the bill 76-17.[38]

Even before the loan basis was increased to 50 percent, plans were being made for immediate payment of the bonus certificates. In 1932 a measure sponsored by Wright Patman of Texas, issuing $2.4 billion in paper money for full and immediate cash payment,[39] passed the House. The Senate refused to pass the bill, primarily because of the vigorous protest of President Hoover. Thereupon occurred the famous "Bonus Expeditionary Force," composed of some 12 to 14,000 jobless veterans marching on Washington. This was accompanied by riots in which two veterans were killed, and by the well known action of General Douglas MacArthur in clearing out a veteran stronghold, Anacostia Flats. To be sure, the bonus agitation was a sign of the deep economic troubles of the day. The veteran, as did many other citizens, looked more and more to Washington for relief, but at least that part of Washington represented by the President sadly related that the full bonus was not the proper method. The bonus question was far from dead in 1932.

Hoover vetoed other veteran legislation, but none was so crucial as the bonus attempts. For example, in 1930 Hoover rejected a disability amendment to the 1924 legislation because he said it would add from 75 to 100,000 men who were not disabled as a result of the war. The bill was "wasteful and extravagant" and it went far beyond the financial necessities of the situation. The House, not yet Democratic in majority, sustained the presidential action 182-188.[40] In February, 1931, he vetoed a bill to extend hospital and soldier home benefits to veterans of the Spanish-American war, the Philippine Insurrection, and the China Relief Expedition. No effort was made to override. Another veto was on granting pension increases to certain regulars of the army and navy who served in wars other than the Civil War. Again, no attempt was made to override. These were in addition to the private relief bills which still made up a large part of the presidential rejections.

Bonus agitation was only a part of the struggle between the Congress and the President reflecting the efforts to expand government relief to areas besides industry. Nowhere was this better illustrated than in the struggle for farm relief. It will be recalled that the first major effort to aid farmers was the Gronna Resolution of 1921, which had passed over Wilson's veto. The Resolution had reactivated the War Finance Corporation, and had issued one billion dollars of debentures to facilitate the export of farm surpluses. The next major proposal to find favor with Congress was derived from a publication, *Equality for Agriculture*, by George N. Peek and Hugh S. Johnson, two Illinois farm machinery manufacturers. The Peek-Johnson proposal was that the government create a farm board whose function would be to sell agricultural surpluses for what could be obtained on the world market.

At first the proposal affected only the wheat crops, but by 1924 cotton, corn, rice, swine, and tobacco were included to make support for it as broad as possible. The McNary-Haugen bill, passed in 1927, was sponsored by a Western-Southern coalition. It provided for the establishment of a Federal Farm Board of 12 members, one from each of the Federal land bank districts, to administer the disposal of surplus crops. A stabilization fund would be created to absorb any losses in the operation, while an equalization fee would be imposed upon the producers to make up for the loss between domestic and the generally lower foreign prices.[41]

Coolidge's veto, on February 25, 1927, was accompanied by a long legal opinion of Attorney-General Sargent, who argued that no matter what might be done, prices are fixed by laws of supply and demand and Congress could never change this fact.[42] Collecting the equalization fee, the creation of which was constitutionally doubtful, would impose severe administrative problems and would be quite expensive.[43] The Attorney-General believed the bill limited the presidential appointing power because of its stipulation that members of the Farm Board be selected from the Federal land districts. According to Sargent, the major purpose of the equalization fee was to fix prices, a function that the Commerce Clause does not give to Congress. With respect to all the commodities included in the bill other than cotton, no provision was made to return to the producers any surplus of the funds derived from the equalization fees. These would be placed in the treasury and used for public purposes. Thus, the equalization fee was in actuality a tax.[44] Other dangers pointed out by Coolidge were that the higher prices contemplated by the bill would result in greater overproduction and greater surpluses. The "dumping" at any price of American produce on the foreign market "would arouse foreign resentment and promote retaliation."[45] In this first attempt at "McNary-Haugenism," no effort was made to override. The veto, called a "sockdolager" by Chief Justice Taft,[46] and the bill were referred to the Senate Committee on Agriculture and Forestry. It was not until the following year, again an election year, that the matter caused great rifts between the Congress and Coolidge.

The second veto of the McNary-Haugen proposal came in May, 1928, a few weeks before the Republican National Convention in Kansas City. The bill and its veto were essentially the same as their predecessors of 1927. Supporters of the bill justified it on grounds that it only applied Republican principles of the tariff to agriculture.[47] Coolidge's objection to the equalization fee was about as sensible as saying there could be a tariff without duties.[48] Thaddeus H. Caraway of Arkansas predicted that the veto would lead to an industrial war between the South and New England. If the latter continued to refuse the farmer, the farmer must of necessity become industrialized. The Arkansas Senator believed the South would ultimately surpass New England in industry because of its unlimited natural resources.[49] The Southern-midwestern bloc in the Senate was still not strong enough to overcome the veto, so it was sustained 50-31.[50] Senator Charles Curtis of Kansas, who had voted for the original measure, now chose to uphold the President's veto. This proved, he said, that he was a friend of the farmer and a friend of the President—in fact, "a friend of everybody." His action was taken to mean that he would be the compromise candidate for the Republicans in the upcoming campaign.[51]

The McNary-Haugen veto was credited with triggering three congressional overriding actions of other Coolidge vetoes. For example, the Tyson-Fitzgerald bill, which granted regular retirement benefits to emergency officers who had served in the war, was repassed 66-14 in the Senate,[52] and in the House, 245-101.[53] The Sproul bill to increase salaries of night employees of the Post Office was approved by the House, 320-42,[54] and 70-9 in the Senate.[55] The measure granted a ten percent increase in the workers' hourly wages.[56] Coolidge had rejected the bill because he believed any additional Post Office expenditures should be accompanied by increased postal rates. Another bill granting governmental allowances to fourth class postmasters was also repassed. Coolidge had pointed out in his rejection that such postmasters usually ran post offices as a sideline to their major occupations, and thus they did not need the $3,000,000 additional appropriation.[57] The House, though, demurred from this position 318-46,[58] and the Senate complied 63-17.[59]

Congress had not been the scene of such events since the days of Andrew Johnson. The Senate overrode four vetoes in one day, May 24, and the only one not approved in the House was the Oddie Road Bill, which had appropriated $3,500,000[60] for building roads on the public domain in the West and on Indian reservations. Leaders of both parties asserted that Coolidge was "running amuck" with his vetoes, and he was liable to "hew down some of the most vital idols of the [congressional] session."[61] Coolidge, on the other hand, believed that his party leaders had purposely doublecrossed him by allowing measures to pass containing provisions "to which he is known to be strongly opposed." All the vetoes, coming as they did just prior to the Republican convention, were sufficient notice that Coolidge assuredly was not looking for another presidential term for himself.[62]

The vetoes, however, especially the one against the McNary-Haugen proposal, made the identity of the Republican candidate highly debatable. Great strife was predicted for the convention as Nebraska governor Andrew McMullin issued a call for 100,000 farmers to march on the Republicans at Kansas City. The *New York Times* chided the governor for this plea, saying that it could see "all roads to Kansas City packed with the cars of the well-to-do sufferers."[63] Because of his negative vote in the reconsideration of the McNary-Haugen bill, many thought Curtis was the most likely candidate since he had now complimented both sides. Others thought that Frank Lowdon of Illinois, longtime champion of agricultural interests, would receive the nomination. Many felt that Herbert Hoover's chances had been irreparably damaged by the McNary-Haugen rejection since, as Secretary of Commerce, he had consistently voiced opinions similar to those contained in the Coolidge veto. When the Republican convention refused to adopt a plan along McNary-Haugen lines, Lowdon withdrew from the race. Eastern Republicans, following the Coolidge program of government, were strong enough to give the nomination to Hoover on the first ballot. Curtis was Hoover's running mate, chosen primarily as a sop to the farmers.

The McNary-Haugen veto also caused Democratic leaders to think about changing their strategy. Before the veto it was generally conceded that the Houston convention would nominate a Southerner for Vice-President to offset some of the prejudice against Al Smith. After the veto, however, the Democrats thought in terms of a Midwesterner for the second place on the ticket. This would enable them to capture one or perhaps two of the disaffected

Corn Belt states. News columnist Arthur Sears Henning, writing in the *Washington Post*, described one of the more excessive interpretations placed on the McNary-Haugen veto. Many believed that a third party would be formed which would represent only the interests of the Midwestern farmer. If this materialized, neither major candidate could obtain an electoral majority and the vote would, of course, go to the House of Representatives. A deadlock would occur in the Lower House and the scene would shift to the Senate. If the Senate had to elect a President, it would choose from among the vice-presidential candidates. Since the Midwestern Republicans held the balance of power in the Senate, the Midwestern Democratic vice-presidential candidate would become the new President on March 4![64] Just before the convention Gilbert Hitchcock of Nebraska, Governor William J. Bulow of South Dakota, John B. Kendrick of Wyoming, and Harry B. Hawes of Missouri were regarded as the most likely candidates. In the end, however, Joseph T. Robinson of Arkansas was selected to round out the Democratic ticket.

Though the McNary-Haugen proposals were defeated, the farming elements had actually gained in strength in their fight for favorable legislation. First, the country's attention was sharply focused on the plight of the farmer and more than ever it was realized that government would ultimately have to act to create higher prices. Thus, McNary-Haugenism "paved the way" for later farm legislation.[65] Second, the McNary-Haugen struggle showed the continuance of Progressivism throughout the 1920's, and the determination to give agriculture the same degree of government benefits that industry was receiving. If industry deserved high protective tariffs, then by the same token agriculture warranted similar assistance. Third, the struggle was important in causing President Hoover, in 1929, to propose and sign the Agricultural Marketing Act. This Act made it possible for a Farm Board to lend money to agricultural cooperatives, and to buy up large quantities of wheat and cotton. This action kept domestic prices slightly above world prices for approximately two years. Finally, however, it became clear that real farm relief would have to be in the form of acreage and production control.

Another intensely provocative issue of the 1920's was the Muscle Shoals dispute, a proposal that brought fire from more than one President. The Muscle Shoals bill of 1928 represented a victory for Senator George W. Norris of Nebraska, who had been fighting for years to create a public corporation to control the waters of the Tennessee River. The bill, known as the Morin-Norris bill, created a government-appointed board to supervise the Muscle Shoals establishment. Research was to be done in fertilizer production, and surplus electric power was to be sold to the public at a reduced rate. Appropriations were also made for the construction of another dam at Cove Creek, Tennessee, "to ensure flood control and a steady flow of water through the Muscle Shoals turbines."[66]

Coolidge made his views on the bill unmistakably clear several days before its passage. In a mid-May speech to the Daughters of the American Revolution, he said there was one field which belonged to the people "upon which they have uniformly insisted that the Federal Government should not trespass. That is the domain of private business."[67] This and similar statements made it inconceivable that anyone could believe Coolidge would do anything except veto the Norris bill.

Congress sent him the bill on May 26, three days before adjournment. Coolidge's failure to return it caused a bitter attack from Senator Norris. Coolidge could not have approved the Muscle Shoals bill, said the Nebraskan, because if he had, it would have dried up the sources of revenue for the presidential race just ahead.[68] The veto's defenders emphasized Coolidge's dislike of "economic principles contained in the bill, particularly the provisions permitting governmental distribution and sale of power directly to municipalities."[69] Coolidge's opponents said the veto reflected the President's desire to "cover up" the excessive rates charged by private power companies.[70]

Despite the pocket veto, Norris and Fiorello LaGuardia hoped that the Muscle Shoals bill would be put into operation. Norris indicated that he would test the pocket veto by asking Congress to appropriate for the Muscle Shoals project, "thus ultimately throwing the question into the courts."[71] This intimation was brought on by another case that at the time was heading for adjudication in the Supreme Court.

This case involved a pocket veto, given by Coolidge at the end of the first session of the Sixty-ninth Congress, allowing certain Indian tribes (Okanogan, Methow, San Poelis, Nespelem, Colville, and Lake) in Washington to submit their claims to the Court of Claims. The bill had been presented to the President on June 24, 1926, and the Congressional session had ended eight days later. Congress did not meet again until December, 1926. Neither house was in session on July 6, the tenth day after the bill had been sent to Coolidge. The Indian tribes believed the bill had become a law because the adjournment was *ad interim* rather than *sine die*. Apparently the Congress agreed, because in December, 1927, it appropriated $463,732 to the Indians, and the President approved it.[72] The Court of Claims, however, prevented payment on the tech-

nicality that the original bill acknowledging the claims had not
been signed by the President. The case dealing with the legitimacy
of the Indian claims was scheduled for argument before the October,
1928, term of the Supreme Court.

Naturally, if the Court ruled in favor of the Indians, Muscle
Shoals still had a chance. Coolidge answered the critics of his
pocket veto in December, 1928, by submitting to Congress a
"list of precedents." Attorney General John G. Sargent compiled
a list of pocket vetoes from James Madison to the present, and
contended that precedent proved the correctness of the Coolidge
position.[73]

The Indian case was argued on March 11, 1929. Attorneys for the
petitioners claimed that each Congress is a single entity and its sessions "have practical unity."[74] The ten days for presidential consideration are legislative, not calendar days. The distinction between
all adjournments of Congress (other than final) "is one of duration and nomenclature only."[75] The Indians claimed that the
failure to return a bill because of congressional adjournment "should
be co-existent with the inability of the Congress thereafter to
consider the objections."[76] Speaking as friend of the Court, Hatton
Sumners of Texas said that the pocket veto gave the President a
greater power over bills presented near the end of a congressional
session than at other times. This in effect endowed the President
with an absolute veto, a power never envisioned by the Constitutional Fathers.[77]

The government's case was argued by Attorney-General William D. Mitchell and Justice Department Attorney Robert P.
Reeder. They contended that there was no basis for inserting
"legislative" in connection with the ten-day period in which to
return bills. If Congress had adjourned, how was a President to
return bills with his objections?[78] The Constitution required that
vetoes be returned to the *House* of origin and not to some secretary
or other designated official. The government attorneys mentioned
that in 1868 a bill that would have allowed congressional secretaries to be recipients of returned bills failed of passage.[79] Finally,
if the petitioners were upheld in this case, at least 120 pocket
vetoed bills of the past would be resurrected and placed on the
statute books.[80]

The Court's decision, delivered by Mr. Justice Sanford, said the
key to the whole question was the word "adjournment." It did
not agree with counsel for the Indians that "adjournment" meant
only "final."[81] Since this was the first case of its kind, the Court
had to rely on practices of the past, and it said that no one had ever
questioned the procedures of a pocket veto until now. Therefore,

the Court sustained the government's position.[82] The ghosts of Henry Clay and Daniel Webster must have frowned deeply at the Court's assertion that no one had ever questioned the procedure of a pocket veto.

The Court's decision, of course, meant that Norris and his followers had lost their bid to establish the project at Muscle Shoals. They would have to wait two more years for another attempt, and again they would meet a President's rejection which was just as cool as that of Coolidge. A Senate-originated Joint Resolution was passed in February, 1931, reenacting the terms of the 1928 legislation. Hoover could have pocketed the measure, but he chose instead to answer the bill's supporters. His veto was delivered to the Senate on March 3, 1931, where it was considered the same day.

The presidential message emphasized most strongly Hoover's belief that government should not compete with private industry.[83] Believing that the Tennessee Valley could best be developed by the residents themselves, he proposed the establishment of a joint Alabama-Tennessee commission "with full authority to lease the Muscle Shoals properties in the interest of the local community and agriculture generally."[84]

In the Senate Hoover came under heavy attack from Hugo Black of Alabama and, of course, from Norris. Black claimed that Hoover had broken campaign pledges made at Elizabethton, Tennessee, that he would support government operation of Muscle Shoals.[85] Claiming again that the veto was a great victory for the power trusts, Norris submitted electric bills from five cities throughout the country which bought power from private companies, and he compared these with what the low cost would be under the Muscle Shoals operation.[86] The opponents of Muscle Shoals still called it a "Socialistic" venture and one that invaded states rights. Representative Charles A. Eaton of New Jersey said it was a "hunk of Sovietism described as a fertilizer bag."[87] When the debate ended in the Senate, Hoover's rejection was upheld, 49-34.[88] The power of the Southern Democrats and the Midwestern Independent Republicans was not yet strong enough to overcome administration forces. Thus, it was not until May, 1933, under a heavily Democratic Congress and a receptive President, that Norris' dream of a government-operated plant at Muscle Shoals was fulfilled.

The fourth major area of vetoes during the period dealt with methods of relief to alleviate the effects of the Great Depression. One of the first general relief bills was pocket vetoed by Hoover at the end of the third session of the Seventy-first Congress. The bill, sponsored by Robert F. Wagner of New York, would have given federal money to enable states to run their own employment agencies. This would have replaced the Federal Employment Service, which had been cooperating with the states. Hoover disliked the measure because it destroyed the federal service, it limited interstate cooperation in obtaining employment which could be had only through the federal government, and he feared that the states would use the new power for purely political purposes.[89] The veto was, of course, in line with Hoover's refusal to approve anything that approached direct aid for deliverance from the depression.

His most important battle with direct aid proponents came in July, 1932, when he was compelled to veto a General Relief bill, the Garner-Wagner bill. It allowed the President to allocate, at his discretion, $100 million in relief money to permit the Reconstruction Finance Corporation to loan money to any needy person, and to finance agricultural exports. The bill also called for the construction of federal buildings in every state and territory, for flood control projects, and for river and harbor improvements. The total cost was $2.2 billion, to be financed by a gas tax.[90] Hoover stated in his veto message of July 11 that "this proposal violates every sound principle of public finance and of government. Never before has so dangerous a suggestion been seriously made to our country."[91]

The President was willing to compromise. Since Congress made no effort to override the veto, work was immediately begun to meet as many of Hoover's demands as possible. Finally, a revised bill was presented to him which permitted financially exhausted states to borrow from a $300 million account in the R.F.C., with repayment to be in the form of reduced highway aid over a five year period. The R.F.C. could also loan $1.5 billion for "publicly or privately constructed self-liquidating public works," and it appropriated $322,224,000 for specific public works.[92] The compromise bill was not entirely satisfactory to Hoover, but he felt more would be gained by approval than by veto. Although it was a "first step" toward direct federal aid for relief, it was not as severe as the bill Hoover had vetoed.

Hoover felt himself obliged in 1932 to stop Democratic attempts to lower the tariff of 1930. Maintaining his protectionist philosophy, he said that at no time in our history was a protective tariff more needed because of the low world wide price levels, which meant in turn that American producers were in great need of protection from foreign competition.[93] The House, after discussing the veto for a short time, sustained it 178-166.[94] In his drive for economy, Hoover also rejected an act pertaining to the wages of laborers and mechanics who worked on public building projects. No effort was made to override.[95] Finally, he pocket vetoed an

Carlton
Presidential vetoes
1792-1945

3g 353.032 Ja12

attempt to advance R.F.C. money to farmers for crop planting or cultivation, and he turned down an emergency appropriation bill because of its excesses.

In addition to the general relief vetoes, Hoover rejected many that were of a private nature. For example, he vetoed attempts to grant money to various Indian tribes. One veto, he said, kept the government from having to reopen Indian problems that had been settled 75 years ago.[96] All of these grants, in Hoover's opinion, belied the Democratic claim of economy which had swept them into a majority in Congress in 1930. The President complained that each time he recommended economies, the Democrats rejected them. On one occasion he asked for a reduction in expenditures of $690 million, but only $150 million was actually eliminated by Congress.[97] The Democrats, he therefore believed, were not interested in economizing, as evidenced by their "pork-barrel" laws and by their tendencies to give money to anyone regardless of need. His vetoes, he claimed, stopped many of the excesses, but the path to "Socialism" was embarked upon in earnest by the Democrats when their candidate won in 1932.

The last significant veto of the period from 1921 to 1933 was Hoover's rejection of Philippine Independence. The Hare-Hawes-Cutting Act, as it was called, was finally passed after months of conferences between the two houses. The chief provisions of the bill were to allow a ten-year period in which American rule would be withdrawn by stages from the Islands, the U.S. tariff would be gradually imposed on Philippine products through an export tax, while immigration from the Philippines would be limited to fifty persons annually during the ten year period.[98]

Hoover's veto was centered on the premise that Philippine independence was in actuality sought to relieve American farmers from competition with Philippine products, chiefly sugar and coconut oil. He believed that the United States was the trustee for Philippine people "and we must not let our selfish interests dominate that trust. . . ."[99] He said the ten-year waiting period was much too short, urging instead a fifteen to twenty-year period and then allowing a plebiscite among the Filipinos. He disliked the possibility, too, that American responsibility for the Philippines would remain, but American authority would not. His Cabinet, especially Secretary of War Patrick Hurley, had warned about the dangers that the infant nation would face from the rising military power of Japan, and from the general instability of the Orient. The Philippine economy was not such that stability could be gained so it could hold its own with the rest of the world.[100]

The House considered the veto on January 13, the same day as it was given. Lloyd Thurston of Iowa said that the Philippine Islands cost the United States between $60 and $90 million a year. They were extremely hard to defend, being located some 6,000 miles from the continental United States, and under treaty arrangements with Japan and England, the already existing defenses could not be expanded. The only selfish interests in the Philippines, said the Iowan, were American business men whose property would be in jeopardy with independence, and the Army and Navy, whose personnel did not want to give up their service in the Islands. Thus, the Secretaries of War and Navy had an unusual influence over the President in his presentation of the veto.[101] Hoover was defended by Charles Underhill of Massachusetts, who said that propaganda from certain paid sources, undoubtedly the sugar interests of Cuba, had convinced the American farmer that Philippine independence with the subsequent sugar tariff would materially aid the sugar farmers of this country.[102] The House had passed the Independence bill under a suspension of the rules (which required two-thirds for approval) so it was clear that a veto would not stop them now. The vote on repassage was 274-94.[103]

The Senate reconsidered the bill on January 17, and little was brought out in the discussion that had not been thoroughly debated before. Opponents of the veto argued that the Philippine question had been a highly significant political factor ever since they were taken at the close of the Spanish-American War, and the veto was an indication of persistent American imperialism. The Philippines had always been more of a liability than an asset, and retention of them would involve us in unnecessary wars.[104] Veto supporters continued to argue for gradual independence by administering the Jones Act of 1916.[105] The pro-independence forces, however, had their way, and the veto was overridden 66-26.[106]

Independence was thus granted to the Philippine Islands in 1934, to take final effect in 1946. Japanese invasion, however, caused many alterations of the planned freedom.[107] Subsequent events, argue some authors, proved the soundness of Hoover's veto.[108] The first evidence of this was the rejection of the Act by the Philippine Legislature because of the harsh provisions relating to trade and immigration. The U. S. Congress, however, pushed through the Tydings-McDuffie Act of 1934, similar to the 1933 legislation, and it was signed by President Roosevelt.[109] Thus, the somewhat unwilling Philippine Republic was scheduled to come into existence in 1946.

There were 93 vetoes during the period narrated in this chapter—6 by Harding, 50 by Coolidge, and 37 by Hoover. They dealt in varying degrees with profound economic and social changes. As stated elsewhere in the chapter, the three Presidents were Hamiltonian in philosophy, possessing the highest faith in industrial development. Accordingly, they concurred in stringent protectionist practices while at the same time they firmly refused the bounty of the government to other fields, especially agriculture. By doing so, they paid homage to the philosophy that grew up largely after the Civil War that corporations should be assisted but not controlled by the government. Of course, prior to the War, corporations had been regulated especially by state governments. Thus, the three Presidents defended the newer system and this made them liberal, not conservative, in the area of their veto policies.

The thesis of Charles Beard that the Civil War was a revolution of fast developing industry against an old, established agriculture, is well known. The 1920's, then, would appear to have seen the climax of an agricultural counter-revolution that had been in the making since the Populist uprising of the 1890's. Before the War agriculture had been centered in the South. After the conflict, the Midwest grew in agricultural prominence and by the 1920's, it had largely taken the historic place of the South in championing the farmers, but with one important difference. The Southerners were usually Jeffersonian, but the Midwesterners thought in terms of Hamiltonianism applied to agriculture. Consequently, the Congresses of the 1920's were by no means averse to governmental aid to certain classes; they merely wanted to shift the aid from industry to agriculture.

Harding, Coolidge, and Hoover's vetoes were similar to those of Franklin Pierce and James Buchanan. The latter had refused government aid in the form of agricultural colleges, homestead laws, and general internal improvements. Yet they did not object to large amounts of assistance to railroad building during the period. Thus, their vetoes did not adequately reflect the prevailing moods of the time, nor did those of Harding, Coolidge, and Hoover. Much negativism must therefore be ascribed to their rejections of legislation. One may admire Coolidge and Hoover for their firmness in holding to principles they thought correct, but this obviously did not solve outstanding problems. There were never any great efforts by these Presidents (except Hoover) to offer alternate plans to Congress' proposals. Thus, the veto was generally used as a closed-end device instead of a way to promote programs mutually acceptable to Congress and the President.

This latter characteristic was particularly true of bonus legislation. Harding and Coolidge did not merely say that finances were inadequate for such proposals—they boldly asserted that the government was under no obligation whatever to the veterans. Payment of a bonus would inevitably increase the national debt or require additional taxes, both of which were naturally opposed by the business community. Thus, if the "business of government was business," there was no place for a soldier bonus. Whether the Presidents were sympathetic to the veteran problem or not, by their vetoes they at least gave the impression that they were not. Such apparent indifference and failure to suggest alternate solutions invariably evoked extreme reactions.

The same motivation which caused presidential vetoes of the bonus and the farm programs also produced the Muscle Shoals rejections. In the thinking of Presidents fully committed to "free enterprise," the government could not compete with private industry. To an extent, the Philippine measure reflected the same principle, since it was widely believed that Hoover wanted to protect American business establishments in the Islands. The most positive of the Presidents was Herbert Hoover because he did suggest compromises in his more important vetoes (Muscle Shoals, General Relief, and Philippine Independence). For the most part, however, the vetoes indicated that there was little in common between the Presidents and the Congresses on several vital issues.

☆ XIV ☆

Franklin D. Roosevelt
1933-1945

MORE vetoes were given by Franklin D. Roosevelt than by any other American President. His rejections numbered 631, which put him 48 above Cleveland's total. According to the number of years served, however, Cleveland still holds the percentage record. In his eight years, Cleveland vetoed an average of 72 bills a year. For Roosevelt's twelve years, the average was 52 annually. Of great importance to Roosevelt, perhaps greater than the veto itself, was his threat to use it unless Congress sent him bills he could approve. He constantly gave party leaders his views on certain pending legislation, letting them know unequivocally whether he would approve or veto. Once in 1934 he suggested that the Congress withdraw an immigration bill from presidential consideration by a concurrent resolution of recall.[1] Thus Roosevelt, through the veto and the threat of it, wielded Executive power over the Congress.

The differences between Roosevelt and Congress leading to major vetoes almost always centered around economic problems. For those who viewed Roosevelt as an incurable "spendthrift," his vetoes of bonus legislation and of relief bills could be cited as proof to the contrary. His most sensational vetoes, the ones that made national and world headlines, dealt primarily with how the government would collect and spend its money and how it would control certain organizations during the perilous days of World War II. The bulk of his vetoes, however, were not exciting or controversial, most dealing with private pension and relief bills.

Individual and corporate relief attempts accounted for 344, or approximately 55 percent, of Roosevelt's vetoes. He began the practice of returning such bills *en masse*, and Congress considered them in the same way. None was overridden. Roosevelt kept hundreds of people busy checking the legitimacy of the relief and pension bills. Invariably, his reasons for vetoes of this type were that the petitioner was not worthy, and that approval would result in reckless finance. For example, in the John B. Brack relief veto, the President pointed out that the bill violated Section 601 of the World War Adjusted Compensation Act. Under the Act, Brack's widow and children were eligible for payment from the government. However, they did not survive him. The bill proposed, therefore, to pay $625.00 to Brack's four brothers and sisters.[2] In another instance, Roosevelt refused aid to the State of Ohio because its officials had not complied with the Social Security Act of 1935.[3]

The only major controversy growing out of a relief question occurred in 1937 when it again became necessary for the Supreme Court to rule on the methods of returning a veto, The case, Wright v United States, originated in a veto given by Roosevelt during the second session of the Seventy-fourth Congress. The bill relieved David A. Wright of Winona, Missouri, who had expanded his manufacturing plant in Chicago during the war to build heavy-duty lathes for the government, but had lost money because of the November, 1918, armistice, and because the War Department had not contracted, but merely promised, to buy from Wright. The Relief Bill was given to President Roosevelt on April 24, 1936, and on May 4 the Senate, the house of origin, took a three-day recess. The House stayed in session during this period. Roosevelt returned the bill to the Senate on May 5, where the Secretary of the Senate, Edwin A. Halsey, was the recipient. Subsequently, on May 7, the day the Senate re-convened, the vetoed bill was referred to the Committee on Military Affairs and was never reconsidered.

The argument for White was that Roosevelt's veto was illegal since it had been referred, not to the Senate, but to an officer of that body. No one could logically maintain that the Congress was in adjournment since the House stayed in session during the Senate recess. However, neither the President nor the Senate had correctly handled the veto, because when it was considered on May 7, the ten-day period for signing or rejecting a bill had expired. Therefore, the bill had become law without the President's signature.[4]

Mr. Chief Justice Hughes delivered the majority opinion of the Court. He said: "There is no greater difficulty in returning a bill to one of the two Houses when it is in recess during the session of Congress than presenting a bill to the President by sending it to the White House in his temporary absence."[5] He noted the Pocket Veto decision of 1929 which asserted that a bill must be returned to the full house of origin. This opinion, however, said the Chief Justice, should not be interpreted so narrowly "as to demand that the President must select a precise moment when the House is within the walls of its chambers. . . ."[6] The Court, therefore, decided for the government by saying that the bill was properly returned by the President, that it was open for consideration by the Congress, and that it did not become a law.[7]

Mr. Justice Stone wrote a dissent to this decision which was concurred in by Mr. Justice Brandeis. Stone said that no authority had ever been conferred on the Secretary of the Senate to receive vetoes from the President and to hold them for senatorial consideration.[8] If the majority decision were correct, the originating house could shorten the period in which a bill could be considered by a President, or it could avoid the veto power altogether by the "simple expedient of adjournment after withdrawing the supposed authority of any officer to receive the vetoed bill."[9]

Perhaps the reason for the return was Roosevelt's claim at the end of the Seventy-third Congress in 1934 that he would always give at least a brief description of his objections to legislation and would return them, even after the adjournment of Congress. This procedure had not been practiced in the past, but Roosevelt wanted "to take a more affirmative position" on the matter of returning bills.[10] Therefore, if the Court's decision in 1936 had been adverse to the government, Roosevelt would have lost considerable prestige. Being sustained by the Court in this instance was another mark of the presidential power.

Four years after this Court decision a bill passed Congress to repeal all legislation that had been pocket-vetoed in the past. Its sponsor, Hatton Sumners of Texas (who had acted as *amicus curiae* in the pocket veto case) said that the present trend of court decisions led him to believe that ultimately the Court would rule that a pocket veto coming after an *ad interim* adjournment was unconstitutional. If this decision were ever rendered, it would bring to life some 500 to 600 bills which had been pocket vetoed. This would create great confusion; his bill, therefore, was only for the purpose of assuring the death of pocket-vetoed legislation of the past.[11] Roosevelt vetoed the Repeal Bill because he thought it would infringe upon the President's power to pocket veto, and he was sustained by the House, 185-105.[12] Sumner's fears have never been fulfilled, but the incident does point out another unanswered question about the veto clause: if the Supreme Court should rule that an *ad interim* pocket veto is illegal, would all bills so treated in the past be resurrected and would they become law?

Other than the Court decision on the relief veto, Roosevelt's rejections of this type did not create many difficulties with the Congress. In addition to questions of relief, pension bills led to 20 of Roosevelt's vetoes. On this subject he used basically the same reasons as had Grover Cleveland. Most of the petitioners for pensions were unworthy of governmental money, he said. Serious mistakes had been made in their applications, indiscriminate pensioning would harm governmental economy, and in most instances, the petitioners were already provided for under the law. An example of his pension reasoning may be seen in his veto of an act granting pensions to certain widows of the Civil War. These widows had married Civil War veterans after the conflict ended. The government had been generous to Civil War veterans, said Roosevelt, and no compelling reason existed to further increase pensions to their widows.[13]

In the area of internal improvements, Roosevelt issued 19 vetoes. These generally dealt with bridge building programs or the enlargement of airports. Here he argued that indiscriminate distribution of funds was too costly and would damage federal-state relations. Indian problems other than relief accounted for 20 of Roosevelt's rejections. These involved attempts by Indians to take their claims to various courts of claims for adjudication, and attempts to acquire government money for building school houses. Again, Roosevelt held that the approval of such bills would lead to a wasteful economy. His vetoes on relief, pension, internal improvements, and Indian claims were motivated by economic considerations. He never questioned the constitutionality of such measures, just their financial inexpediency.

The first major dispute between Roosevelt and the Congress over a veto was in March, 1934. This came on an independent offices appropriation bill containing provisions to gradually restore a 15 percent pay reduction to government employees, adopted earlier as an economy measure. The plan was to restore 5 percent of the cut as of February 1, 1934, 5 percent on July 1, and the remaining 5 percent during the following fiscal year.[14] The appropriation bill also restored "presumptive" pensions (non-service disabilities) at approximately 75 percent of their original value to Spanish-American War veterans.

Roosevelt vetoed the bill because its costs would be around $228 million and this sum had not been included in the budget. The proposed raises were larger than the cost of living index; thus, they were excessive. He hoped, too, to balance the budget by 1936 but this could not be accomplished with pay restorations. Roosevelt also objected to the features of the bill dealing with veterans. He opposed general service pensions, believing they should be only for service connected disabilities.[15] Moreover, he held that the pensions could be restored in a more efficient manner by executive order than by legislation.[16]

The House considered the veto on March 27, the same day as it was given. Discussion centered mostly around the veteran pension provisions. After a brief debate, the House overrode the presidential action, 31-72.[17] It was reported that when the President heard of the House action, he "expressed himself with a colloquial monosyllable of contempt."[18] He hoped that the House's conduct would be negated by the forthcoming Senate vote.

Such was not to be, though, for on the next day the Senate, after considerable discussion, overrode the veto, 63-27.[19] The Senators, like the Congressmen, dwelt on the pension features of the bill. Arthur Robinson, Republican of Indiana, said the pension question was too "sacred" for politics. Whether the veteran was a "Republican or a Democrat," he should have an adequate pension. Finance Committee Chairman Pat Harrison of Mississippi, however, asked the Senate not to destroy the President's economy program. Carter Glass of Virginia said that House members had "masqueraded behind the veterans," and he hoped the Senate would not act in a similar manner. Josiah W. Bailey, North Carolina Democrat, said the veterans were already well provided for, and that "the American people haven't a ray of a chance to get out of this depression until the Government balances the budget."[20] The Democrats and Republicans were almost equally divided in casting their votes to override the veto, 29 for the former, and 33 for the latter.[21]

Congress's overriding action was the first defeat suffered by Roosevelt since becoming President. The veterans' lobby had much influence on the way the lawmakers voted, and 1934 was, of course, a congressional election year. Columnist David Lawrence said "for political purposes the members of both houses wish to assure a certain group of their constituents that the Congress wants to give them the financial benefits they once had, but that only the President is opposed to such a course."[22] The incident showed, said Lawrence, that the President would have to educate the public against extravagant spending before he could keep Congress from constantly threatening the budget.[23]

The destruction of the independent offices veto was only a temporary rupture between the Congress and President Roosevelt. For more than a year after the incident, no attempt was made to override a veto, and dozens were given during the period. It was not until May, 1935, that the Congress, primarily the House, rebelled once more against the Chief Executive. The subject of the uprising was an old one—the bonus question, with which every President since Wilson had dealt.

It will be recalled that Hoover rejected a bill in 1931 to increase to 50 percent the borrowing privileges of the adjusted service certificates. The veto was overridden by the Congress. The following year attempts had been made to redeem the certificates immediately, but Hoover had used his influence to stop the bill in the Senate. Now in 1935, Representative Patman was able to get his bill through Congress and presented to the President. The proposal called for the issuance of $2.2 billion in unsupported currency to give full payment for the service certificates, although they were not due to mature until 1945.[24]

The bill was antagonistic to Roosevelt's New Deal program of reform, so it was well known that a veto would be forthcoming. Patman's followers were confident that any veto would be destroyed in the House. Democratic Whip Patrick J. Boland of Pennsylvania predicted that no more than 125 of the 432 House members would vote to sustain a presidential rejection. The real test on a veto would come from the Senate, although the Patmanites were hopeful that a presidential rejection could be overthrown in that body. He spoke of the endorsement of his bill by the New York Board of Aldermen, and he believed this would have a favorable influence. Some observers believed a deal was in the making between the President and Patmanites whereby Roosevelt would write a "lukewarm" veto to give the impression that he did not care whether the veto was sustained or overridden. Others forecast the strongest possible veto to indicate Roosevelt's belief in a sound currency. By this move, Roosevelt could ingratiate himself with the country's financial circles. The veto, however, did not reflect any "deal making" between the opposing factions.[25]

President Roosevelt adopted a precedent shattering manner of delivering his veto of the Patman Bonus Bill. He dramatically announced to a group of newsmen at the White House that he would deliver the veto in person to a joint session of Congress. His personal appearance, he hoped, would sway the opinions of many who would otherwise vote against him. In the news conference of May 18, 1935, he said he would use the "strongest possible language" in the veto and he "hoped with all his heart" that it would be sustained.[26] The announcement caught Congress, especially the bonus advocates, off-guard.[27]

Arrangements for a congressional joint session produced some problems when the question was discussed in the Senate. Oregon's Frederick Steiwer and Huey Long of Louisiana maintained that the joint session would be unconstitutional. The veto was directed to the House of Representatives and it was that body to which it should be delivered. The two Senators said that Roosevelt's personal appearance would give his views greater influence than they should have. "What's the idea," asked Long, "of going over there [to the House] to listen to a message when he [the President] has already sent you word what the message is going to be?"[28] Steiwer said the President had a right to deliver the veto in person if he desired, but only to the House of origin. If the Senate attended the presentation, a stage would be set for a more forceful veto than it would have been ordinarily.[29] Long was suspected of filibustering to prevent a vote on the resolution for a joint session. He left the Senate, however, during what he thought was a quorum call, only to return to find that he had lost the floor. Thus, the resolution passed.

The President's chief objection to the Patman bill was that the government should not spend $2.2 billion for the benefit of 4 percent of the population. The bill gave to this 4 percent nearly half as much Treasury cash as the recently passed omnibus relief bill gave to the entire population.[30] The measure was undesirable, and if Congress insisted on passing it, it should appropriate additional taxes.[31] Roosevelt gave these objections to Congress on May 22 when he addressed the joint session, and also to the country through a nation-wide radio hook-up. It is interesting to note that his reasons for disapproval were almost exactly the same as those of Coolidge and Hoover before him.

Since the bill had originally passed the House 318-90, or 3½ to 1, it was clear that not even F.D.R.'s personal appearance would prevent an overriding. The Senate, though, had originally passed the bill 55-33, so there was a good chance that the House action would be nullified. The House vote on overriding was 322-98, with Speaker Joseph Byrns voting in the negative.[32] The veto was considered in the Senate on May 23. Only one Senator, Peter Norbeck of South Dakota, was absent. The galleries were packed with spectators, many of them veterans in khaki uniforms. J. W. Elmer Thomas of Oklahoma argued that the beneficiaries of the bill would probably be in small numbers by 1945 when the certificates matured. The certificates had already depreciated 40 percent from their original value, and he feared continued depreciation. Other Senators claimed that the bill was not inflationary, but was a controlled expansion of the currency. It would, in their opinion, stimulate the economy.[33] Argument for the bill, however, was not sufficient, and the veto was sustained, 54-40.[34]

The veto was flayed by Father Charles Coughlin. He likened Roosevelt to "money changers," and bitterly denounced "plutocratic capitalism." He said that it was not merely the American soldier who had been vetoed, but the whole American people. Bankers were accused of regulating the country's money, a function that the Constitution gave only to Congress.[35] On the other hand, conservatives "warmly applauded what they interpreted as an outright declaration against 'printing press money.' "[36]

The *New York Times* supported the President's veto, and suggested that the country should flood Washington with telegrams, letters, and resolutions in favor of it.[37] The influential *Washington Evening Star* also upheld the President. Editorially, it said that a vote to override was "an expression of political realism as distinct from statesmanship." Those who voted to override were definitely looking forward to the next congressional elections. Writing in the *Star*, columnist Lawrence said: "The trend toward spending and huge borrowings has proved a Frankenstein for this administration. That's why, although Mr. Roosevelt can be sustained on the veto of the Patman bill, the Congress will pass over his veto another type of measure clearing up the bonus question through the issuance of Government bonds."[38] Thus, Lawrence accurately predicted the situation of about eight months later when the "baby bond" issue came before the Congress, the President, and the country.

The "baby bond" bill included some changes in the efforts at immediate cash payment of the service certificates. It eliminated the issuance of unsupported currency, but substituted interest-bearing bonds which could be converted into cash at any time. It also forgave all unpaid interest on service-certificate loans since October, 1931.[39] The effect of the bill would be to pay $2 billion of adjusted service certificates in $50.00 cashable bonds. In addition, the forgiven interest would amount to approximately $268,000,-000.[40] In vetoing the measure, Roosevelt used the same reasons as he used for the Patman veto the year before.[41]

Since 1936 was an election year, most observers forecast destruction of the "baby bond" veto. In the House, on January 24, 1936, John Bankhead of Alabama tried to postpone a vote on the veto because the Senate was in recess, and several House members were absent because they had not expected a vote to be taken so quickly. Proponents of the bill, however, defeated Bankhead's motion, and the veto was overridden without discussion, 322-61.[42]

The Senate debated the veto on January 27. The Democratic leadership deserted Roosevelt as Majority Leader Robinson and Finance Committee Chairman Harrison used their influence for the bill. Total Senate membership was represented in the vote, a situation that caused Vice-President Garner to congratulate, rather facetiously, all of the members for their excellent health.[43] The debate centered mostly around the prior veto of the bonus bill, and neither side brought out anything new on the subject. The vote was 76-1,[44] so the "baby bond" bill became law.

With the overriding action, a drive was consummated that began in 1924, shortly after the passage of the first adjusted compensation bill. The question was motivated more by political considerations than by the Progressive tendencies of Congress during the 1920's and early 30's. This is seen by the fact that bonus advocates were always more in abundance during election years than at any other time. The veteran population amounted to around four percent of the total, and the bonus issue was not necessarily for relief, although bonus advocates utilized this idea to a great extent. The bonus represented a voluntary debt which the United States contracted in 1924. With the borrowing privileges under the service certificates, the veteran was probably in a better condition economically than his non-veteran neighbor. In addition to this, the veteran qualified for all the other assistance programs offered by the government. The veteran lobby, however, tended to overlook the amount of money spent for rehabilitation, for hospitals, and indeed for coming to the aid of the genuinely needy veteran. To vote for a full bonus was to be on the popular side of a question; the blame could easily be shifted to the President for "heartless" vetoes, and much of the same type of opprobrium directed against Cleveland for his pension vetoes now descended upon the 20th century Presidents for their rejections of bonus legislation. In the view of Harding, Coolidge, and Hoover the bonus was simply bad finance, something that would hamper their cherished programs of business and industrial supremacy. Roosevelt was willing to unbalance the budget if general relief were the goal. Bonus bills, however, would not aid general relief, but would disproportionately favor a small portion of the American citizenry over the others. Veteran relief from the depression, believed Roosevelt, depended upon general recovery. The veteran groups, and ultimately the Congress, could not accept this view. Thus, the whole series of events must be ascribed more to politics than to progressive philosophy.

The veteran problem was still present even after the overriding of the "baby bond" veto. In June, 1937, Roosevelt disapproved a bill extending the five-year term insurance policies held by veterans under the War Risk Act. This Act had enabled veterans to pay low insurance rates into a special Treasury Department fund, with the understanding that the insurance would be converted into permanent policies five years after the formal end of World War I. The term insurance had been renewed three times, and the bill vetoed by Roosevelt called for the fourth extension.

Roosevelt claimed that a continuance of the wartime low rates to the term insurance holders would be a disservice to the 85 percent of the veterans who had already converted to permanent life or endowment insurance. The reserves built up by those who had converted would be used to pay claims on the term policies. This, in Roosevelt's view, was favoritism.[45] In the House, on June 1, John Rankin of Mississippi fought for passage of the bill over the veto, saying that no form of Government life insurance placed a charge on the Treasury. The holders of the five-year policies simply constituted a subdivision of the Government life-insurance fund.[46] He said that the number of veterans in question came to 23,000, and if they were forced to convert, many would be unable to obtain old-line insurance policies because of infirmities. Moreover, many who could qualify on the health requirements were not financially capable of paying the higher costs after conversion.[47] If the veto were sustained, said Rankin, at least 2,000 veterans would be without insurance of any kind.[48] When the vote was taken, the Congressmen were almost unanimous in overriding the veto. The count was 372-13.[49]

The Senate considered the veto on June 1. There, the cause for the veterans was argued by Walter George of Georgia, who repeated essentially what Rankin had said in the House. Sherman Minton of Indiana defended the veto. The Senate vote, 69-12,[50] like the one in the House, was highly favorable to the veteran bill. Thus, another presidential veto against veteran legislation was overturned. This was the last of the important veteran vetoes given by Roosevelt. There were other vetoes of specific veteran legislation for relief and pension after this, but only one, the Philippine Travel veto, was overridden.[51]

In addition to being faced with demands for extending veteran term insurance, Roosevelt tried to combat the same tendencies in regard to federal farm loans. A bill was passed in July, 1937, to extend for one year 3½ percent interest rates on loans for farmers. Roosevelt disliked the bill because he thought the economic emergency for farmers was ended. He believed that farmers could now pay the higher interest rates because of increased farm prices and farm income.[52] Also, the bill would impede his efforts to balance the budget.

Several members of Congress, however, differed sharply with Roosevelt's estimate of the farmers' condition. They argued that floods and drought had erased many of the gains made by the agricultural community during the past several months. The average farm income was much less than that of city dwellers, and many farmers were at the time facing foreclosures. Extension of the low interest rates would be helpful to the economy because it would keep thousands of farmers off the relief rolls.[53] The House overrode the veto on July 13, 260-98.[54] The Senate complied nine days later, 71-19.[55] The Senate vote showed 53 Democrats, 15 Republicans, and 3 Independents favoring the interest rate extension.[56]

In June of the following year, Congress passed another extension, this time to 1940, of the low interest rates. Again Roosevelt vetoed the measure on the same grounds as the year before. He said the bill would cost $208,700,000, a sum that was not conducive to the much needed retrenchment in spending. The Congress was no more impressed now with the President's reasoning than it had been in 1937, so the veto was overridden. The House vote was 244-87, and the Senate's was 57-18.[57] Thus the government continued its assistance to farmers in the face of strong opposition from the President.

Roosevelt's efforts to refuse government assistance to what he considered special interest groups continued in 1940. A bill was sent to him in June of that year altering the General Bridge Act of 1906. The earlier bill had stated that whenever the Secretary of War found it feasible, he could require the owners of bridges, at their expense, to make necessary alterations for safety and convenience. The later bill committed the government to pay for that part of the alterations which did not immediately accrue to the benefit of the owner.[58]

The President's veto of June 10 argued that owners of railway and highway bridges over navigable waters knew when they gained the construction contract that the government could force them, under certain conditions, to make alterations at their own expense. The Supreme Court had sustained the 1906 law on several occasions, ruling that its enforcement did not constitute the seizure of private property without just compensation.[59] The veto intimated that the owners should consider it a privilege to be permitted to build bridges over navigable waters, and should therefore be willing to pay the full cost of required alterations.

The bridge owners, however, were amply represented in Congress. Clarence Lea of California said that the President's "Committee of Six," appointed to recommend transportation legislation, supported the Bridge Bill. Though the bridges were privately owned, in the case of railroads at least, their functions were public. The old rule embodied in the 1906 legislation was too harsh against the owners, especially the railroads, which were now operating at a loss.[60] Lea also hinted that the President's veto was based on *ex parte* information, hurriedly handed to him by the War Department.[61] Everett Dirksen of Illinois argued that it would be unfair to assess a railroad for bridge alterations if the railroad received no benefit from it. If the War Department said, "This is the kind of bridge you must build . . . then certainly in all equity and good conscience it is fair to apportion properly the total cost on an equitable basis and assess everybody accordingly."[62] The veto was supported by John Cochran of Missouri. He claimed that the railroads had launched a propaganda campaign to get the veto overridden. The financial benefits of the bill would help a few at the expense of the general population who would have to pay for it through taxes.[63] Adolph Sabath of Illinois agreed with Cochran by asserting that the government had been more than generous to railroads in times past and the Bridge Bill would be favoritism.[64] Supporters of the bill, however, won their case in the House, and the veto was overridden on June 19 by a vote of 324-68.[65]

The Senate reconsidered the Bridge Bill two days later. There, the bill was favored by Harry Truman of Missouri. He and Senator Reed of Kansas said the bill had been approved by the appropriate committees in both houses, and the public interest was adequately protected. An example was given to show why the government should share costs of alterations. It had been suggested that the long bridge across the Potomac be raised two feet wholly for scenic purposes. The bridge was safe and completely adequate for railroad use. It would therefore be unfair for the railroads to bear the total cost of any such alterations. Very few Senators spoke against the bill; so when the vote was taken, it was repassed 65-17. Again, Roosevelt had lost an argument, albeit a relatively minor one, with his Congress over the matter of distributing the government's money.

The same type of dispute was present a year later when a Highway Defense Bill was passed and sent to the President. Roosevelt had asked for $125,000,000, which the House raised to $287,-000,000. Afterwards, a Senate-House conference set the sum at $320,000,000.[66] Opponents of the bill referred to it as pork-barrel legislation.

The President objected to apportioning the money according to the population of the states under the Federal Highway Act. The money should be spent, in his opinion, where the need was greatest. Other objectionable features to the bill were the provisions to build off-street parking facilities, and to reimburse local communities for damages resulting from army maneuvers.[67]

The Senate overrode the veto on August 6, 1941, 57-19,[68] placing "themselves and the states above the national interest."[69] The House, however, was not totally impressed, even after the presentation of statistics by Oklahoma's Wilburn Cartwright. He said that of the 234,000 miles of roads on the Federal aid system there were 78,000 which had military value; on those 78,000 miles there were over 2,400 weak bridges that would not carry medium army tanks; and there were over 5,000 miles of highways less than 18 feet wide, and 14,000 miles were too narrow. To do the job properly, averred the Oklahoman, $458,000,000 was actually needed.[70] James W. Mott of Oregon said that the War Department and others concerned with national defense strongly favored the bill. The only agency against it, he said, was the Budget Bureau, which knew nothing of building and maintaining roads.[71] The vote was so close that Speaker Sam Rayburn called for a recapitulation.[72] The result was 251-128.[73] This was approximately 66.20 percent favoring the bill, just a fraction short of the necessary two-thirds to override. Thus, the House, unlike the Senate, recognized "the inflationary trends and the necessity for cutting expenses."[74]

The veto of the Defense Highway Bill did not necessarily mean that Roosevelt did not think the money should be spent. The question was more on how governmental finances would be expended, and by whom. One of Congressman Cartwright's chief objections to the veto was that it was given only because the bill prevented the President from spending money exactly as he chose. Certainly, there was no constitutional problem involved with the bill or its veto. It was essentially a matter of a strong-willed President, determined to be the chief arbiter on the allocation of funds, being seriously challenged, at least on this occasion, by business and local government interests as reflected by Congress. This, of course, did not happen too often.

The remainder of President Roosevelt's significant vetoes dealt directly with World War II. It was here that his power was greatest, rarely being threatened by the Congress. But when the latter did choose to gainsay Roosevelt's actions on matters relating to the war, its reaction was usually as powerful as the veto which brought it into being in the first place. The first serious disagreement between Roosevelt and Congress over the war was in finding a way to prevent strikes in war-related industries. Unions had taken a "no-strike" pledge shortly after America's entry into the war, but some had threatened to break it unless wages remained compatible with the cost of living. In July, 1942, the National War Labor Board had issued the "Little Steel Formula," granting a 15 percent wage increase to meet higher prices. Then, in April, 1943, the President brought out his "hold the line" order, hoping to stop inflationary spirals. The only labor leader of note to disregard the no-strike pledge and the "hold the line" directive was John L. Lewis, head of the United Mine Workers of America. On

May 1, 1943, he called a half million miners off their jobs. This resulted in the government's taking over many of the coal mines. Accordingly, the strike was called off, and Lewis presented his case to the War Labor Board. The latter refused to alter the Little Steel formula for the miners; so Lewis called another strike on June 11. The second strike set off a tremendous reaction, both in Congress and throughout the country.

The Congress and the President differed sharply over the best methods of bringing the strike to an end. Roosevelt wanted a law that would draft miners up to age 65 into the army and put them into coal mines as soldiers. The Congress, however had other ideas. It passed the War Labor Disputes Act, known as the Smith-Connally-Harness Act. This authorized the government's seizure of plants where strikes threatened the output of war materials, and it required 30 days notice by a Union of intention to strike, at the end of which time the workers, by secret ballot, would decide whether or not to stop war production.[75] Roosevelt disliked the latter section, and it was the chief reason for his veto of June 25.

He said that this section would encourage strikes rather than prevent them. "In wartime," he argued, "we cannot sanction strikes with or without notice."[76] The 30 days waiting period might become, in his judgment, a "boiling period" instead of a "cooling off" time, in which "the thought and energies of the workers would be diverted from war production to vote-getting."[77] The ninth section of the bill, said the President, contained material irrelevant to the problem at hand, such as prohibiting labor unions from making political contributions for the duration of the war. If there was merit in the prohibition, Roosevelt believed it should not be restricted to times of war.[78]

The veto made Roosevelt the hero of organized labor. Many observers charged that the President was making a play for labor support during the next presidential campaign, but in the opinion of columnist G. Gould Lincoln the veto would probably cost Roosevelt millions of votes.[79] Labor leaders, terming the Smith-Connally Act as "fascist," and as a bill to "crucify labor," had brought their full pressure to bear on the President to reject the measure.[80] The mood of the country, however, and that of Congress, was a sullen one, and in only a few minutes on June 25 the Senate overrode the veto 56-25.[81] The House quickly did likewise on the same day, 244-108.[82] This action of Congress was so strenuous that labor leaders referred to it as a "major disaster."[83]

The defeat of the Smith-Connally veto was "indicative of a deep and significant change in the temper of the American people and their representatives."[84] It indicated that there would be no toleration of strikes in the basic industries while the war was still in progress. There were some strong intimations from labor leaders that they would not comply with the Act until the Supreme Court had tested its constitutionality. These inclinations did not materialize, however, for it was feared that such tactics would bring even sterner laws from Congress.[85] The overriding action was also interpreted as a protest against Roosevelt's labor policies. The President had argued that the time spent in the coal strike was small in comparison with the time of work put out by all industries. The effect of the strike, however, on the state of mind of the people had been exceedingly bad, "and neither the President nor the labor leaders seem to have grasped this fact."[86]

Columnist Lawrence viciously assailed the President for having around him "smart-alec leftwingers," who "misled and misinformed [him] about the state of public opinion on the strike issue."[87] Lawrence believed that the President should fire his "stupid" advisers and "get in tune with the Congress and the rest of the country," because "on the subject of prohibiting strikes in wartime, the Nation is virtually unanimous."[88] Many people believed that a deal had been made between the President and John L. Lewis, whereby in return for Lewis' allowing the mines to operate under the W.L.B., Roosevelt would veto any strike legislation.[89] This view carried along with it the belief that Roosevelt's wish to draft recalcitrant workers was in error because the draft should not be used as a "club" to prevent labor disputes. This was the most disastrous defeat handed to Roosevelt by the Congress since he became President. The Congress and the country were asking in essence: "Who is bigger? John L. Lewis or the United States government?"[90] The Congress answered in terms which could not be mistaken by anyone.

Within less than a fortnight after Congress handed Roosevelt his defeat on the War Labor Disputes Act, another veto controversy arose. In a House originated bill continuing the Commodity Credit Corporation for two years, the Congress prohibited any further government subsidies to hold down retail food prices. This was in opposition to Roosevelt's rollback program which he wanted to make possible through continued and increased government subsidies, and which he believed was necessary to arrest inflation. The congressional subsidy ban would end the existing rollback on meats and butter on August 1, with subsidies on the vital foods continuing until the end of the 1943 crop year. Further subsidies of any kind would have to receive the specific approval of the Congress.[91]

Roosevelt's strongly worded veto of July 2 called the bill an inflationary measure because it would increase the cost of living. Although it continued the C.C.C., the agency was "hamstrung" to the extent that it could not effectively carry out its responsibilities. The bill took away the Executive power of purchasing farm products for re-sale at a loss, or of making incentive payments to obtain increased production of foodstuffs. Roosevelt believed that the government could not stabilize the cost of living if it could not stabilize the cost of necessary foods. The measure would cause an immediate and sharp increase in food prices, and thus another inflationary spiral would be started. Therefore, the bill would become law "only over my strenuous objection and protest."[92]

The *New York Times* was critical of Roosevelt's veto of the C.C.C. bill. Government subsidies, it said, were not a primary weapon against inflation. In the veto, however, Roosevelt seemed to consider them as the most important safeguard against high retail prices. Moreover, the veto implied that Congress should approve any subsidy suggested by the President and if it failed to do so, it would bear full responsibility for inflation.[93]

House members expressed their opinions of the bill and its veto. Representative Patman feared that the bill would lead to inflation because Congress was eliminating the rollback program without substituting any safeguards against price spiraling. Representative Hamilton Fish, Jr., of New York suggested the creation of a seven member House committee to study prices, rents, wages, and all other phases of inflation, but Jesse Wolcott of Michigan, ranking minority member of the House Banking Committee, said the only increase in the cost of living because of the bill would be the difference between the President's rollback and the actual cost of the commodities. Thus, the increased prices were not sufficient to cause one to fear uncontrolled inflation.[94] Proponents of the measure were not plentiful enough to pass it over the veto. On July 2 it was upheld in the House, 228-154.[95] Possibly, the chief reason for this action was Roosevelt's statement in the veto that the bill would "compel every housewife to pay more for each pound of butter bought, [and] every ounce of beef. . . ."[96] House members apparently thought it would be easier to obscure the taxes which made subsidies possible than to force an immediate upward trend in the price of food. Accordingly, subsidies were continued in the form desired by the President.

It was not until February, 1944, that another of Roosevelt's vetoes created the greatest amount of excitement. This was against a Revenue Bill, in which Roosevelt had requested Congress to raise

$10.5 billion over and above the existing taxes. The bill, however, raised the revenue by only $2.3 billion.[97] In a sarcastic mood, Roosevelt angrily objected to the bill in his veto message of February 22.

The bill canceled Social Security increases that would have yielded $1.1 billion, and it granted relief from existing taxes to several businesses and corporations. Thus the bill was "not a tax bill but a tax relief bill providing relief not for the needy but for the greedy." Specifically, the bill gave benefits to corporations reorganized in bankruptcy by permitting them to retain the high excess-profits credit and depreciation basis "attributable to the contributions of stockholders who were usually eliminated in the reorganization." Percentage depletion allowances were extended to the distributors of several widely used minerals. The lumber industry was allowed to treat income from cutting of timber as capital gain rather than annual income. Natural gas lines were exempted from the excess-profits tax, which would probably cause the oil companies to demand similar advantages. Commercial airlines were granted an extension of the tax subsidy on their airmail contracts. The bill failed to simplify the procedures by which citizens filed their income returns, and it continued the "clumsy" Victory Tax. The President said that several people had urged him to sign the bill because, "having asked the Congress for a loaf of bread . . . I should be content with a small piece of crust. I might have done so if I had not noted that the small piece of crust contained so many extraneous and inedible materials."[98]

The veto was criticized by the *Washington Evening Star* because its langauge would contribute to resentment. It asserted that Roosevelt had not consulted Robert L. Doughton of North Carolina, Chairman of the House Ways and Means Committee, nor Senator Walter George of the Senate Finance Committee, two of the leading supporters of the Revenue Bill. The President tried to "saddle" Congress with the complexities of the tax system, but for these the Treasury Department must share a large part of the blame. Under the Constitution, the Congress must originate tax legislation, but apparently Roosevelt had forgotten this fact.[99] On the other hand, the *St. Louis Post-Dispatch* favored the veto. The revenue provided by the bill came to only one-fourth of the $10.5 billion increase needed by the government.[100]

The House reconsidered the vetoed bill on February 22. There was some irony in the fact that Roosevelt's veto was read just after the annual presentation of Washington's Farewell Address. After the veto was read, Doughton moved that its consideration be postponed for two days. On February 24, 1944, in only a few minutes, the House destroyed the veto, 299-95.[101] The real drama, however, was not in the House of Representatives, but in the Senate where, on the 23rd, Majority Leader Alben Barkley made a speech, the subject of which was the Revenue veto.

"For 12 years," he shouted, "I have carried to the best of my ability the flag of Franklin Delano Roosevelt. For the past seven years I have carried the flag of the administration as Majority Leader of this Senate. . . . Sometimes I have carried it with little help here on the Senate floor and more often with less help from the other end of Pennsylvania Avenue. . . . This is the first time during that long service, which I thought was honorable, that I have been accused deliberately of voting for a bill impoverishing the needy and enriching the greedy."[102] Roosevelt's veto was therefore a "deliberate and calculated assault upon the honesty and integrity" of Congress. If the legislators had any self respect left, they would override the veto and enact the Revenue bill into law.[103] Barkley then announced his intention to resign as Majority Leader of the Senate.

When his speech was over, both Democrats and Republicans crowded around the Majority Leader's desk to congratulate him, and there were several demonstrations of approval from the tightly packed galleries. In interpreting Barkley's speech and subsequent resignation, some anti New-Deal Democrats forecast a split in the party and felt that Barkley's action imperiled Roosevelt's chances for a fourth term. Republicans claimed that if the resignation caused Roosevelt to stop ignoring Congress, Barkley would have performed a tremendous service to the country. Almost everyone agreed that the speech cleared the atmosphere and tended to set things straight again between the Congress and the President.[104] European papers followed the events closely, with representatives of small countries which had governments in exile "endeavoring to read into the squabble the possible future attitude of Mr. Roosevelt in regard to their countries."[105]

The President was at Hyde Park when Barkley gave his speech. Hearing of its contents, he remarked, "Alben must be suffering from shell shock."[106] He then wrote to the Majority Leader, the now famous "Dear Alben" letter. He regretted that Barkley thought the veto was a personal attack against the Congress. "Such you must know was not my intention. You and I may differ, and have differed on important measures, but that does not mean we question one another's good faith." He went on to say that he had made certain changes in the veto at the insistence of Barkley, but that Barkley had not tried to change the President's basic decision once the former learned how strongly the latter felt about the Revenue

Bill. Roosevelt hoped that Barkley would not persist in his intention to resign as Majority Leader. "If you do, however, I hope your colleagues will not accept your resignation; but if they do, I sincerely hope that they will immediately and unanimously re-elect you."[107]

This was, of course, what happened. On the 24th, a Democratic caucus met in the office of Senator Kenneth McKellar of Tennessee, and Barkley was unanimously re-elected. Many believed that the entire incident put Barkley in the front ranks for the Democratic nomination in 1944. Others, though, held later that the incident in actuality prevented Barkley from becoming President. Up to the time of the disagreement, Roosevelt had speculated about the possibility of Barkley's succeeding him, and Barkley believed that "if Henry Wallace were discarded for renomination for Vice President in 1944, I would be acceptable to Mr. Roosevelt as a running mate." After the breach, however, Roosevelt's attitude was one of coolness "which did not completely thaw until after the 1944 convention."[108]

The day after Barkley's re-election as Majority Leader, the Senate overrode the Revenue veto, 72-14,[109] and thus it became law. Though it was far less than what Roosevelt wanted, the amount of increased revenue in the bill was more than the entire national debt of pre-war days.[110] The overriding action was indicative of the loss of confidence by many legislators in the President's domestic leadership, while it demonstrated that Congress would ultimately rebel against the inroads made on its constitutional prerogative to lay and collect taxes.[111] It was an indication of congressional displeasure with the Treasury policymakers, who were largely blamed for the veto, and many lawmakers called for a complete "shake-up" in that Department. And, finally, it showed the "capriciousness of history," as Barkley put it, for if his resignation caused Roosevelt to veer away from him as Vice-Presidential candidate and ultimately select Harry Truman (and Barkley is careful to point out that this is mere speculation), it did indeed cost him the Presidency.[112]

An analysis of Roosevelt's vetoes shows that he was most like Andrew Jackson, since both Presidents were tremendously influential with the Congress while retaining the support of the general populace. Like Jackson's veto messages Roosevelt's were addressed to the American people as much as, and in some instance more than, to the Congress. Also like Jackson, he was a pragmatic President, not committing himself to inflexible programs, and not making apologies for apparent inconsistencies. There were jobs to do—the depression had to be ended, the war had to be won—

and Roosevelt, as had Jackson, believed that Congress should respond to Executive initiative rather than the reverse.

Roosevelt obtained the desired response from Congress in most instances. Through legislators friendly to the New Deal, through his personal charm, and through his sincerity in wanting to help the "little man," he could get things accomplished. But if these advantages should happen not to work on a given occasion, there was always the veto which he used without hesitation. However, he still did not represent the veto at its greatest power during the period covered by this survey. In the first place, his power was great even without the veto, and in the second place, too many of his major vetoes were overridden. Taking into account the context in which they occurred, John Tyler's rejections still reflect the veto power at its peak.

In his use of the veto, Roosevelt was a political, and even an economic, conservative. He devised a reform program and quickly rejected most ideas that differed from it. He objected to Congress' spending more than he thought it should, and with equal facility he disliked it when Congress, in his opinion, did not spend enough. He used much of his energy combatting special interest appropriations, and it was this area which accounted for the major vetoes. Therefore, his vetoes helped him to consolidate a reform movement that had been long in the making.

The veto rose to its greatest heights under Tyler and sank to its lowest depths under Johnson. The Presidents following Roosevelt have generally conformed to the various veto patterns set by their predecessors. Since Roosevelt, vetos have rarely become the objects of great interest and controversy.

Notes

CHAPTER I

1. Many plans of representation have been similar to the Apportionment Act of 1792, the one created by the German Weimar Republic in November, 1918, being prominent.

2. Douglas Southall Freeman, *George Washington*, pp. 345-48.

3. *National Gazette*, April 7, 1792.

4. *Ibid.*

5. Freeman, p. 346. In expressing this opinion, Hamilton probably allowed his desire to see a dominant Federalist Party momentarily sway his wishes for a strong central government.

6. *Annals of Congress*, 2 Cong., 1 Sess., p. 539.

7. *National Gazette*, April 9, 1792.

8. *Providence Gazette and Country Journal*, May 5, 1792.

9. *Ibid.*

10. James Richardson, ed., *Messages of the Presidents*, I, p. 211. Hereafter cited as *Messages*.

11. *Annals of Congress*, 4 Cong., 2 Sess., pp. 2331-2332.

12. *Annals of Congress*, 11 Cong., 3 Sess., p. 995.

13. *Messages*, I, p. 489.

14. *Annals of Congress*, pp. 983-84.

15. *Ibid.*, p. 984.

16. *Ibid.*

17. *National Intelligencer*, February 12, 1811.

18. *Annals of Congress*, p. 1104.

19. *Ibid.*, 12 Cong., 1 Sess., p. 1252.

20. *Messages*, I, p. 511.

21. *National Intelligencer*, April 9, 1812.

22. *Annals of Congress*, pp. 1275-77.

23. *National Intelligencer*, November 17, 1812.

24. *Annals of Congress*, p. 1561.

25. *Ibid.*, p. 1571.

26. *Messages*, I, p. 523.

27. *National Intelligencer*, November 19, 1812.

28. *New York Herald*, February 1, 1815.

29. *Messages*, I, p. 555. It is interesting to note that the prescriptive process seemed to be in conflict with Madison's earlier stated system of minority checks in which a number of large interest groups in the country each possessed a veto against numerical majorities. His statement here pointed out a vast difference between Madison "the father of the Constitution," and Madison, the President. An interesting discussion on the Madisonian formula of government is given in James Mac-Gregor Burns, *The Deadlock of Democracy*, pp. 8-23.

30. *Messages*, I, p. 555.

31. *Ibid.*, p. 557.

32. *Annals*, 13 Cong., 3 Sess., p. 212.

33. *Ibid.*, p. 213.

34. *Ibid.*

35. *Maryland Gazette*, February 16, 1815.

36. *Ibid.*, February 9, 1815.

37. *Messages*, I, p. 556.

38. Edward Mason, *The Veto Power*, p. 74.

39. *National Intelligencer*, February 27, 1817.

40. *Ibid.*, February 22, 1817.

41. *Ibid.*, March 3, 1817.

42. *Messages*, I, p. 584.

43. *Ibid.*

44. *National Intelligencer*, March 4, 1817.

45. *Ibid.*, April 13, 1822.

46. *Ibid.*, April 21 and May 3, 1822.

47. *Messages*, II, p. 142.

48. *National Intelligencer*, May 29, 1822.

49. *Ibid.*, May 13, 1822.

50. *Ibid.*, May 13 and May 20, 1822.

51. W. P. Cresson, *James Monroe*, p. 392.

52. *Ibid.*, p. 396.

CHAPTER II

1. May 31, 1830, for example, he approved an appropriation of eight thousand dollars toward the construction of a road from Detroit to Chicago. He stipulated, though, that the use of the money authorized by the act must be confined to Michigan territory. *Gales and Seaton Register*, 21 Cong., 1 Sess., p. 1148.

2. William MacDonald, *Jacksonian Democracy*, p. 141.

3. *Ibid.*, p. 139.

4. John Spencer Bassett, *The Life of Andrew Jackson*, p. 485.

5. *National Intelligencer*, May 21, 1830.

6. Bassett, p. 486.

7. Glyndon G. Van Deusen, *The Jacksonian Era*, p. 52.

8. *National Intelligencer*, September 1, 1830.

9. *Messages*, II. p. 484.

10. *National Intelligencer*, June 24, 1830.

11. *Messages*, II, p. 489.

12. Bassett, p. 493.

13. *Messages*, II, p. 486.

14. *Ibid.*

15. Bassett, p. 494.

16. *Ibid.*

17. *Ibid.*, p. 495.

18. *Messages*, II, p. 486.

19. *Ibid.*, p. 492.

20. Bassett, p. 495.

21. *National Intelligencer*, September 1, 1830.

22. *Ibid.*, June 24, 1830.

23. *Messages*, II, p. 484.

24. *National Intelligencer*, June 24, 1830.

25. *Gales and Seaton Register*, 21 Cong., 1 Sess., p. 1138. Hereafter cited as *Register*.

26. *Ibid.*, p. 1140.

27. *Ibid.*

28. *National Intelligencer*, June 24, 1830.

29. *Register*, pp. 1140-41.

30. *National Intelligencer*, June 19, 1830.

31. *Register*, p. 1141.

32. *Ibid.*, p. 1142.

33. *Ibid.*

34. *Ibid.*

35. *Ibid.*

36. *National Intelligencer*, June 24, 1830.

37. *Ibid.*, July 3, 1830.

38. *National Intelligencer*, June 18, 1830, quoting the *Farmer's Chronicle*.

39. *Alabama Journal*, June 25, 1831.

40. Jackson's affirmative votes on the bill to procure "the necessary surveys, plans, and estimates upon the subject of rivers and canals," April 23, 1824; the bill to "improve the navigation of the Ohio and Mississippi Rivers," May 19, 1824; and the bill "subscribing stock in the Chesapeake and Delaware Canal Company," February 24, 1826, were cited from the *National Intelligencer*, August 28, 1830.

41. *Register*, pp. 1147-48.

42. *National Intelligencer*, June 24, 1830.

43. *Ibid.*, July 3, 1830.

44. *The Washington Globe*, December 11, 1830.

45. *National Intelligencer*, July 2, 1830.

46. *Ibid.*

47. *Ibid.*, July 12 and August 3, 1830.

48. Statistics were compiled from a chart in David M. Potter and Thomas G. Manning, *Nationalism and Sectionalism in America 1775-1877*, p. 149. Southern states included in the bonus bill analysis: Georgia, Louisiana, North Carolina, South Carolina, Tennessee, and Virginia; Northern states: Connecticut, Maine, Massachusetts, New Hampshire, New Jersey, New York, Pennsylvania, Rhode Island, and Vermont. In the Maysville analysis, the Southern states of Alabama and Mississippi were added. The Northern states remained the same as for the Bonus bill.

49. *National Intelligencer*, June 1, 1830.

50. *Ibid.*, June 4, 1830.

51. *Ibid.*, July 3, 1830.

52. *Ibid.*, June 24, 1830.

53. *Messages*, II, pp. 508-517.

54. *Ibid.*

55. *Ibid.*, p. 638.

56. Mason, *Veto Power*, p. 98.

57. Bassett, p. 496.

CHAPTER III

1. The best sources are: Bassett, *The Life of Andrew Jackson;* MacDonald, *Jacksonian Democracy;* Bowers, *Party Battles of the Jackson Period;* Schlesinger, *The Age of Jackson;* and Van Deusen, *The Jacksonian Era.*
2. *National Intelligencer,* June 11, 1832.
3. *Ibid.*
4. *Ibid.,* June 13, 1832.
5. *Ibid.*
6. *Messages,* II, p. 576.
7. *Ibid. National Intelligencer,* July 11, 1832.
8. *Messages,* II, p. 577.
9. *Ibid.*
10. *Ibid.,* p. 578.
11. *Ibid.,* p. 579.
12. *Ibid.*
13. *Ibid.,* p. 580.
14. *Ibid.*
15. *Ibid.,* p. 581.
16. *Ibid.*
17. *Ibid.,* pp. 581-582.
18. Specifically in *McCulloch vs Maryland* in which Chief Justice Marshall ruled that states did not possess the power to tax the branches of the national bank. The decision supposedly settled the constitutional question regarding the bank.
19. *Messages,* II, p. 582.
20. *Ibid.*
21. He had failed to enforce the celebrated Supreme Court Decision of *Worcester vs Georgia,* given by Chief Justice Marshall early in 1832. Also, in September, 1832, Jackson discontinued surveys for the New York and Erie Railroad in Ohio after funds had been duly appropriated for that purpose. But he assuredly did not make a practice of "picking and choosing" the laws he would enforce. *National Intelligencer,* Sept. 4, 1832.
22. *Messages,* II, p. 583.
23. *Ibid.,* p. 584.
24. *Ibid.*
25. *Ibid.,* p. 585.
26. *Ibid.,* p. 586.
27. *Ibid.,* p. 589.
28. Mason, p. 33.
29. *Messages,* II, p. 590.
30. *Register,* 1 Sess., 22 Cong., pp. 1226-7.
31. *Ibid.,* pp. 1252-53.
32. *Ibid.,* pp. 1223.
33. *Ibid.,* p. 1242.
34. *Ibid.,* p. 1254.
35. *Ibid.,* p. 1228.
36. *Ibid.*
37. *Ibid.,* p. 1229.
38. *Ibid.*
39. *Ibid.,* pp. 1245-1246.
40. *Ibid.,* pp. 1269-1270.
41. *Ibid.,* p. 1240.
42. *Ibid.,* p. 1257.
43. *Ibid.,* p. 1224.
44. *Ibid.,* p. 1255.
45. *Ibid.,* p. 1263.
46. *National Intelligencer,* August 9, 1832.
47. *Register,* p. 1230.
48. *Ibid.,* p. 1231.
49. My italics.
50. *Register,* p. 1244.
51. See p. 9 on Madison's bank veto of 1815 and his belief in the prescriptive process.
52. *Register,* p. 1264.
53. *Ibid.,* pp. 1272-1273.
54. *Ibid.,* p. 1237.
55. *Ibid.,* p. 1235.
56. *Ibid.,* p. 1266.
57. *Ibid.,* p. 1293.
58. *Ibid.,* p. 1294.
59. *Ibid.,* 1296. *National Intelligencer,* July 19, 1832.
60. *National Intelligencer,* July 19, 1832.
61. *Ibid.,* August 13, 1832.
62. Jackson's electoral vote was 219, Clay's was 49. Jackson collected 157,313 votes out of 1,217,691 votes cast.
63. Bassett, *Correspondence of Andrew Jackson,* IV, p. 458.

CHAPTER IV

1. *Register,* 22 Cong., 1 Sess., p. 48.
2. *Ibid.,* p. 49.
3. *Ibid.*
4. *Messages,* II, p. 637.
5. *Ibid.,* III, p. 64.
6. *Ibid.,* pp. 57-62.
7. *Ibid.,* pp. 60-62.
8. *Federal Constitution,* Article Four, Section Three; *Messages,* III, p. 60.
9. *Messages,* III, p. 64.
10. *Ibid.,* p. 65.
11. *Ibid.*
12. *Ibid.,* p. 67.
13. *Ibid.,* p. 69.
14. *Ibid.,* p. 57. *Register,* 22 Cong., 2 Sess., p. 14.

15. *Register*, p. 18.
16. *Ibid. National Intelligencer*, December 5, 1833.
17. *National Intelligencer*, April 2, 1835.
18. *National Intelligencer*, April 2, 1835.
19. *Ibid.*
20. *Ibid.*
21. *Ibid.*
22. *Ibid. Register*, 23 Cong., 2 Sess., pp. 540-551.
23. *Register*, 23 Cong., 2 Sess., pp. 540-551.
24. Mason, p. 36.
25. *Messages*, III, p. 146.
26. *Ibid.*, p. 232.
27. *Ibid.*
28. *Ibid.*
29. Mason, pp. 26-27.
30. *Ibid.*, p. 79.
31. *National Intelligencer*, March 3, 1837.
32. *Messages*, III, p. 284.
33. *National Intelligencer*, March 6, 1837.
34. Clinton Rossiter, *The American Presidency*, pp. 62-63.
35. *Ibid.*, p. 72.
36. *Ibid.*
37. Edward S. Corwin, *The President: Office and Powers*, p. 24.
38. *Ibid.*, pp. 29-30.

CHAPTER V

1. *National Intelligencer*, July 21, 1841.
2. *Jonesborough Whig* (Tennessee), April 28, 1841.
3. *Ibid.*
4. *Ibid.*, July 15, 1841.
5. Mason, *Veto Power*, p. 76; *Jonesborough Whig*, July 15, 1841.
6. *Jonesborough Whig*, July 15, 1841.
7. Oliver P. Chitwood, *John Tyler: Champion of the Old South*, p. 223.
8. *Messages*, IV., p. 63.
9. *Ibid.*
10. *Ibid.*
11. *Ibid.*, p. 66.
12. *Ibid.*
13. *Congressional Globe*, 27 Cong., 1 Sess., p. 338 (hereafter cited as *Globe*); Chitwood, p. 227.
14. *Globe*, 27 Cong., 1 Sess., p. 339.
15. *Ibid.*, p. 340.

16. *Ibid.*, p. 342.
17. *Ibid.*, p. 346.
18. *Jonesborough Whig*, August 25, 1841.
19. *Ibid.*, September 1, 1841.
20. *Ibid.*
21. *National Intelligencer*, August 17, 1841.
22. *Jonesborough Whig*, September 1, 1841. The paper now changed its mast head to read "one term, a National Bank, No one man power, No Virginia abstractions."
23. These various press reports were gleaned from the *Jonesborough Whig* in its editions from September 1 to September 8, 1841.
24. Peter R. Levin, *Seven By Chance*, p. 35.
25. *Alabama Journal*, September 1, 1841.
26. *Messages*, IV, pp. 68-72. Chitwood, p. 245. Mason p. 76.
27. *Messages*, IV, p. 68.
28. *Ibid.*
29. *Globe*, 27 Cong., 1 Sess., p. 447.
30. *Ibid.*, p. 448.
31. *Ibid.*, p. 449
32. *Jonesborough Whig*, September 22, 1841.
33. *Ibid.*, September 29, 1841.
34. *National Intelligencer*, September 10, 1841.
35. *Jonesborough Whig*, October 13, 1841.
36. *Alabama Journal*, October 27, 1841.
37. William B. Hesseltine, *A History of the South, 1607-1936*, p. 295.
38. This tariff had been enacted in 1833 as a way out of the nullification crisis with South Carolina. By its terms, the tariff was to be gradually lowered until it was uniformly twenty percent *ad valorem*.
39. Charles M. Wiltse, *John C. Calhoun, Sectionalist*, p. 76.
40. William M. Meigs, *The Life of John Caldwell Calhoun*, p. 234.
41. Wiltse, p. 78. Meigs, p. 234; Arthur Styron, *The Cast-Iron Man: John C. Calhoun and American Democracy*, p. 252; *Globe*, 27 Cong., 1 Sess., p. 266.
42. Meigs, p. 234.
43. *Ibid.*, p. 235.

44. Styron, p. 252. Calhoun's theory of concurrent majorities was quite similar to Madison's belief in the constitutional convention of Minority Checks.

45. Styron, p. 253.

46. Margaret L. Coit, *John C. Calhoun, American Patriot*, p. 350.

47. Levin, pp. 44-45.

48. *Messages*, IV. pp. 180-183.

49. *Jonesborough Whig*, July 13, 1842.

50. *Ibid.*, July 20, 1842.

51. *National Intelligencer*, June 30, 1842.

52. *Globe*, 27 Cong., 2 Sess., p. 695.

53. *Ibid.*, p. 702.

54. *Ibid.*, p. 703.

55. *Ibid.*, p. 704.

56. *Ibid.*, p. 707.

57. *Ibid.*, p. 709.

58. *Ibid.*, p. 710.

59. *Messages*, IV, pp. 183-189.

60. *Globe*, 27 Cong., 2 Sess., p. 873.

61. *Ibid.*, p. 273.

62. *Ibid.*, p. 880.

63. *Ibid.*, p. 882.

64. *Alabama Journal*, August 17, 1842.

65. *Jonesborough Whig*, August 24, 1842.

66. *Alabama Journal*, November 16, 1842.

67. *National Intelligencer*, August 10, 1842.

68. *Jacksonville Republican*, August 17, 1842.

69. *Ibid.*, *August 24*, 1842.

70. *Globe*, 27 Cong., 2 Sess., p. 895.

71. *National Intelligencer*, August 17, 1842.

72. *Globe*, 27 Cong., 2 Sess., p. 899.

73. *Ibid.*, pp. 900-901.

74. *Ibid.*, p. 905.

75. In January, 1843, Botts "felt out" the House members on several articles of impeachment only to have them decisively defeated.

76. Chitwood, p. 249.

77. *Ibid.*

78. Chitwood discussed the charge in *Ibid.*, pp. 259-268, *passim*.

79. *Ibid.*

CHAPTER VI

1. *Globe*, 27 Cong., 2 Sess., p. 939.

2. *Ibid.*, p. 940.

3. *Ibid.*, p. 948.

4. *Ibid.*

5. See pp. 65-66 for his reasons for rejecting the two tariff bills.

6. *National Intelligencer*, November 28, 1842.

7. *Globe*, 27 Cong., 2 Sess., p. 862.

8. *Ibid.*, p. 861.

9. *Ibid.*, p. 860.

10. *Ibid.*, p. 861.

11. *Ibid.*, p. 862.

12. *Ibid.*, p. 949.

13. *Messages*, IV, p. 256.

14. *Ibid.*

15. *National Intelligencer*, November 28, 1842.

16. *Globe*, 28 Cong., 1 Sess., p. 668.

17. *Messages*, IV, p. 329.

18. *Ibid.*

19. *Ibid.*

20. *Federal Constitution*, Article 1, Section 7.

21. See p. 50.

22. *Messages*, IV, p. 330.

23. *Ibid.*

24. *Ibid.*, p. 332.

25. *Ibid.*

26. *Globe*, 28 Cong., 1 Sess., p. 675.

27. *Ibid.*, p. 676.

28. *Ibid.*

29. *Ibid.*

30. *National Intelligencer*, June 12, 1844.

31. *Baltimore Sun*, June 12, 1844.

32. *Richmond Enquirer*, June 18, 1844.

33. *Ibid.*, March 7, 1845.

34. *Messages*, IV, p. 366.

35. *Ibid.*, p. 367.

36. *Baltimore Sun*, March 5, 1845.

37. *Richmond Enquirer*, March 7, 1845.

38. *Globe*, 28 Cong., 2 Sess., p. 396.

39. *Ibid.*, p. 396. *Baltimore Sun*, March 5, 1845. *Richmond Enquirer*, March 7, 1845.

40. *Baltimore Sun*, March 5, 1845.

41. *Globe*, 28 Cong., 2 Sess., p. 396.

42. Mason, *Veto Power*, p. 147.

CHAPTER VII

1. See p. 21.

2. *Messages*, IV, p. 460.

3. *Jonesborough Whig*, August 19, 1846.

4. *Messages*, IV, p. 462.

5. *Ibid.*, p. 464.

6. *Ibid.*

7. *Ibid.,* p. 463.
8. See pp. 26-27.
9. *Messages,* IV, p. 465.
10. *Globe,* 29 Cong., 1 Sess., p. 1183.
11. See pp _____.
12. *Globe,* 29 Cong., 1 Sess., p. 1184.
13. *Ibid.,* p. 1185.
14. The Walker Tariff.
15. *Globe,* 29 Cong., 1 Sess., pp. 1185-1186.
16. *Ibid.,* p. 1188.
17. *Ibid.,* p. 1189.
18. *National Intelligencer,* August 3, 1846.
19. *Ibid.,* August 5, 1846.
20. *Jonesborough Whig,* August 19, 1846.
21. *Ibid.,* September 2, 1846.
22. *Baltimore Sun,* August 4, 1846.
23. *Richmond Enquirer,* August 7, 1846.
24. *Ibid.,* August 4, 1846.
25. *Ibid.,* August 7, 1846.
26. *Ibid.*
27. *Ibid.,* August 8, 1846.
28. *Ibid.*
29. *Ibid.,* August 7, 1846.
30. *Jacksonville Republican,* September 9, 1846.
31. *National Intelligencer,* August 6, 1846.
32. *Richmond Enquirer,* September 12, 1846.
33. *Ibid.*
34. *Messages,* IV, p. 467.
35. *Ibid.,* p. 468.
36. *Ibid.,* pp. 468-469.
37. *Globe,* 29 Cong., 1 Sess., p. 1219.
38. See pp. 3-4.
39. *Globe,* 29 Cong., 1 Sess., p. 1219.
40. *Ibid.,* p. 1220.
41. *Ibid.*
42. *National Intelligencer,* August 11, 1846.
43. *Baltimore Sun,* August 12, 1846.
44. *Ibid.,* August 10, 1846.
45. *Ibid.,* August 12, 1846,
46. *Jonesborough Whig,* September 9, 1846.
47. *Ibid.*
48. *Richmond Enquirer,* September 26, 1846.
49. *Ibid.*
50. *Messages,* IV, pp. 615-620.
51. *Ibid.,* p. 613.
52. *Ibid.,* pp. 616-618.
53. *Ibid.,* p. 626.
54. *Globe,* 30 Cong., 1 Sess., p. 34.
55. *Ibid.,* p. 36.
56. *Ibid.,* p. 37.
57. *Ibid.*
58. *Richmond Enquirer,* March 11, 1847.

CHAPTER VIII

1. *Eufaula* (Alabama) *Democrat,* August 1, 1848.
2. Holman Hamilton, *Zachary Taylor, Soldier in the White House,* p. 383.
3. See pp. 83-84.
4. *Messages,* V, p. 248.
5. *Ibid.;* Roy F. Nichols, *Franklin Pierce: Young Hickory from the Granite Hills,* p. 349.
6. See pp. _____.
7. *Messages,* V, p. 253.
8. *Ibid.* Nichols, p. 349.
9. *Messages,* V, pp. 253-254.
10. *Globe,* 33 Cong., 1 Sess., p. 1064.
11. *New York Times,* May 3, 1854.
12. *Richmond Enquirer,* May 6, 1854.
13. *Messages,* V. p. 260.
14. *Ibid.,* p. 270.
15. *Ibid.,* p. 271.
16. *Richmond Enquirer,* August 7, 1854.
17. *Messages,* V, p. 308.
18. *Nichols,* p. 377.
19. *New York Times,* February 20, 1855.
20. *Richmond Enquirer,* February 20, 1855.
21. *New York Times,* February 20, 1855.
22. Nichols, p. 377.
23. *New York Times,* March 5, 1855.
24. Nichols, p. 377.
25. *New York Times,* March 6. 1855.
26. *Ibid.*
27. *Richmond Enquirer,* March 9, 1855.
28. See p. 102.
29. *Messages,* V, pp. 386-388.
30. *Globe,* 34 Cong., 2 Sess., p. 1270.
31. *New York Times,* May 23, 1856.
32. *Ibid.,* July 10, 1856.
33. *Globe,* 34 Cong., 2 Sess., p. 1550.
34. Mason, pp. 148-149.
35. *New York Times,* July 9, 1856.
36. *Messages,* V, p. 543.
37. *Globe,* 35 Cong., 1 Sess., p. 3002.
38. *Messages,* V, p. 543.
39. *Ibid.,* p. 544.
40. *Ibid.,* p. 545.
41. *Ibid.,* p. 546.

42. *Ibid.*, p. 547.
43. *Ibid.*, p. 548.
44. *Ibid.*, p. 550.
45. *Globe*, 35 Cong., 2 Sess., p. 1414.
46. *Ibid.*, *New York Times*, February 26, 1859.
47. *Globe*, 35 Cong., 2 Sess., p. 1414.
48. *Messages*, V, pp. 600-601.
49. *Ibid.*, p. 602.
50. *Ibid.*, p. 605.
51. *Globe*, 35 Cong., 1 Sess., p. 670.
52. *Ibid.*, p. 672.
53. *Ibid.*, p. 674.
54. *Ibid.*, pp. 673-677, *passim.*
55. *Ibid.*, p. 676.
56. *New York Times*, February 9, 1860.
57. *Messages*, V, pp. 607-608.
58. Known today as "way-pouch" mail, the term referred to bags of mail opened at substations between the points of origin and destination. Mail belonging to residents served by the substation would be taken out, mail being sent by residents would be placed in the bag and then carried to the next substation. Through mail was not opened between origin and destination.
59. *New York Times*, June 30, 1860.
60. *Globe*, 36 Cong., 1 Sess., p. 1775.
61. *Messages*, V, pp. 608-609.
62. See pp. 107-108.
63. *Messages*, V, pp. 608-614.
64. *New York Times*, June 25, 1860.
65. *Brownlow's Knoxville Whig*, July 14, 1860.
66. Philip S. Klien, *President James Buchanan*, p. 346.
67. *Ibid.*, p. 347.
68. *Messages*, V, pp. 670-672.

CHAPTER IX

1. *Messages*, VI, p. 88.
2. *Ibid.*
3. *Ibid.*, p. 271.
4. J. G. Randall, *Lincoln the President: Springfield to Gettysburg*, Vol. II, p. 228.
5. *Ibid.*
6. J. G. Randall, *Lincoln the President: Midstream*, Vol. III, p. 120.
7. *New York Times*, July 10, 1864.
8. See pp. 24-25.
9. *Messages*, VI, p. 536. The resolution placed certain troops of Missouri on an equal footing with others as to bounties. The veto was never returned to Congress, but deposited with the State Department.
10. Mason, *Veto Power*, p. 47.
11. Corwin, *The Presidency*, p. 27.
12. *Messages*, VI, pp. 398-399.
13. *Ibid.*, pp. 399-403.
14. *New York Times*, February 20 and 21, 1866.
15. *Globe*, 39 Cong., 1 Sess., pp. 3839-3840.
16. *New York Times*, February 21, 1866.
17. *Ibid.*, February 22, 1866.
18. *Messages*, VI, pp. 405-413.
19. *Globe*, 39 Cong., 1 Sess., p. 1801.
20. Lloyd P. Stryker, *Andrew Johnson: A Study in Courage*, p. 291.
21. *New York Times*, March 28, 1866.
22. *Brownlow's Knoxville Whig and Rebel Ventilator*, April 18 and 25, 1866.
23. *Messages*, VI, pp. 414-416.
24. *Globe*, 39 Cong., 1 Sess., p. 2713.
25. *Messages*, VI, pp. 418-421.
26. *New York Times*, June 16, 1866.
27. *Messages*, VI, p. 423.
28. *New York Times*, July 17, 1866.
29. Claude Bowers, *The Tragic Era*, p. 115.
30. *Messages*, VI, pp. 473-481.
31. *Globe*, 39 Cong., 1 Sess., p. 306.
32. *Ibid.*, p. 309.
33. *New York Times*, January 8, 1867.
34. Stryker, pp. 418-419.
35. *Messages*, VI, p. 484.
36. *New York Times*, January 29, 1867.
37. *Messages*, VI, p. 490.
38. J. G. Randall and David Donald, *Civil War and Reconstruction*, p. 609.
39. Mason, p. 43.
40. Stryker, p. 431. Bowers, p. 156.
41. *Messages*, VI, p. 494.
42. *Ibid.*, p. 498.
43. *Ibid.*, pp. 498-500.
44. *New York Times*, March 3, 1867.
45. *Ibid.*, March 4, 1867.
46. *Messages*, VI, pp. 531-535.
47. *New York Times*, March 25, 1867.
48. *Messages*, VI, pp. 537-545.
49. Randall and Donald, *Civil War and Reconstruction*, p. 600.
50. *Messages*, VI, pp. 646-647.
51. *Globe*, 40 Cong., 2 Sess., pp. 2096-2097.

52. *Ibid.*, p. 2097.
53. *Messages*, VI, p. 648.
54. *New York Times*, June 21, 1868.
55. *Messages*, VI, pp. 650-651.
56. *New York Times*, June 26, 1868.
57. *Messages*, VI, pp. 651-652.
58. *Ibid.*, p. 654.
59. *Ibid.*, p. 705.
60. Mason, p. 72.
61. *Knoxville Weekly Whig*, March 3, 1869.
62. See pp. 24-25, 34.
63. Corwin, p. 27.
64. *Federal Constitution*, Article 1, Section 7.

PART II

CHAPTER X

1. Henry M. Lewis, Jr., *The Veto Power of the President*, pp. 3-20.
2. *Messages*, VII, p. 80.
3. *Hartford Daily Courant*, January 12, 1870.
4. *Congressional Globe*, 41 Cong., 1 Sess., pp. 1500-01.
5. *Ibid*, p. 3950.
6. Mason, p. 155.
7. *Messages*, VII, pp. 389-390.
8. *Ibid.*, p. 388.
9. *Globe*, 44 Cong., 1 Sess., p. 5664.
10. *Ibid.*, p. 5665.
11. Mason, p. 160.
12. *Messages*, VII, p. 172
13. *New York Times*, June 3, 1872.
14. *Messages*, VII, p. 174.
15. *Ibid.*, p. 215.
16. *Ibid.*
17. *Ibid.*, p. 216.
18. A. Barton Hepburn, *A History of Currency in the United States*, p. 221.
19. Don C. Barrett, *The Greenbacks and Resumption of Specie Payment, 1862-1879*, p. 179.
20. William B. Hesseltine, *Ulysses S. Grant: Politician*, p. 333.
21. Barrett, p. 178.
22. W. E. Woodward, *Meet General Grant*, p. 453.
23. Hesseltine, p. 334.
24. Hepburn, p. 221.
25. Woodward, p. 453.
26. Barrett, p. 178.
27. Irwin Unger, *The Greenback Era: A Social and Political History of American Finance, 1865-1879*, p. 241.
28. Woodward, p. 454.
29. *Messages*, VII, pp. 269-270.
30. *Ibid.*, p. 271.
31. Unger, p. 243.
32. *New York Times*, April 23, 1874.
33. *Ibid.*
34. *Hartford Courant*, April 24, 1874.
35. *New York Times*, April 24, 1874.
36. Unger, p. 243.
37. *New York Times*, April 24, 1874.
38. *Hartford Courant*, April 25, 1874.
39. *New York Times*, April 24, 1874.
40. Mason, p. 158.
41. Unger, p. 244.
42. Hesseltine, p. 337.
43. Woodward, p. 454.
44. Unger, 248.
45. H. J. Eckenrode, *Rutherford B. Hayes: Statesman of Reunion*, p. 293.
46. *Ibid.*, p. 294. Hepburn, pp. 280-281. Charles R. Williams, *The Life of Rutherford Birchard Hayes: Nineteenth President of the United States*, pp. 120-121.
47. T. Harry Williams, (ed.), *Hayes: The Diary of a President, 1875-1881*, pp. 115-116. Hereafter cited as *Diary*.
48. Eckenrode, p. 287.
49. *Diary*, pp. 121-122.
50. *Ibid.*, p. 122.
51. The Secretary of the Treasury had changed his mind on the bill after the Senate amendment was added to it. He felt that the limited coinage would not have any adverse effects. Since the silver bill was widely supported by the American public, he thought it wise to make no strong objections to its passage. *Sherman's Recollections*. Chapter XXXII. Quoted in Charles Williams, p. 121.
52. *Diary*, p. 122.
53. *Messages*, VII, pp. 486-488.
54. *Congressional Record*, 45 Cong., 2 Sess., p. 1420. Hereafter cited as *Record*.
55. *Ibid.*, p. 1411.
56. Hepburn, p. 281. Eckenrode, p. 297.
57. Eckenrode, p. 296.
58. *Ibid.*, p. 297.
59. *Messages*, VII., p. 380.
60. *Ibid.*, p. 381.
61. *New York Times*, April 19, 1876.
62. *Hartford Courant*, April 19, 1876.
63. *Messages*, VII, pp. 430-1.

64. *Ibid.*, p. 432.

65. Of course, there is not, and never was, a Republic of Pretoria. That city is the capital of the Transvaal region, and since 1910 it has been the administrative capital of the Union of South Africa.

66. *Messages*, VII, p. 524.

67. *Diary*, p. 197.

68. *Ibid.*, p. 199.

69. *Ibid.*, p. 217.

70. *Messages*, VII, p. 528.

71. *Ibid.*, p. 531.

72. Mason, p. 162.

73. *Hartford Courant*, April 29, 1879.

74. Charles Williams, p. 195.

75. *Messages*, VII, p. 535.

76. *Diary*, p. 219. Charles Williams, p. 195.

77. *Diary*, pp. 219-220.

78. Mason, p. 163.

79. Charles Williams, p. 198.

80. *Messages*, VII, p. 540.

81. Record, 46 Cong., 1 Sess., pp. 1710-1711.

82. *Messages*, VII, p. 542.

83. *Diary*, p. 232.

84. Mason, p. 163.

85. *Messages*, VII, p. 546.

86. *Record*, 46 Cong., 1 Sess., p. 2442.

87. *Messages*, VII, p. 591.

88. *Diary*, p. 276.

89. *Ibid.*, pp. 596-97.

90. *Record*, 48 Cong., 1 Sess., pp. 5933-34; George Frederick Howe, *Chester A. Arthur: A Quarter Century of Machine Politics*, pp. 251-52.

91. Howe, p. 252.

92. *Record*, 48 Cong., 1 Sess., p. 5933. *Hartford Courant*, July 3, 1884.

93. *Record*, 48 Cong., 1 Sess., p. 5933.

94. *Hartford Courant*, July 3, 1884.

95. Mason, p. 165.

96. Samuel Flagg Bemis (ed.) *The American Secretaries of State and Their Diplomacy*, p. 251.

97. *Ibid.*

98. George M. Stephenson, *A History of American Immigration, 1820-1924*, p. 260.

99. Bemis, p. 252.

100. *Diary*, p. 189.

101. Bemis, p. 253.

102. *Messages*, VII, pp. 518-19.

103. Mason, p. 162.

104. Bemis, p. 254.

105. Stephenson, p. 261.

106. *Ibid.*, p. 262.

107. *Record*, 47 Cong., 1 Sess., pp. 2553-2562.

108. *Messages*, VIII, p. 112.

109. *Ibid.*, p. 116.

110. *Ibid.*, p. 118.

111. *Record*, 47 Cong., 1 Sess., p. 2607.

112. *Ibid.*, p. 2616.

113. *Ibid.*, p. 2608.

114. *Ibid.*, p. 2611.

115. *Ibid.*, p. 2617.

116. Stephenson, p. 262.

117. *Messages*, VIII, p. 118. Howe, p. 169.

118. *Messages*, VIII, p. 119.

119. *San Francisco Daily Examiner*, July 2, 1882.

CHAPTER XI

1. Allan Nevins, *Grover Cleveland: A Study in Courage*, p. 328.

2. *Ibid.*, p. 327.

3. *Ibid.*

4. *Hartford Courant*, July 7, 1888.

5. Horace Samuel Merrill, *Bourbon Leader: Grover Cleveland and the Democratic Party*, p. 106.

6. *Hartford Courant*, July 6, 1888.

7. *Ibid.*

8. Nevins, p. 327.

9. *Ibid.*

10. *Cleveland Plain Dealer*, August 5, 1886.

11. *Record*, 49 Cong., 1 Sess., p. 6694.

12. *Ibid.*

13. *Ibid.*, p. 7058.

14. *Ibid.*, p. 7059.

15. *Ibid.*, p. 7060.

16. *Ibid.*, p. 7907.

17. Merrill, p. 106.

18. F. E. Goodrich, *The Life and Public Services of Grover Cleveland*, p. 447.

19. *Ibid.*

20. *Record*, 49 Cong., 2 Sess., pp. 1639-40.

21. *Ibid.*, p. 1639.

22. *Ibid.*

23. *Ibid.*, p. 2222.

24. *Ibid.*, p. 2223.

25. *Ibid.*

26. *Ibid.*, p. 2226.

27. Merrill, p. 107.

28. Nevins, p. 331.

29. *Record*, 49 Cong., 2 Sess., p. 1875.

30. *Ibid.*

31. Nevins, p. 331.

32. *Record,* 49 Cong., 2 Sess., p. 1876.

33. *Ibid.,* 49 Cong., 1 Sess., p. 2297.

34. *Cleveland Plain Dealer,* July 2, 1886.

35. *Ibid.*

36. *Record,* 50 Cong., 2 Sess., p. 2550.

37. *Ibid.,* p. 2552.

38. *Ibid.,* p. 2553.

39. *Ibid.,* pp. 2556-7.

40. *Ibid.,* p. 2562.

41. *Ibid.,* 49 Cong., 1 Sess. p. 2616.

42. *Cleveland Plain Dealer,* July 3, 1886.

43. *Ibid.,* July 12, 1886.

44. *Record,* 49 Cong., 1 Sess., p. 6719.

45. *Ibid.,* p. 2613-14.

46. *Ibid.,* p. 2616.

47. *Ibid.,* p. 2719.

48. *Cleveland Plain Dealer,* July 13, 1886.

49. *Record,* 52 Cong., 1 Sess., p. 630.

50. *Cleveland Plain Dealer,* July 28, 1892.

51. *Washington Post,* July 30, 1892.

52. *Omaha World Herald,* July 31, 1892.

53. *Cleveland Plain Dealer,* July 30, 1892.

54. *Washington Post,* March 4, 1893.

55. *Record,* 52 Cong., 2 Sess., p. 2433.

56. *Ibid.,* p. 2435.

57. *Ibid.*

58. *Ibid.,* p. 2524.

59. Nevins, p. 600.

60. *Ibid.*

61. *Ibid.*

62. *Record,* 53 Cong., 1 Sess., pp. 3352-53.

63. *Ibid.,* pp. 3351-53.

64. Allan Nevins records in his biography of Cleveland that the President summoned Speaker Crisp to the White House the night before the veto was to be considered. Cleveland told Crisp that the veto could be sustained if the question were voted upon immediately without any debate. The President had already picked a man to move the previous question and he wanted Crisp to recognize him and refuse all who wanted to debate. At first, Crisp refused, saying that his political career would be endangered because Georgians generally favored free silver. When Cleveland convinced the Speaker that the fortunes of the country were more important than anyone's political future, Crisp agreed to the President's request. This incident, of course, explains the acrimony of the next day's session. Nevins, pp. 602-03.

65. *Record,* 53 Cong., 1 Sess., pp. 3459-60.

66. *Ibid.,* 54 Cong., 1 Sess., p. 2296.

67. *Ibid.*

68. *Ibid.,* p. 2301.

69. *Ibid.,* p. 5520.

70. *Ibid.*

71. *Ibid.,* p. 5521.

72. *Ibid.,* p. 5524.

73. *Ibid.,* p. 5526.

74. *Ibid.,* p. 6381.

75. *Ibid.,* 54 Cong., 2 Sess., p. 1678.

76. *Record,* 54 Cong., 2 Sess., pp. 1678-79.

77. *Ibid.,* p. 1680.

78. *Ibid.,* p. 1681.

79. *Ibid.,* 54 Cong., 1 Sess., p. 1682.

80. *Ibid.,* p. 1683. *New York Daily Tribune,* February 10, 1897.

81. *Record,* 54 Cong., 1 Sess., p. 6027.

82. *Washington Post,* June 4, 1896.

83. *Record,* 54 Cong., 1 Sess., p. 6011.

84. *New York Daily Tribune,* June 3, 1896.

85. *Record,* 54 Cong., 1 Sess., pp. 6029-30.

86. *Ibid.,* p. 6030.

87. *Ibid.,* p. 6039.

88. *Ibid.,* p. 6035.

89. *Ibid.,* p. 6042.

90. *Ibid.,* p. 6038.

91. *Ibid.,* p. 6040.

92. *Ibid.,* p. 6045.

93. Nevins, p. 725.

94. *Ibid.*

95. Margaret Leech, *In The Days of McKinley,* p. 384.

96. *Messages,* X, pp. 186-188.

97. *Ibid.,* XV, pp. 7151-52.

98. *Washington Evening Star,* May 24, 1908.

99. *Ibid. Record,* 60 Cong., 1 Sess., p. 6866.

100. *Washington Evening Star,* February 6, 1909.

101. *Cleveland Plain Dealer,* February 6, 1909.

102. *Washington Post,* February 4, 1909.

103. *New York Tribune,* February 6, 1909. *Messages,* XV, pp. 7176-78.

CHAPTER XII

1. Henry F. Pringle, *The Life and Times of William Howard Taft*, pp. 418-431.

2. *Ibid.*, p. 421.

3. *Ibid.*, p. 419.

4. *Messages*, XVI, p. 7622.

5. *Record*, 62 Cong., 1 Sess., pp. 4167-68.

6. *Messages*, XVI, p. 7619.

7. *Ibid.*, pp. 7619-7625.

8. *San Francisco Examiner*, August 18, 1911.

9. *Record*, 62 Cong., 1 Sess., p. 4145.

10. *Ibid.*, p. 4146.

11. *Ibid.*, pp. 4146-47.

12. *Ibid.*, pp. 4146-4170.

13. *Ibid.*, p. 4170.

14. *Messages*, XVI, pp. 7626-7629.

15. *Record*, 62 Cong., 1 Sess., pp. 4172-3.

16. *Ibid.*, p. 4174.

17. *San Francisco Examiner*, August 19, 1911.

18. *Messages*, XVI, p. 7636.

19. *Record*, 62 Cong., 2 Sess., pp. 10834-45.

20. *Ibid.*, p. 10845.

21. *Ibid.*, p. 10943.

22. *San Francisco Examiner*, August 23, 1911.

23. *Messages*, XVI, pp. 7638-39.

24. *Ibid.*, p. 7640.

25. *Ibid.*, pp. 7641-42.

26. *San Francisco Examiner*, August 16, 1911.

27. *Ibid.*, August 19, 1911.

28. *Ibid.*

29. *Ibid.*

30. *Ibid.*

31. *Messages*, XVI, pp. 7752-58.

32. *Record*, 62 Cong., 2 Sess., p. 11027.

33. *Ibid.*, p. 11035.

34. *Ibid.*, 62 Cong., 3 Sess., p. 4838.

35. *Ibid.*

36. *Ibid.*, 62 Cong., 2 Sess., p. 10318.

37. *Ibid.*, p. 11796.

38. Stephenson, p. 154.

39. *Record*, 62 Cong., 3 Sess., p. 3412.

40. *Messages*, XVII, pp. 7847-51.

41. *Record*, 62 Cong., 3 Sess., p. 3309 and pp. 3312-13.

42. *Ibid.*, p. 3307.

43. *Ibid.*, p. 3310.

44. *Ibid.*, p. 3318.

45. *Atlanta Constitution*, February 15, 1913.

46. *San Francisco Examiner*, February 15, 1913.

47. *Atlanta Constitution*, February 15, 1913.

48. *Record*, 62 Cong., 3 Sess., p. 3421.

49. *Ibid.*, p. 3429.

50. *Atlanta Constitution*, February 28, 1913.

51. *Record*, 62 Cong., 3 Sess., pp. 4292-96.

52. *Ibid.*, p. 4297.

53. *Atlanta Constitution*, February 28, 1913.

54. *Record*, 62 Cong., 3 Sess., p. 4299.

55. *Ibid.*, p. 4434.

56. *Ibid.*, pp. 4434-42.

57. *Ibid.*, p. 4447.

58. *Messages*, XVII, pp. 8043-44.

59. *Record*, 63 Cong., 3 Sess., p. 3031.

60. *San Francisco Examiner*, February 3, 1915.

61. Arthur S. Link, *Woodrow Wilson and the Progressive Era: 1900-1917*, p. 61.

62. *Record*, 63 Cong., 3 Sess., pp. 3013-77, *passim*.

63. *Ibid.*

64. Link, *The New Freedom*, Vol. 2., p. 276.

65. *Record*, 63 Cong., 3 Sess., p. 3077.

66. *Washington Evening Star*, February 5, 1915.

67. *Record*, 64 Cong., 2 Sess., p. 2443.

68. *Ibid.*, p. 2619.

69. *Ibid.*

70. *Ibid.*, p. 2456-7.

71. *San Francisco Examiner*, February 2, 1917.

72. *Washington Evening Star*, February 5, 1917.

73. *Record*, 64 Cong., 2 Sess., p. 2629.

74. Stephenson, pp. 169-170.

75. *Record*, 66 Cong., 1 Sess., p. 4008.

76. *Messages*, XVIII, p. 8758.

77. *Ibid.*, pp. 8760-61.

78. *Record*, 66 Cong., 1 Sess., p. 4009.

79. *Messages*, XVIII, p. 8799.

80. *Washington Evening Star*, October 28, 1919.

81. *Atlanta Constitution*, October 28, 1919.

82. *Ibid.*

83. *Record,* 66 Cong., 1 Sess., p. 7611.
84. *Ibid.,* pp. 7631-34.
85. *Ibid.,* p. 7634.
86. *Washington Evening Star,* October 28, 1919; *Atlanta Constitution,* October 28, 1919.
87. *Record,* 66 Cong., 2 Sess., p. 7805.
88. *Washington Evening Star,* May 21, 1920.
89. *Record,* 66 Cong., 2 Sess., p. 7805.
90. *Washington Evening Star,* May 28, 1920.
91. *Record,* 66 Cong., 2 Sess., p. 7806.
92. *Ibid.,* pp. 7806-7.
93. *Ibid.,* p. 7809.
94. *Washington Evening Star,* January 2, 1921.
95. *Record,* 66 Cong., 3 Sess., p. 876.
96. *Ibid.,* p. 878.
97. *Ibid.,* p. 949.
98. *Washington Evening Star,* January 4, 1921.
99. *Record,* 66 Cong., 3 Sess., p. 2684; *Washington Evening Star,* February 5, 1921.
100. *Atlanta Constitution,* February 6, 1921.
101. *Record,* 66 Cong., 3 Sess., p. 2685.
102. *Ibid.,* p. 2719.

CHAPTER XIII

1. *New York Times,* May 21, 1928.
2. John D. Hicks. *Republican Ascendancy, 1921-1933,* p. 52.
3. *Ibid.*
4. *Record,* 67 Cong., 2 Sess., pp. 12981-82.
5. *Ibid.,* p. 12981.
6. *Ibid.,* p. 12982.
7. *Ibid.,* p. 13004.
8. *New York Times,* September 19 & 20, 1922.
9. *Ibid.,* September 16, 1922.
10. *Ibid.,* September 21, 1922.
11. *Record,* 67 Cong., 2 Sess.. p. 12986.
12. *Ibid.,* p. 12983.
13. *Ibid.,* p. 12998.
14. *Ibid.,* p. 12990. *New York Times,* September 21, 1922.
15. *Record,* 67 Cong., 2 Sess., pp. 12999-13000.
16. *New York Times,* September 20, 1922.
17. *Ibid.,* September 21, 1922.
18. *Record,* 68 Cong., 1 Sess., pp. 7755-56.
19. *Washington Evening Star,* May 15, 1924.
20. *Ibid.,* May 16, 1924. *Record,* 68 Cong., 1 Sess., pp. 8870-8871.
21. *Record,* 68 Cong., 1 Sess., p. 8809.
22. *Ibid.,* p. 8812.
23. *Ibid.,* p. 8813.
24. *Ibid.,* pp. 8813-14.
25. *Washington Evening Star,* May 16, 1924.
26. *Atlanta Constitution,* May 16, 1924.
27. *Record,* 68 Cong., 1 Sess., p. 8871.
28. *Record,* 71 Cong., 2 Sess., p. 9911.
29. *Chicago Herald-Examiner,* June 3, 1930.
30. *Ibid.*
31. *Record,* 71 Cong., 2 Sess., p. 9876.
32. *Ibid.,* p. 9914.
33. *Ibid.,* 71 Cong., 3 Sess., pp. 6168-6170; Harris G. Warren, *Herbert Hoover and the Great Depression,* pp. 225-226.
34. *Washington Evening Star,* February 23, 1931.
35. *Ibid.,* February 24, 1931.
36. *Record,* 71 Cong., 3 Sess., p. 6171.
37. *Washington Evening Star,* February 26, 1931.
38. *Record,* 71 Cong., 3 Sess., p. 6230.
39. Arthur S. Link, *American Epoch,* p. 363.
40. *Record,* 71 Cong., 2 Sess., pp. 11827-28.
41. Hicks, *Republican Ascendancy,* pp. 198-199; Hicks, *Populist Revolt,* p. 417; Howard H. Quint and Robert H. Ferrell (eds.), *The Talkative President: The Off-the-Record Press Conferences of Calvin Coolidge,* p. 141.
42. *Record,* 69 Cong., 2 Sess., p. 4771.
43. *Ibid.,* p. 4772.
44. *Ibid.,* p. 4777.
45. Hicks, *Republican Ascendancy,* p. 199.
46. Claude M. Fuess, *Coolidge: The Man From Vermont,* p. 388.
47. *Record,* 70 Cong., 1 Sess., p. 9874.
48. *New York Times,* May 24, 1928.
49. *Record,* 70 Cong., 1 Sess., p. 9877.
50. *Ibid.,* p. 9879.

51. *Washington Post*, May 26, 1928.
52. *Record*, 70 Cong., 1 Sess., p. 9674.
53. *Ibid.*, p. 9769.
54. *Ibid.*, p. 9481.
55. *Ibid.*, 9667.
56. *Washington Post*, May 19, 1928.
57. *Ibid.*, May 25, 1928.
58. *Record*, 70 Cong., 1 Sess., p. 9482.
59. *Ibid.*, p. 9667.
60. *Washington Post*, May 19, 1928.
61. *Atlanta Constitution*, May 23, 1928.
62. *Ibid.*
63. *New York Times*, May 25, 1928.
64. *Washington Post*, May 28, 1928.
65. Hicks, *Republican Ascendancy*, p. 200.
66. Link, *American Epoch*, p. 271; Preston J. Hubbard, *Origins of the TVA: The Muscle Shoals Controversy, 1920-1932.*, pp. 217, 226, 235; *Washington Post*, May 23, 1928; Alfred Lief, *Democracy's Norris: The Biography of a Lonely Crusader*, p. 316.
67. *Washington Post*, May 14, 1928.
68. Lief, p. 316.
69. Hubbard, p. 235.
70. *Ibid.*
71. *New York Times*, June 9, 1928.
72. *New York Times*, January 22, 1929.
73. *Ibid.*, December 23, 1928.
74. *United States Reports*, vol. 279, p. 657.
75. *Ibid.*, pp. 657-58.
76. *Ibid.*, p. 659.
77. *Ibid.*, pp. 668-69. *New York Times*, March 12, 1929.
78. *United States Reports*, vol. 279, p. 662.
79. *Ibid.*
80. *Ibid.*, p. 664.
81. *Ibid.*, p. 680.
82. *Ibid.*, p. 692. *New York Times*, May 28, 1929.
83. Hubbard, p. 295. David Hinshaw, *Herbert Hoover: American Quaker*, p. 194.
84. Hubbard, p. 293.
85. *Ibid.*, p. 294.
86. Richard L. Neuberger and Stephen B. Kahn, *Integrity: The Life of George W. Norris*, p. 224.
87. *Washington Evening Star*, February 21, 1931.
88. *Record*, 71 Cong., 3 Sess., p. 7098.

89. William S. Myers and Walter H. Newton, *The Hoover Administration: A Documented Narrative.*, p. 472.
90. Warren, p. 205; *Record*, 72 Cong., p. 15040.
91. *Ibid.*, p. 15041.
92. Warren, p. 206.
93. *Record*, 72 Cong., 1 Sess., p. 10035.
94. *Ibid.*, p. 10039.
95. *Record*, 72 Cong., 1 Sess., p. 14589.
96. Herbert Hoover, *The Memoirs of Herbert Hoover: The Cabinet and the Presidency, 1920-1933.*, p. 276. Cited hereafter as *Hoover Memoirs*.
97. *Ibid.*, p. 134.
98. Grayson L. Kirk, *Philippine Independence: Motives, Problems, and Prospects*, p. 119.
99. *Hoover Memoirs*, p. 360.
100. *Ibid.;* Kirk, p. 120; *Record*, 72 Cong., 2 Sess., pp. 1759-61. Of course, Hoover was deeply criticized for his rejection of Philippine independence. Although he had sympathized with the objective, he made little headway in getting the opposition to agree that now was not the propitious time for the freedom of the Islands. In his memoirs he relates that while the Independence bill was being discussed in Congress, he was visited by Manuel Quezon, President of the Philippine Senate, and by Sergio Osmena, President Pro-tem of the Philippine Senate, who told him that they hoped he would veto it. The reasons for their request were that they were not economically prepared for independence, and they did not want to stand alone against the threat of China and Japan. When Hoover asked why, then, they were lobbying publicly for independence, they said "that independence was their political issue in the Philippines and that unless they promoted it, their leadership would be lost to more dangerous elements. Disgusted, Hoover threatened to expose them, but they said they would claim that Hoover had entirely misunderstood them. Without evidence to support him, then, Hoover chose not to make an issue of their visit and of their statements. *Hoover Memoirs*, p. 361.
101. *Washington Evening Star*, Jan-

uary 13, 1933. *Record*, 72 Cong., 2 Sess., pp. 1761-1762.

102. *Ibid.*, p. 1762.

103. *Ibid.*, pp. 1768-69.

104. *Ibid.*, pp. 1911-1924.

105. This Act had created an elective Senate for the Philippines, had lowered voting requirements, and had allowed the Governor-General, with the advice of the Senate, to appoint heads of executive departments, except that of public instruction. The measure had come close to giving the Philippines a dominion status under United States sovereignty.

106. *Record*, 72 Cong., 2 Sess., pp. 1924-5.

107. *Hoover Memoirs*, p. 361.

108. William S. Myers, *The Foreign Policies of Herbert Hoover: 1929-1933*, p. 178.

109. Link, *American Epoch*, p. 460.

CHAPTER XIV

1. James MacGregor Burns, *Roosevelt: The Lion and the Fox*, p. 187.

2. *Record*, 76 Cong., 1 Sess., pp. 10718-19.

3. *Ibid.*, 3 Sess., pp. 649-650.

4. There were precedents now for returning bills in this manner. In March, 1934, on a bill for the reimbursement of Edward Wheeler for the loss of certain lands, and in July, 1935, on a relief bill for the Fidelity Trust Company of Baltimore, similar situations had arisen. The Senate Secretary, "in order to protect the interests of the Senate so that it might have the opportunity to reconsider the bill," accepted the vetoes and presented them to the Senate when it reconvened after a three day recess. *Veto Messages*, p. 111. This procedure was apparently unchallenged in 1934 and 1935.

5. *United States Reports*, Vol. 302, 1937, p. 590.

6. *Ibid.*, p. 594.

7. *Ibid.*, p. 598.

8. *Ibid.*, p. 599.

9. *Ibid.*, p. 606.

10. *Veto Messages*, p. 107.

11. *Record*, 76 Cong., 3 Sess., p. 9885.

12. *Ibid.*, p. 9889.

13. *Ibid.*, p. 5116.

14. *Washington Evening Star*, March 26, 1934.

15. *Ibid.*, March 27, 1934. *Record*, 73 Cong., 2 Sess., pp. 5540-5541.

16. *Washington Evening Star*, March 27, 1934.

17. *Record*, 73 Cong., 2 Sess., p. 5544.

18. *Washington Evening Star*, March 29, 1934.

19. *Record*, 73 Cong., 2 Sess., p. 5606.

20. *Washington Evening Star*, March 29, 1934.

21. *Ibid.*

22. *Ibid.*

23. *Ibid.*

24. *Ibid.*, May 17, 1935.

25. *New York Times*, May 17, 1935.

26. *Ibid.*, May 20, 1935; *Washington Evening Star*, May 18, 1935.

27. *The Daily Oklahoman*, May 18, 1935.

28. *St. Louis Post Dispatch*, May 21, 1935; *Washington Evening Star*, May 21, 1935.

29. *Washington Evening Star*, May 21, 1935.

30. *The Daily Oklahoman*, May 23, 1935.

31. *Washington Evening Star*, May 18, 1935.

32. *Ibid.*, May 22, 1935.

33. *Ibid.*, May 19, 23, 1935. *Record*, 74 Cong., 1 Sess., p. 8066.

34. *Record*, 74 Cong., 1 Sess., 8066; *Washington Evening Star*, May 23, 1935.

35. *Washington Evening Star*, May 23, 1935.

36. *Ibid.*

37. *New York Times*, May 21, 1935.

38. *Washington Evening Star*, May 23, 1935.

39. *Ibid.*, January 21, 27, 1936; *Record*, 74 Cong., 2 Sess., p. 975.

40. *Record*, 74 Cong., 2 Sess., p. 975; *Washington Evening Star*, January 21, 1936.

41. This veto was written in longhand by President Roosevelt, a device that had not been employed since Theodore Roosevelt. Copies of the veto message were given out "casually" by White House Secretary Stephen Early. He announced to news correspondents that he wanted to give out

a "little story." He then handed the newsmen a batch of mimeographed sheets, among which was included F.D.R.'s veto message. The reporters at first gave only a casual glance at the papers—and then there "was a mad rush for the telephones." *Washington Evening Star*, January 24, 1936.

42. *Record*, 74 Cong., 2 Sess., pp. 975-76; *Washington Evening Star*, January 24, 1936.

43. *Washington Evening Star*, January 27, 1936.

44. *Record*, 74 Cong., 2 Sess., p. 1015.

45. *Ibid.*, 75 Cong., 1 Sess., p. 5142.

46. *Ibid.*

47. *Ibid.*, p. 5160.

48. *Washington Evening Star*, June 1, 1937.

49. *Record*, 75 Cong., 1 Sess., p. 5165.

50. *Ibid.*, p. 5146.

51. This bill made beneficiaries of approximately 15,000 volunteers who had been in the Philippines at the close of the Spanish-American War. These personnel, having been instrumental in putting down the uprising led by Emiliano Acquinaldo, had re-enlisted in 1899 on the promise that they would receive the same travel pay as soldiers of the regular army. Roosevelt's veto of April 23, 1940, however, said that the cost would be one day's pay and one ration for each twenty miles covered between the Philippines and San Francisco, a distance of about 8,000 miles. The total cost of all this would be around $7 million. The men in question had already received transportation home by the government plus two extra months of pay at the time they were mustered out of service. Therefore, Roosevelt believed the Travel Bill would unduly favor the volunteer over the regular army personnel. Congress did not agree, however, and the veto was destroyed in the House 275-83, and in the Senate, 76-3. *Record*, 76 Cong., 3 Sess., pp. 5030, 5033, 5383.

52. *Record*, 75 Cong., 1 Sess., p. 7127.

53. *Ibid.*, pp. 7121-7132, *passim*.

54. *Ibid.*, p. 7132.

55. *Ibid.*, p. 7374.

56. *St. Louis Post Dispatch*, July 22, 1937.

57. *Ibid.*, June 16, 1938; *Record*, 75 Cong., 3 Sess., p. 9501, 9513.

58. *Record*, 76 Cong., 3 Sess., p. 7874.

59. *Ibid.*

60. *Ibid.*, pp. 8647-48.

61. *Ibid.*, p. 8648.

62. *Ibid.*, p. 8650.

63. *Ibid.*, p. 8649.

64. *Ibid.*, pp. 8650-51.

65. *Ibid.*, p. 8655.

66. *New York Times*, August 8, 1941.

67. *Record*, 77 Cong., 1 Sess., p. 6886.

68. *Ibid.*, p. 6810.

69. *New York Times*, August 8, 1941.

70. *Record*, 77 Cong., 1 Sess., p. 6886.

71. *Ibid.*, p. 6890.

72. *Ibid.*, p. 6896; *Washington Evening Star*, August 7, 1941.

73. *Record*, 77 Cong., 1 Sess. pp. 6895-96.

74. *New York Times*, August 8, 1941.

75. *Record*, 78 Cong., 1 Sess., p. 6488.

76. *Ibid.*

77. *Ibid.*

78. *Ibid.*

79. *Washington Evening Star*, June 26, 1943.

80. *Ibid.*, June 25, 1943.

81. *Record*, 78 Cong., 1 Sess., p. 6489.

82. *Ibid.*, pp. 6548-49.

83. *St. Louis Post Dispatch*, June 26, 1943.

84. *Washington Evening Star*, June 26, 1943.

85. *Ibid.*

86. *Ibid.*

87. *Ibid.*

88. *Ibid.*

89. *Ibid.*, June 25, 1943.

90. *St. Louis Post Dispatch*, June 21, 1943.

91. *Washington Evening Star*, July 11, 1943.

92. *Record*, 78 Cong., 1 Sess., pp. 7051-53.

93. *New York Times*, July 5, 1943.

94. *Washington Evening Star*, July 1, 1943.

95. *Record*, 78 Cong., 1 Sess., pp. 7054-55.

96. *New York Times,* July 3, 1943.

97. *Record,* 78 Cong., 2 Sess., p. 1959; *Washington Evening Star,* February 23, 1944; *St. Louis Post Dispatch,* February 17, 1944.

98. *Record,* 78 Cong., 2 Sess., pp. 1958-59; Donald Day, *Franklin D. Roosevelt's Own Story: Told in his Own Words from his Private and Public Papers,* p. 412; William D. Hassett, *Off the Record with F.D.R.: 1942-1945,* p. 235; Alben Barkley, *That Reminds Me,* p. 171.

99. *Washington Evening Star,* February 23, 1944.

100. *St. Louis Post Dispatch,* February 22, 1944.

101. *Record,* 78 Cong., 2 Sess., p. 2013.

102. *Washington Evening Star,* February 23, 1944.

103. *Ibid.; St. Louis Post Dispatch,* February 23, 1944.

104. *Washington Evening Star,* February 24, 1944.

105. *Ibid.,* February 25, 1944.

106. Hassett, p. 235.

107. *Washington Evening Star,* February 24, 1944.

108. Barkley, pp. 169-170.

109. *Record,* 78 Cong., 2 Sess., p. 2050.

110. *Washington Evening Star,* February 23, 1944.

111. *Ibid.,* February 24, 1944.

112. Barkley, p. 170.

Selected Bibliography

Alabama Journal, 1841-1842.

Annals of Congress: Containing the debates and proceedings of the first session of the Second Congress, the second session of the Fourth Congress, the third session of the Eleventh Congress, the first session of the Twelfth Congress, and the third session of the Thirteenth Congress. Washington: Gales and Seaton, (1792-1822).

Atlanta Constitution, 1913-1928.

Baltimore Sun, 1844-1846.

Barkley, Alben, *That Reminds Me.* Garden City, N.Y.: Doubleday and Co., Inc., 1954.

Barrett, Don C., *The Greenbacks and Resumption of Specie Payments, 1862-1879.* Cambridge: Harvard University Press, 1931.

Bassett, John Spencer, ed., *Correspondence of Andrew Jackson.* Vol. 4. Washington: Carnegie Institute of Washington, 1926.

————*The Life of Andrew Jackson.* New York: Macmillan Co., 1928.

Bemis, Samuel Flagg, ed., *The American Secretaries of State and Their Diplomacy.* Vol. 7. New York: Pageant Book Co., 1958.

Bowers, Claude, *Party Battles of the Jackson Period.* New York: Chautauqua Printers, 1922.

————*The Tragic Era.* Sentry edition. Boston: Houghton Mifflin Co., 1962.

Brownlow's Knoxville Whig, 1860.

Brownlow's Knoxville Whig and Rebel Ventilator, 1866.

Burns, James MacGregor, *Roosevelt: The Lion and the Fox.* New York: Harcourt, Brace, and World, Inc., 1956.

————*The Deadlock of Democracy: Four Party Politics in America.* Englewood Cliffs, New Jersey: Prentice-Hall, 1963.

Chicago Herald-Examiner, 1930.

Chitwood, Oliver P., *John Tyler: Champion of the Old South.* New York: D. Appleton Century Co., 1939.

Cleveland Plain Dealer, 1886, 1892, 1909.

Coit, Margaret L., *John C. Calhoun, American Patriot.* Sentry edition. Boston: Houghton Mifflin Co., 1961.

Congressional Globe: Washington: Blair and Rives, *et al,* 1841-1870.

Congressional Record. Washington: Government Printing Office, 1871-1945.

Corwin, Edwin S., *The President: Offices and Powers*. 2nd ed. New York: New York University Press, 1941.

Cresson, W. P. *James Monroe*. Chapel Hill: University of North Carolina Press, 1946.

Daily Oklahoman, 1935.

Day, Donald, *Franklin D. Roosevelt's Own Story: Told In His Own Words From His Private and Public Papers*. Boston: Little, Brown and Co., 1951.

Eckenrode, H. J., *Rutherford B. Hayes: Statesman of Reform*. Port Washington, New York: Kennikat Press, Inc., 1963.

Eufaula (Alabama) *Democrat*, 1848.

Federal Constitution. Article Four, Section Three, and Article One, Section Seven.

Freeman, Douglas Southall, *George Washington*. Vol. 4. New York: Charles Scribner, 1954.

Fuess, Claude M., *Coolidge: The Man From Vermont*. Boston: Little, Brown and Co., 1940.

Gale and Seaton Register: Containing the debates and proceedings of the first and second sessions of the Twenty-second Congress; and the second session of the Twenty-third Congress. Washington: Gale and Seaton. (1830-1837).

Goodrich, F. E., *The Life and Public Services of Grover Cleveland*. Cincinnati: Forshee Co., 1888.

Hamilton, Holman, *Zachary Taylor: Soldier in the White House*. Indianapolis: Bobbs-Merrill Co., 1951.

Hartford Courant, 1870-1888.

Hassett, William D., *Off the Record with F.D.R.: 1942-1945*. New Brunswick, New Jersey: Rutgers University Press, 1958.

Hepburn, A. Barton, *A History of Currency in the United States*. Rev. ed. New York: Macmillan Co., 1924.

Hesseltine, William B., *A History of the South, 1607-1936*. New York: Prentice-Hall, 1936.

————*Ulysses S. Grant: Politician*: New York: Dodd, Mead and Co., 1935.

Hicks, John D., *Populist Revolt: A History of the Farmers' Alliance and the People's Party*. Minneapolis: University of Minnesota Press, 1931.

————*Republican Ascendancy, 1921-1933*. New American Nation Series. New York: Harper and Row, 1960.

Hinshaw, David, *Herbert Hoover: American Quaker*. New York: Farrar, Straus and Co., 1950.

Hoover, Herbert, *The Memoirs of Herbert Hoover: The Great Depression, 1929-1941*. New York: Macmillian Co., 1952.

Howe, George Frederick, *Chester A. Arthur: A Quarter Century of Machine Politics*. New York: Dodd, Mead and Co., 1934.

Hubbard, Preston J., *Origins of the TVA: The Muscle Shoals Controversy, 1920-1932*. Nashville: Vanderbilt University Press, 1961.

Jacksonville (Alabama)*Republican*, 1842-1846.

Jonesborough Whig, 1841-1846.

Kirk, Grayson L., *Philippine Independence*: *Motives, Problems, and Prospects*. New York: Farrar and Rinehart Co., 1936.

Klien, Philip S., *President James Buchanan*. Philadelphia: University of Pennsylvania Press, 1962.

Knoxville Weekly Whig, 1869.

Leech, Margaret, *In The Days of McKinley*. New York: Harper Bros., 1959.

Levin, Peter, *Seven By Chance*. New York: Farrar and Straus, 1948.

Lewis, Henry M., Jr., *The Veto Power of the President*. Unpublished Dr. of Civil Laws dissertation, American University, 1927.

Lief, Alfred, *Democracy's Norris*: *The Biography of a Lonely Crusader*. New York: Stackpole Co., 1939.

Link, Arthur S., *American Epoch*: *A History of the United States Since the 1890's*. New York: Alfred A. Knopf, 1959.

————*Wilson*: *The New Freedom*. Vol. 2. Princeton: Princeton University Press, 1956.

————*Woodrow Wilson and the Progressive Era*: *1900-1917*. New American National Series. New York: Harper and Row, 1954.

MacDonald, William, *Jacksonian Democracy*. New York: Harper Bros., 1906.

Maryland Gazette, 1815.

Mason, Edward, *The Veto Power*. Boston: Ginn and Co., 1891.

Meigs, William M. *The Life of John Caldwell Calhoun*. New York: G. E. Steckart, 1917.

Merrill, Horace Samuel, *Bourbon Leader*: *Grover Cleveland and the Democratic Party*. Boston: Little, Brown and Co., 1957.

Myers, William Starr, *The Foreign Policies of Herbert Hoover*: *1929-1933*. New York: Charles Scribner's Sons, 1940.

Myers, William Starr, and Newton, Walter H., *The Hoover Administration*: *A Documented Narrative*: New York: Charles Scribner's Sons, 1936.

National Gazette, 1792.

National Intelligencer, 1811-1848.

Neuberger, Richard L., and Kahn, Stephen B., *Integrity*: *The Life of George W. Norris*. New York: The Vanguard Press, 1937.

Nevins, Alan, *Grover Cleveland*: *A Study in Courage*. New York: Dodd, Mead and Co., 1934.

New York Herald, 1815.

New York Daily Tribune, 1896, 1897, 1909.

New York Times, 1854-1868, 1872-1876, 1922-1943.

Nichols, Roy F., *Franklin Pierce*: *Young Hickory of the Granite Hills*. Philadelphia: University of Pennsylvania Press, 1931.

Omaha World Herald, 1892.

Potter, David M., and Manning, Thomas G., *Nationalism and Sectionalism in America*, *1775-1877*. New York: Holt, Rinehart and Winston, 1949.

Presidential Vetoes. List of Bills vetoed and Action Taken Thereon by the Senate and the House of Representatives, first Congress through the eighty-sixth Congress, 1789-1961. Washington: Government Printing Office, 1961.

Pringle, Henry F., *The Life and Times of William Howard Taft.* 2 vols. New York: Farrar and Rinehart, Inc., 1939.

Providence Gazette and County Journal, 1792.

Quint, Howard H., and Ferrell, Robert H., eds., *The Talkative President: The Off-the-Record Press Conferences of Calvin Coolidge.* Amherst: University of Massachuetts Press, 1964.

Randall, J. G., *Lincoln the President: Midstream.* Vol. 3. New York: Dodd, Mead and Co., 1945-1955.

——————*Lincoln the President: Springfield to Gettysburg.* Vol. 2. New York: Dodd, Mead and Co., 1945.

Randall, J. G., and Donald, David., *Civil War and Reconstruction.* 2nd ed. Boston: D. C. Heath and Co., 1961.

Richardson, James, ed., *Messages of the Presidents.* Vols. 1-8, 10, 15-18. Washington: Bureau of National Literature and Art, 1897.

Richmond Enquirer, 1844-1855.

Rossiter, Clinton, *The American Presidency.* New York: Harcourt and Brace, 1956.

St. Louis Post-Dispatch, 1935, 1937, 1943, 1944.

San Francisco Examiner, 1882, 1911, 1913, 1915, 1917.

Schlesinger, Arthur M., Jr., *The Age of Jackson.* Boston: Little, Brown and Co., 1953

Stephenson, George M., *A History of American Immigration, 1820-1924.* Boston: Ginn and Co., 1926.

Stryker, Lloyd P., *Andrew Johnson: A Study in Courage,* New York: Macmillan Co., 1929.

Styron, Arthur, *The Cast Iron Man: John C. Calhoun and American Democracy.* New York: Longman, Green and Co., 1935.

Unger, Irwin, *The Greenback Era: A Social and Political History of American Finance, 1865-1879.* Princeton: Princeton University Press, 1964.

United States Reports. Vol. 279: Cases adjudged from February, 1929 to June, 1929. Vol. 302: Cases adjudged from October, 1937 to January, 1938. Washington: Government Printing Office.

Van Deusen, Glyndon G., *The Jacksonian Era.* New York: Harper and Row, 1959.

Warren, Harris G., *Herbert Hoover and the Great Depression.* New York: Oxford University Press, 1959.

Washington Evening Star, 1908-1944.

Washington Globe, 1830.

Washington Post, 1892-93, 1896, 1909, 1928.

Williams, Charles R., *The Life of Rutherford Birchard Hayes: Nineteenth President of the United States.* Vol. 2. Boston: Houghton Mifflin Co., 1914.

Williams, T. Harry, ed., *Hayes: The Diary of a President, 1875-1881*. New York: David MacKay Co., Inc., 1964.

Wiltse, Charles M., *John C. Calhoun, Sectionalist*. Indianapolis: Bobbs-Merrill Co., 1951.

Woodward, W. E., *Meet General Grant*. Literary Guild of America, 1928.

Index

Adams, John Quincy, and "corrupt bargain" charges, 16; and Eastern Harbor veto, 1844, 82; and Internal Improvements, 21; mentioned by Pierce, 102; mentioned by Polk, 95; and National Republican Party, 14

Adjournment of Congress veto, 1836, 52-54

Adjusted Compensation veto, of 1924, 189-90; of 1931, 191-92; of 1935, 209-11

Agricultural Marketing Act of 1929, 196

Alabama Journal, and Bank veto, 1841, 63; and Maysville veto, 22; and Tariff veto, 1842, 70

Alien veto, 1812, 8-9

Allison, William B. (Iowa), 137, 138, 139

Amendments to curb veto power, 50-52; 64

American System, and Henry Clay, 16, 35; identification with Bank of United States, 43-44; and Land Bill, 1832, 49-50

Amonson, Louis S., quoted, 176

Anderson, Charles M. (Ohio), 156

Apportionment veto, 1792, 1-3

Argentine and "Pretorian Republic" veto, 1877, 140-41

Arizona School veto, 1896, 159-60

Arizona Statehood veto, 1911, 172-74

Arkansas veto, 1868, 124

Army Appropriation vetoes, 1879, 141-42

Army Reduction veto, 1921, 184-86

Arnold, Thomas D. (Tenn.), 76

Arthur, Chester A., as a veto president, 148; and Chinese Immigration, 146-47; and Fitz-John Porter veto, 1884, 145; and Steamship veto, 147

Ashley, James M. (Ohio), 121

Ashurst, Henry F. (Ariz.), and Soldier Bonus bill, 188-90; and Spanish-American veto, 191

Attorneys veto, 1893, 157-58

"Baby bond" bill, 212-13

Bagby, Arthur (Ala.), 97

Bailey, Josiah (N.C.), 209

Baltimore Sun, and Eastern Harbor veto, 1844, 82; and French Spoliation Claims, 1846, 93; and Internal Improvement veto, 1846, 89-90

Bank Note veto, 1862, 114

Bank of the United States, and Daniel Webster, 29, 36, 37, 38, 39, 40, 41, 42, 43; and Fiscal Bank, 1841, 57-64; and Henry Clay, 29, 35, 36, 38, 39, 42, 43; identified with American System, 35; Jackson's veto, 1832, 29-44; McCulloch v. Maryland, 34, 40; Madison's veto, 1815, 9-10; and Nicholas Biddle, 29

Bankhead, John (Ala.), 212

Baptist veto, 1811, 7

Barkley, Alben (Ky.), 222-23

Bartlett, Franklin (N.Y.), 161

Bassett, Burwell (Va.), 6

Bate, William (Tenn.), 163

Bayard, Richard (Del.), 57

Bayard, Thomas (Del.), 147

Bayley, Thomas (Va.), and Eastern Harbor veto, 1844, 82; and Internal Improvement veto, 1846, 89; and Revenue Cutter veto, 1845, 84

Beard, Charles, mentioned, 203

Bede, J. Adam (Minn.), 165

Bell, John (Tenn.), 22

Belser, James E. (Ala.), 84

Benjamin, Judah P. (La.), 104

Benton, Thomas H. (Mo.), and Bank veto, 1832, 36, 42, 43; and Bank veto, 1841, 58, 59; and Land Bill veto, 1832, 49

Berrien, John (Ga.), 59

Best veto, 1872, 133-34

Bibb, George M. (Ky.), 22

Biddle, Nicholas, 29

"Black codes," 116-17

Black, Hugo (Ala.), 199

Blaine, James G. (Me.), 137

Blair, Henry W., 151-52

Bland-Allison veto, 1878, 137-39

Bland, Richard P. (Mo.), and Free Silver, 137, 139; and Seigniorage bill, 159

Boland, Patrick J. (Pa.), 210

Bonus Bill, 1817, compared with Maysville veto, 24; vetoed, 11-12

Bonus Expeditionary Force, 192

Borah, William E. (Idaho), 191

Botts, John Minor (Va.), and Bank veto, 1841, 145-46; and Tariff veto, 1842, 69, 70, 72

Boutelle, Charles (Me.), 159

Brack Relief veto, 205-06

Brandeis, Louis, 207